Britain at the Polls 1983

A Study of the General Election

EDITED BY AUSTIN RANNEY

An American Enterprise Institute Book,
Published by Duke University Press
1985

Contents

Preface   Austin Ranney   ix

1   Thatcher's First Term   ANTHONY KING   1

2   The Conservative Campaign   MICHAEL PINTO-DUSCHINSKY   39

3   The Labour Campaign   PETER KELLNER   65

4   The Alliance Campaign, Watersheds, and Landslides: Was 1983 a Fault Line in British Politics?   JORGEN RASMUSSEN   81

5   Opinion Polls as Feedback Mechanisms: From Cavalry Charge to Electronic Warfare   RICHARD ROSE   108

6   The Ethnic Minorities' Vote   MONICA CHARLOT   139

7   How to Win a Landslide without Really Trying: Why the Conservatives Won in 1983   IVOR CREWE   155

Appendix   197

Notes   201

Index   223

Contributors   227

Tables and Figures

TABLES

P.1 British parliamentary constituencies, 1979–83   x
P.2 Votes and seats in the 1983 British general election   xi
1.1 Public standings of government, Conservative party, Thatcher, 1979–82   10
1.2 Inflation and unemployment, 1979–82   11
1.3 Public standings of Labour party, Callaghan, Foot, 1979–82   23
1.4 Public standings of Liberal party, Liberal-SDP Alliance, 1979–82   29
1.5 Public standings of government, parties, and leaders, inflation and unemployment, 1982–83   33
2.1 Conservative party central income and expenditure, 1979–83   62
2.2 Conservative party central precampaign and campaign expenditures   63
5.1 Nationwide polls during the 1983 general election campaign   113
5.2 Accuracy of the final poll forecasts, 1983   120
5.3 Influence of the polls   131
5.4 Accuracy of 1983 polls compared to polls in previous elections   132
5.5 Popular views about the banning of opinion polls   137
6.1 Places of birth of electors outside the United Kingdom   140
6.2 Registration by sex and age of Asians and Afro-Caribbeans, 1983   142
6.3 Turnout by ethnic group, 1983   147
6.4 Voting intentions of Asians and Afro-Caribbeans   148
6.5 Social class and voting intention of Asians and Afro-Caribbeans, 1983   149
6.6 Voting intention of first-time voters among Asians and Afro-Caribbeans, 1983   149
7.1 Party support in the opinion polls during the campaign   158
7.2 Impact of campaigning   163

7.3   Campaign's effect on vote choice   164
7.4   Flow of the vote from 1979 to 1983   166
7.5   Vote by age and sex   168
7.6   Vote by social class   170
7.7   Vote by sector of employment and housing   171
7.8   Defection rates among 1979 Labour voters   172
7.9   Two working classes and the 1983 vote   173
7.10 Motivation of party choice   174
7.11 Party preferences on various criteria   176
7.12 The issues that mattered, 1983   178
7.13 Expectation of the effect of each party   180
7.14 The best (and worst) person for prime minister   181
7.15 Popular attitudes toward elements of "Thatcherism"   185
7.16 Thatcherism and vote switching, 1979–83   186
7.17 Attitudes toward Conservative economic positions   189
7.18 Conservative and Labour party identification, 1964–83   190
7.19 Strength of the parties' vote   193
7.20 Why the Alliance did not do better   194

FIGURES AND MAPS

1.1   Party voting support, 1979–82   37
4.1   Alliance support in polls, 1981–83   83
4.2   Alliance strength in polls, May–June 1983   93
4.3   Alliance distance behind Labour, May–June 1983   94
A.1   Electoral map of the United Kingdom   200

Preface

AUSTIN RANNEY

———— On 9 June 1983 the United Kingdom of Great Britain and Northern Ireland held its twenty-third general election in the twentieth century. A total of 30,670,905 voters cast valid ballots. This constituted a turnout of 76.3 percent of the registered voters, slightly up from the 76 percent in the 1979 general election but slightly below the mean turnout of 77 percent in general elections since 1945.

This book is the third produced by the American Enterprise Institute for Public Policy Research on recent British general elections; the previous two were under the editorship of Howard R. Penniman.[1] As in the previous volumes, this book has a multinational roster of authors: one is French, two are American, and four are British.

Under Howard Penniman's direction, I contributed to the volume on the 1979 election an introductory chapter seeking to introduce to non-British readers, mainly Americans, the principal features of the British system for conducting general elections. In this preface I shall update some of that information and highlight the most noteworthy 1983 developments.

Dates and Dissolutions

The first Conservative government led by Margaret Thatcher took office on 4 May 1979. By law there had to be a general election no later than five years from that date, but Thatcher, like every British prime minister, had the power to ask the queen for a dissolution of Parliament and a new general election at any time before 1 June 1984. After discussing alternative dates with her party colleagues and weighing the advantages and disadvantages of each (a process described well by Michael Pinto-Duschinsky in chapter 2), on 9 May 1983 the prime minister announced that Parliament would be dissolved on 13 May and the election would be held on 9 June.

Table P.1 British parliamentary constituencies, 1979–83

	Population (est. 1977)	Number of constituencies		Mean population of constituencies	
		1979	1983	1979	1983
England	46,351,300	516	523	88,830	88,626
Scotland	5,195,600	71	72	73,180	72,161
Wales	2,768,200	36	38	76,890	72,847
Northern Ireland	1,537,300	12	17	128,100	90,429
United Kingdom	55,852,400	635	650	87,960	85,927

Source: The figures for 1979 come from Howard R. Penniman, ed., *Britain at the Polls 1979* (Washington, D.C.: American Enterprise Institute for Public Policy Research, 1981), table 1-2, p. 5. The figures for 1983 are taken from the appendix to this volume by Richard M. Scammon.

The first Thatcher government thus lasted four years and one month, a period almost identical to the median duration of four years and no months for all Parliaments from 1945 to 1979.[2]

The Constituencies

The 1983 general election was the first fought after the post-1979 redistribution of seats,[3] called by one scholar, "the most sweeping since the granting of universal suffrage in 1918."[4] The total number of constituencies was increased from 635 in 1979 to 650 in 1983, and only 66 constituencies remained exactly as they had been in 1979. All the others were altered in some way, many of them substantially. The changes are summarized in table P.1.

There were two main reasons for such a sweeping redistribution. The first was that there had been considerable population movement within Great Britain since the previous redistribution, which was recommended in 1969 but did not go into effect until 1971. The main trends were declining populations in the core big cities and increasing populations in the suburbs and in the rural "shire" counties, especially in the south of England. Thus most of the big cities lost seats, the biggest losers being London (−8), Manchester (−3), Glasgow (−3), Liverpool (−2), and Birmingham, Bristol, Edinburgh, and Salford (−1 each).

The second reason was the changes in the boundaries of the counties wrought by the local government reforms of the early 1970s. The Boundary Commission, which drew up and recommended the redistribution, adhered strictly to the tradition of permitting no constituency to cross county lines. Accordingly, since so many county lines had been changed, the boundaries of the constituencies were bound to change as well, and many old seats were broken up or even eliminated because their boundaries crossed the new county lines.

Table P.2 Votes and seats in the 1983 British general election

Party	Popular vote	Percent of vote	Seats	Percent of seats	Percentage point difference
Conservative	13,012,602	42.4	397	61.1	+18.7
Labour	8,457,124	27.6	209	32.2	+4.6
Alliance	7,780,587	25.4	23	3.5	−21.9
Other	1,420,592	4.6	21	3.2	−1.4

Source: Calculated from the appendix to this volume by Richard M. Scammon.

Any such sweeping change in the allocation and boundaries of constituencies is bound to favor some parties and disadvantage others. Most observers concluded that the redistribution damaged the Labour party more than the others, especially by reducing the number of its safe seats in the core big cities and in the heavy-industry areas of the Midlands and Scotland. Labour's leaders evidently shared this view, for in 1982 a suit in the name of Party Leader Michael Foot, General Secretary Jim Mortimer, Chief Whip Michael Cocks, and National Agent David Hughes was brought in the Queen's Bench division court. It charged that Parliament's enactment of the Boundary Commission's new scheme did not fulfill the legal requirement of establishing electorates of equal size both within counties and between seats in different counties and London boroughs.

In December 1982 the court held that the commission had acted properly and added that courts should be reluctant to interfere in a matter so clearly within Parliament's jurisdiction. In January 1983 a division of the appeal court upheld the lower court's ruling, and in February the House of Lords, acting as Britain's supreme court, refused to hear a further appeal.

The redistribution appears to have made a significant difference in the outcome of the election: several analysts concluded that the Conservatives won around thirty more seats in 1983 than they would have won under the old distribution.[5]

Votes and Seats

The 1983 election produced the greatest differences in the conversion of shares of the popular vote into shares of parliamentary seats in any general election in this century.[6] The parties' shares of each are shown in table P.2.

The British system for electing members of Parliament combines single-member districts with a first-past-the-post rule for determining winners. Observers have long noted the tendency of this system (and all like it) to give the first and second parties shares of the seats that are substantially greater than their shares of the popular votes—and to give the third party and smaller parties disproportionately small shares of the seats for their votes. This tendency operated with a vengeance in 1983: the Conservatives won 42.4 percent of the popular votes but 61.1 percent of the seats. This 18.7 point "bonus" was the second greatest for any party in this century; it was exceeded only by the Conservatives' windfall in the 1924 general election, in which 48.3 percent of the popular vote brought them 68.1 percent of the seats—a bonus of 19.8 points.

The other side of the picture was equally striking. The Liberal-Social Democratic Alliance won 25.4 percent of the popular vote, but only 3.5 percent of the seats. Their "penalty" of 21.9 points was the largest in this century; it was approached only in 1906, when the Conservatives' 43.6 percent of the votes brought them only 23.4 percent of the seats, a penalty of 20.2 points.

The discrepancy between the Alliance's shares of the votes and seats is even more striking when it is compared with Labour's performance. With 27.6 percent of the popular votes—only 2.2 points higher than the Alliance's share—Labour still won 209 seats (32.2 percent of the total), over *nine times* the Alliance's total of 23 seats. Accordingly, despite its precipitous drop in popular support (see Ivor Crewe's analysis in chapter 7), Labour nevertheless remained, by a wide margin, the official opposition party, and the Alliance still had a long way to go to equal or surpass Labour where it counts—in the House of Commons.

In the light of these discrepancies, it is not surprising that perhaps the leading item on the Alliance's policy agenda, as Jorgen Rasmussen makes clear in chapter 4, continues to be reform of the electoral system leading to some form of proportional representation.

Winners and Losers

One apparently inevitable postlude to a major national election in any democratic country consists of election analysts' comments on who "really won" and who "really lost"—a calculation that often turns out to be more complicated than one would suppose from a first glance at how many votes and offices went to each of the contending parties. The British general election of 1983 was certainly no exception, as the chapters to follow will show.

Perhaps we should begin our assessment of these comments by recognizing that, at the simplest and most obvious level of analysis, there is no question whatever about who won in Britain in 1983. The greatest of all prizes in the British political system is control of a majority of the seats in the House of Commons for, given the high cohesion and strong discipline of all the parties, such a majority gives the winning party the power to form the government, fill all the top political policy-making offices, and largely determine what public policies Britain will follow during the life of the new Parliament. In short,

British government is, to a degree far beyond anything known in the United States, government by the majority *party*.

By this first and most basic standard, the Conservative party and the government led by Prime Minister Margaret Thatcher won the 1983 election and won it big. They increased their number of seats in the House of Commons from 334 (out of 635, or 52.6 percent of the total) at the dissolution to 397 (out of 650, or 61.1 percent of the total). This not only returned them to power for another four or five years, but it increased their majority over all other parties from 33 seats at the dissolution to 144 seats in the new Parliament.

Seen in historical perspective, this was an impressive achievement. Of the twenty-three general elections held in this century, only ten have returned the incumbent government to power while eleven have brought in a new government (the others continued coalition governments in power). Of the twelve elections held since 1935, six have returned governments to power and six have forced changes in governments. Moreover, the Conservatives' increase-in-majority of 111 seats in 1983 is the greatest increase by a reelected government in the twentieth century; only the Labour increase of 92 seats in 1966 comes even close.

Thus 1983 was a Conservative landslide and a complete vindication of the Thatcher government's performance in office. Or was it? The answer depends upon what measure one uses: yes, if one looks only at the number of seats won; no, if one looks only at the shares of the popular votes. In 1983 the Conservatives won a total of 13,012,602 votes, which constituted 42.4 percent of the total. But this was 685,088 *fewer* votes than they had won in 1979, and their 42.4 percent of the total in 1983 was the lowest for any Conservative government taking office since Bonar Law became prime minister in 1922. Accordingly, while Thatcher and the Conservatives were big winners in terms of parliamentary seats and power, their victory certainly did not come from any great upsurge of popularity among the voters.

However, while the Conservative party's victory was somewhat clouded, the Labour party's loss was downright disastrous. Labour's total popular vote in 1983 was 8,457,124, which constituted 27.6 percent of all votes cast. This was over 3 million votes fewer than the 11,532,148 they had won in 1979. Indeed, it was the smallest vote Labour had won in any general election since 1935. Moreover, their 27.6 percent of the votes was the lowest share Labour had received in a general election since it first became a serious contender in the 1922 election. If one uses the criterion of the average share of constituency votes going to Labour candidates (which holds constant the factor of the number of constituencies contested), Labour's showing in 1983 was its poorest in *any* general election since the party was founded in 1900. The London *Economist* summed it up well:

Labour was forced back into its recession-racked city redoubts, and even there it was not always safe. In Wales and the north of England its share fell by almost 10%. South [of England apart from inner London] Labour barely exists, with just three seats to its name (Bristol, Ipswich and Thurrock). An aspiring Labour member of parliament must now find a decaying city centre with high unemployment, an ageing population and an air of despair. It is not much of a basis for a party of the future.[7]

What brought Labour so low and what, if any, are its prospects for recovery are discussed by Peter Kellner in chapter 3.

In many respects, the most interesting question prior to the election was, Would the new force in British politics, the alliance between the Liberal party and the new Social Democratic party (SDP), win enough votes and seats to replace Labour as the Conservatives' main opposition and perhaps even become the official opposition party? The election results gave the answers: votes, almost but not quite; seats, not a chance. Alliance candidates won a total of 7,780,587 votes, or 25.4 percent of the total—by far the best showing of any third party since World War II. They came close to passing Labour in popularity, but not quite close enough. In terms of seats, however, the British electoral system did them in. Before the dissolution, the Alliance held 42 seats, 29 by Social Democrats and 13 by Liberals. After the election they held only 23 seats, and two of the SDP's "Gang of Four" founders—Shirley Williams and Bill Rodgers—lost their seats. In chapter 4 Jorgen Rasmussen portrays in detail the Alliance's hopes, strategies, failures, and prospects.

This is already too much for a preface, so I shall add only that in the chapters to follow Anthony King surveys the events between the 1979 and 1983 elections; Michael Pinto-Duschinsky, Peter Kellner, and Jorgen Rasmussen describe, respectively, the Conservative, Labour, and Alliance campaigns; Richard Rose analyzes the unusually powerful impact of the public opinion polls; Monica Charlot describes the special behavior and role of immigrant voters; and Ivor Crewe analyzes the voters' attitudes, motivations, and choices. In the appendix Richard M. Scammon provides a breakdown of the election results.

Margaret Thatcher's First Term

ANTHONY KING

──────── The four years leading up to the 1983 general election were among the most turbulent in British political history. They saw the Conservative party sink to its lowest level ever in terms of popular support, only to recover spectacularly in the aftermath of the Falklands war in the South Atlantic. They saw Labour suffer its worst electoral defeats since the formation of the party at the beginning of this century. They also saw the formation of an entirely new political party, the Social Democrats, and the forging of a close alliance between this new organization and the long-established Liberals. Between 1979 and 1983, millions of British voters abandoned, or seriously considered abandoning, their traditional party allegiances (without, however, in the great majority of cases, forming new ones). By the time the 1983 election was over, Britain's traditional two-party system had all but been transformed.

"Can the Tories Win Again"?

On the afternoon of 4 May 1979, Britain's newly elected prime minister, Margaret Thatcher, stood on the steps of 10 Downing Street and quoted words attributed to St. Francis of Assisi:

> Where there is discord may we bring harmony;
>   where there is error may we bring truth.
> Where there is doubt may we bring faith;
>   where there is despair may we bring hope.

This was an odd passage for the new prime minister to have chosen. If the world's leaders are divided into a class of "warriors" and a class of "healers," St. Francis was indubitably a healer; Thatcher, by contrast, is a warrior—and has always acknowledged herself to be such. As she said in an interview shortly before her 1979 election triumph, "I'm not a consensus politician or a pragmatic politician. I'm a conviction politician."[1] From the beginning her intention as prime minister was not to be emollient; it was to impose her will on the government and the country and to bring about, if she could, nothing less than a total reorientation of British public policy and the content of British political debate.

The need for her to impose her will arose from two sources. The first was her minority position within her own party. British prime ministers reach the highest office because they have been chosen, in the first instance, as leader of their own political party. Usually they have been chosen as leader of their party because they are well respected within it but also, more important, because their political views coincide with those of a majority of the party's members. So it was with Sir Anthony Eden, Harold Macmillan, Sir Alec Douglas-Home, and Edward Heath. But Thatcher became Conservative leader in a most unusual set of circumstances. The majority of Conservative members of Parliament in the winter of 1974–75 wanted to depose as leader Edward Heath, who was personally remote from them and who by this time had led them to defeat in two general elections in a row. At the same time, Heath's obvious successors, like William Whitelaw and James Prior, had served in Heath's government, felt ties of loyalty to him, and had no desire to make themselves the instruments of his political destruction. They accordingly refused to stand against him when the first ballot in the election for the Tory leadership was held in February 1975. Margaret Thatcher, however, had no such inhibitions. She stood against Heath, even though, like the others, she had served under him, and in the first ballot she won more votes than Heath, who at once resigned. Several other candidates, including Whitelaw and Prior, entered the contest in time for the second ballot, but by then it was too late. Thatcher's lead was commanding, and it was she who gained the credit for displaying the political courage that the others seemingly lacked. In the decisive ballot, she polled 146 votes, 70 more than Whitelaw, the runner-up.[2]

The upshot was that the Conservative party, in its anxiety to rid itself of Edward Heath, elected a leader that it knew astonishingly little about. Most Conservative MPs were only dimly aware in 1975 of the content of Thatcher's economic ideas; only a handful were aware of the depths of her personal determination. If they had suspected the extent of her radicalism and known how single-minded she could be, many of them might not have voted for her. Even after their party's election victory in 1979, most Conservatives—including most leading Conservatives—were agnostic with regard to many of Thatcher's economic views or else were positively hostile toward them. Thus, if Thatcher were to succeed in translating those views into public policy, she was going to have to fight hard, inside her government as well as out.[3]

The second reason she was going to have to impose her will was related to the first. It is easy to overlook the fact that Margaret Thatcher was unusual—and is unusual—among British prime ministers in the very wide range of subjects on which she holds strong opinions. Most British prime ministers, like most American presidents, are content to give a general political tone to their administrations and to settle disputes among their colleagues and subordinates. Major crises apart, their involvement in the details of policy tends to be intermittent, and they are not usually in the business of leading personal crusades. In practice, their own goals are seldom distinct from the goals of their party or their administration generally. For instance, when the Conservative Home succeeded the Conservative Macmillan in 1963, few changes of policy or political direction were apparent. It was the same when Labour's James Callaghan succeeded Labour's Harold Wilson in 1976. But—and this is crucial to an understanding of her prime ministership—Thatcher is different. She holds views on a remarkably wide range of subjects: monetary policy, fiscal policy, public expenditure, the appropriate economic role of the state, defense, Britain's relations with America, Britain's relations with the Soviet Union, Britain's relations with the European Community, education, immigration, crime and punishment, police methods, and many, many more. Not only does she hold views on all these subjects, she holds strong views; and she has an immense capacity for immersing herself in the detail of them. Furthermore, these views are her own views. They are personal to her. They are not merely emanations from her party, her government, or wherever. Thatcher's determination to assert as many of these views as possible, together with her minority position within her own party and government, determined from the outset her characteristic prime ministerial style.[4]

The cabinet that Margaret Thatcher appointed in May 1979 contained many members who were not "Thatcherites"—men (all of Thatcher's cabinet colleagues were men) who were skeptical of the feasibility, or even the desirability, of changing radically the overall direction of British economic policy. Thatcher, however, took care to appoint her supporters to most of the key economic positions. In particular, a Thatcher loyalist, Sir Geoffrey Howe, became chancellor of the exchequer, and he and the prime minister worked closely together throughout her first term. For purposes of economic policy making, they constituted, in effect, a duopoly inside the government.[5]

Theirs was a bold strategy. One specific aim, though not necessarily their most important one, was to reduce the rate of inflation, running when the Conservatives came to power at an annual rate of approximately 11 percent.[6] The desired reduction was to be achieved by two principal means. First, the government sought a gradual scaling down in the rate of growth of money supply. This would act on inflation directly and also would reduce the overall level of demand in the economy. Second, the government intended to cut public expenditures drastically. This would permit substantial reductions in public-sector borrowing, thereby reducing pressure on interest rates and also making possible further reductions in the rate of growth of money supply. Thatcher and Howe, in addition to their broadly "monetarist" strategy, also wanted to see a reduction in the level of wage increases, but they were not interested in operating incomes policies of the type that had been characteristic of the Heath government and the Wilson and Callaghan Labour governments. On the contrary, they believed that such policies, applying uniformly to the whole labor force, led inevitably to economic distortions and also to unnecessarily high levels of industrial unrest, as traditional wage differentials were eroded and as workers employed in profitable firms saw their incomes squeezed to the benefit of workers in less profitable firms and the public sector. Thatcher's ministers instead set out to impose strict cash limits on spending in the public sector. With regard to the private sector, they were content to allow market forces to operate freely.[7]

This concentration on combating inflation constituted in itself a revolution in British economic policy. All previous postwar governments, Conservative as well as Labour, had given top priority to maintaining full or nearly full employment. Now, tacitly, this commitment was dropped. Restoring full employment was from now on to be a goal of policy, but by no means the only goal.[8]

Thatcher and her allies were, moreover, determined to carry their revolution into other fields. They believed in the necessity of creating greater economic incentives for both managers and workers, and they were emphatic that the proportion of British economic activity subject to market forces should be vastly increased, not just in the single field of pay bargaining. The Conservatives' 1979 election manifesto promised cuts in the higher marginal rates of income tax and also a pronounced shift from taxes on income and capital to taxes on spending (i.e., from so-called direct to so-called indirect taxation).[9] Government intervention in the economy was to be reduced across the board. Residual price controls introduced by the Labour government were to be removed, and state agencies such as the National Enterprise Board—whose borrowing limit in 1979 was set at £4,500 million—would have their activities reviewed, possibly with a view to some agencies being abolished altogether. In the same spirit, the manifesto looked forward to the "privatization" of nationalized industries:

> We will offer to sell back to private ownership the recently nationalized aerospace and shipbuilding concerns, giving their employees the opportunity to purchase shares. We aim to sell shares in the National Freight Corporation to the general public in order to achieve substantial private investment in it. We will also relax the Traffic Commissioner licensing regulations to enable new bus and other services to develop . . . and we will encourage new private operators.[10]

Thatcher and those around her also were bent on reducing the power of Britain's trade unions, partly on economic grounds (to make it harder for individual unions to exploit their monopoly position in the labor market), but partly also on libertarian grounds (to make it more difficult for trade unions to impose

closed shops and operate in ways that the Conservatives maintained were undemocratic).

The Tories' 1979 manifesto was, on paper, a radical document. It foreshad-
owed a series of sharp breaks with the policies pursued by all previous postwar
governments.[11] But what makes the 1979–83 Thatcher government remarkable
is that it not only fulfilled the majority of its manifesto commitments, in many
fields it went well beyond them. It somehow contrived, as the Soviet planners
say, to "overfulfill its norms." One factor was undoubtedly the logic of the revolutionary process itself: if one nationalized industry could be successfully sold
off to the private sector, why not another, and another, and another? But a
crucial factor was also the force of personality and the sheer determination of
the prime minister herself. She often had to compromise. More than once she
was defeated by her own cabinet (for example, in November 1980 when it refused to accede to public expenditure cuts on the scale that she and Howe were
demanding),[12] but she went on undaunted, and she frequently got her way.
Given her minority position in the government, it is inconceivable that so much
would have been accomplished so quickly without her constant prodding, ex-
horting, maneuvering, and cajoling. In its first term, the Thatcher government
was "the Thatcher government" more than just in name.[13]

Within weeks of the government's taking office, Sir Geoffrey Howe in his
first budget cut the standard rate of income tax from 33p in the pound to 30p
and at the same time, as promised, cut the highest marginal rate of income tax
from 83p to 60p (bringing it into line with that of other European countries).
To recover the revenue lost as the result of these measures, the two existing
rates of value-added tax, 8 percent and 12.5 percent, were both raised to a
standard rate of 15 percent. Targets for the rate of growth of money supply
were announced for 1979–80 and subsequently for later years, and some £2.5
billion were lopped off the spending plans of the outgoing Callaghan administration. Going further than anyone had anticipated, Howe in October 1979
announced the total abolition of the system of exchange controls that had
helped to protect the international position of sterling ever since the Second
World War. Partly as the result of the government's tough anti-inflation stance,
partly as the result of rises in the value of Britain's North Sea oil, the value
of the pound against the United States dollar soared, from $2.06 when the
Thatcher government first took office to $2.40 in little over a year. The outside
world, it seemed, had confidence in Britain and in the British government.

But it was in the field of privatization that the prime minister and her colleagues went furthest, fastest. The commitments contained in their manifesto
were relatively modest, amounting to little more than a reversal of Labour's
most recent acts of nationalization and a loosening of controls over competition between state-owned and privately owned firms. Once in power, however,

the government discovered that the process of privatization was easier and encountered less resistance than had been anticipated.[14] Although ministers said little in public, they also seem to have realized that, once it had been carried far enough, the process of privatization would be extremely difficult for any future government to reverse. In other words, the Tories could not only effect a revolution in the ownership of British industry, but could ensure that that revolution was permanent, or nearly so. Whatever its precise motives, the Thatcher government proceeded between 1979 and 1983 to sell all or large proportions of the shares of British Aerospace, Associated British Ports, the National Freight Corporation, Amersham International (a state-owned biotechnology concern), Cable and Wireless (a large international telecommunications company), British Petroleum, British Sugar, and the production side of the British Oil Corporation. It required Labour's National Enterprise Board (renamed the British Technology Group) to sell its interests in Ferranti, Fairey, International Computers Limited (ICL), and other companies. It also required British Steel, British Rail, British Gas, the Central Electricity Generating Board, British Leyland (the state-owned car company), British Telecom, and the Post Office either to sell off parts of their businesses or to permit competition where the state-owned concerns had previously had a monopoly. Private companies, in addition, were allowed to tender for the provision of public services such as refuse collection and cleaning in hospitals. At the time of the 1983 election, the government had plans for the sale to the private sector of all of British Airways and approximately half the shares in British Telecom.[15] The whole enterprise was on a colossal scale, without precedent in any Western democracy.

The government's moves in the field of trade union law were considerably more tentative, if only because of the Heath government's failure to impose its across-the-board trade union reforms in the early 1970s.[16] The Thatcher government adopted, in its own words, a "step-by-step approach." The Employment Act of 1980 restricted lawful picketing to the pickets' own place of work, provided compensation for people unreasonably excluded or expelled from a union in a closed shop, required that proposed new closed shops be approved in a secret ballot by four-fifths of the workers to be covered, and made available public funds for the holding of secret ballots on issues such as strikes and the election of union officers. The subsequent Employment Act of 1982 toughened up the 1980 act's closed shop provisions. More important, it made whole trade unions, not just individual union officials, liable to be sued for participating in unlawful industrial action, and it effectively outlawed secondary industrial action (i.e., the taking of sympathy strikes in the absence of any direct dispute between the employer struck and his own employees). Unlike the Heath legislation, the Thatcher legislation usually put the onus of taking legal action on the employers or employees concerned, not on the government. As in the case of privatization, Thatcher and her colleagues had announced further plans for the reform of trade union law by the time of the 1983 election. These plans included the requirement that trade union officials be elected by secret ballot, that secret ballots should also be held prior to strikes, and that a secret ballot should be held among the members of any union seeking to maintain, or to institute, a political fund (political funds usually being used for purposes of affiliation to the Labour party).

Two other important domestic commitments were honored. The first was to give higher priority to tackling the problem of law and order. The Conservatives' victory in the 1979 election owed something to their success in identifying themselves in voters' minds with the law and order issue, and between 1979 and 1983 the Thatcher government increased spending on the police and prisons by 27.7 percent in real terms, while police numbers were increased by more than 9,500 to some 120,000 in England and Wales. The government also honored its pledge to give council-house tenants (the equivalent of people living in public housing in the United States) the right to buy their own homes. Discounts were offered to tenants who had been in their houses for more than three years, and those unable to buy outright were given the option, on payment of £100, to buy in two years at the original price. Between 1979 and 1983, some 500,000 council houses were sold to their occupants, far more than passed into private hands in the whole of the period from 1945 to 1979. Altogether the number of owner-occupied dwellings in Britain increased by a million during Thatcher's first four years. The Conservatives' motives in selling council houses were partly ideological: they wanted to see property ownership in the society spread more widely. But they were also partly electoral: they believed that a householder, somebody who had acquired "a stake in the community," would be more likely to vote Conservative than somebody who depended for his or her housing on the beneficence of the (quite possibly Labour-controlled) local authority. Just how successful in electoral terms the Tories were is suggested by Ivor Crewe in the final chapter of this book.

The Thatcher government in its first term was unusually determined and single-minded, but the picture should not be overdrawn. Thatcher may not have been a pragmatist by instinct, but she could be pragmatic on occasion, and in any case the non-Thatcherite majority in the cabinet ensured that, whenever the Thatcherites threatened to become (as their opponents saw it) too doctrinaire, they could be held in some kind of check. Moreover, the very word "Thatcherism," while it accurately caught the prime minister's personal preferences for hard work, self-reliance, and free-market economics, for stern monetary discipline combined with stern social discipline, and for the robust assertion of British interests overseas, was misleading if it conveyed the impression that the prime minister and her allies were in possession of an ideology that was coherent and fully thought through. They were not. Thatcherism was actually something of a ragbag—like Reaganism, socialism, and most other -isms.

The result was that the government's policies were by no means all of one piece. On the one hand, the Thatcherites protested that firms, including nationalized firms, should be made to pay their own way. On the other, huge sums of taxpayers' money were poured into the National Coal Board, into British Steel (even though its work force was cut by nearly half during these years), into British Shipbuilders (which, in the event, was not sold off for the good reason that nobody wanted to buy it), and into British Leyland (which, making good use of £1.3 billion of taxpayers' money, cut its work force by more than half between 1979 and 1983, increased productivity by some 70 percent, and turned massive operating losses into a minute but encouraging operating profit). Likewise, whereas on the one hand the Thatcher government looked to private enterprise and private capital to play the predominant part in the revival of Britain's economy, on the other it promoted expensive schemes to assist small businesses and even more expensive schemes (£250 million in 1983–84 alone) to assist innovation in high-technology fields such as microelectronics, fiber optics, information technology, and space (not for nothing was Thatcher Britain's first prime minister with a natural sciences degree).[17] Needless to say, political prudence was a prime factor in many of these decisions and in others like them. In February 1981, for example, faced with the possibility of a national coal strike (of exactly the kind that had toppled Edward Heath in 1974), the prime minister rapidly retreated and agreed that twenty-three pits, threatened with closure, should remain open. In December 1982, only six months before the general election, the government decided to reject the British Steel Corporation's recommendation to shut down a loss-making plant in one of Scotland's most depressed areas. After the first of these episodes, a Thatcher ally, Treasury minister John Biffen, said that he had not gone into politics to be "a kamikaze pilot." Thatcher was of the same view. Forcefulness and determination in Thatcher should never be mistaken for rashness. She was, and remains, an extremely cautious politician.[18]

The government's main concerns initially had to do with domestic policy. Indeed the prime minister herself began by being impatient with the rituals and endless verbiage of big international meetings (though in time, like most heads of government, she came rather to enjoy them). Nevertheless, the government throughout its first term (and after) found itself forced to fight a long running battle—half domestic, half foreign—with the other member countries of the European Community (EC). Britain maintained that its net contributions to the community's budget were far too high, especially since Britain was one of the poorest countries in Europe, and also that far too much was being spent on the EC's common agricultural policy, encouraging Europe's farmers to produce vast quantities of food and wine that nobody could afford to buy at the community's inflated prices. Thatcher's negotiating tactics were aggressive to the point of unpleasantness. Whether because of them or in spite of them (views differed), the other countries' leaders conceded to Britain a series of substantial rebates.[19]

The government's determination to take a tough stance in foreign affairs was also reflected in its staunch backing of President Ronald Reagan's foreign policy, in its twin decisions to buy the Trident nuclear missile system from the United States and to allow American Cruise missiles to be sited on British soil, and, not least, in its strict adherence to the NATO commitment to increase defense spending by 3 percent each year in real terms. Between 1979 and 1983, British defense spending in real terms increased by no less than 16.7 percent; by 1983, Britain was spending a larger proportion of its gross domestic product on defense—and more on defense in absolute terms—than any other major European country. Paradoxically, given its generally tough anti-Communist stance, the Thatcher government also in its first term granted legal independence to Rhodesia / Zimbabwe in conditions that made it highly probable that a Marxist or quasi-Marxist government would come to power. In this, as in so much else, Thatcher manifested her essential caution and realism. The white-backed government of Bishop Abel Muzorewa could not win its civil war against the Marxist guerrillas in Rhodesia / Zimbabwe. Most black African countries were sympathetic to the guerrillas and in many of them Britain had substantial business interests. So a deal had better be struck. And one was, at the 1980 Lancaster House conference in London under the aegis of the British foreign secretary, Lord Carrington.

The Thatcher government's policies were thus radical in their content and sweeping in their effects, especially in the domestic sphere. Merely to summarize them, however, is to risk missing part of the point. Thatcher and her allies were not content merely to alter the policies pursued by a single government during a single four-year period; they wanted to change the whole intellectual and moral framework within which public policy in Britain was discussed. "We have to move this country," Thatcher told the 1979 Tory conference, "in a new direction—to change the way we look at things, to create a wholly new attitude of mind."[20] She and those closest to her believed that ever since the Second World War a kind of "ratchet" had operated, making people more and more dependent on the state, more and more disposed to look to the state to solve their own and the country's problems. The Thatcherites wanted to reverse that ratchet.[21] They wanted to persuade firms that got into trouble through indolence or incompetence or even just bad luck that the government had no intention of bailing them out. They wanted to persuade trade unions that, if higher wages led to higher unemployment, the government would be sorry, of course, but it would otherwise do nothing to protect people from the consequences of their own actions. They wanted to persuade the nation as a whole that no one owed Britain a living, that the disciplines of the marketplace were healthy (and in any case were inescapable), and that wealth must be cre-

Table 1.1   Public standings of government, Conservative
party, Thatcher (quarterly averages, 1979–82)

	Percent approving of government's record to date	Percent intending to vote Conservative	Percent satisfied with Thatcher as prime minister
1979			
June–September	36	42	43
October–December	35	39	43
1980			
January–March	31	37	38
April–June	36	39	43
July–September	32	38	40
October–December	29	37	36
1981			
January–March	26	33	35
April–June	26	31	33
July–September	24	30	30
October–December	22	27	26
1982			
January–March	26	29	32

Source: Gallop Political Index.
Note: The first question was worded, "Do you approve or disapprove of the government's record to date?" The voting-intention question was worded, "If there were a general election tomorrow, which party would you support?" Respondents replying "don't know" to this question were then asked, "Which party would you be most inclined to vote for?" Responses to both questions have been merged in the second column. The final question was worded, "Are you satisfied or dissatisfied with Mrs. Thatcher as prime minister?"

ated before it could be distributed (let alone, as the socialists wanted, redistributed). The new government accordingly did not in general intervene in industrial disputes and did not erect barriers to the importation of foreign goods; but it did place strict limits on the state funding of such institutions as art galleries, opera companies, and universities, thus requiring them, if they wished to remain in existence, to look more to the private sector for support. These messages were conveyed less by words (though many words were used) than by actions. The government did not just talk tough (governments had done that before), it acted tough. Its long-term aim was to lower people's inflation expectations (to use the economists' jargon) but also, more generally, to lower their expectations of the state. There is every reason to believe that by 1983 it had achieved a considerable measure of success. The climate of opinion could be seen to be changing, slowly but in the desired direction.[22]

Table 1.2 Inflation and unemployment (quarterly averages, 1979–82)

	Percentage increase in retail price index during previous twelve months	Percent of labor force unemployed
1979		
June–September	15	6
October–December	17	5
1980		
January–March	19	6
April–June	22	6
July–September	16	8
October–December	15	8
1981		
January–March	13	10
April–June	12	10
July–September	11	11
October–December	12	12
1982		
January–March	11	12

Source: Calculated from *The Campaign Guide 1983* (London: Conservative Research Department, 1983), chap. 9.

At this point, the reader could be forgiven for supposing that the Thatcher government in the middle of its first term was a considerable success, that it was well respected by both the general public and its own supporters, with the prime minister accorded the sort of esteem normally reserved only for national leaders in wartime. The truth, in fact, was nearly the opposite. In December 1981, fewer people, 18 percent, approved of the incumbent government's record than on any occasion since the Gallup Poll started to ask the relevant question in 1945. In that same month, fewer people, 23 percent, said they would vote Conservative in an early election than had ever said they would vote for either major party since the Gallup Poll began in the late 1930s. Only two months earlier, in October 1981, Margaret Thatcher became the most unpopular prime minister since records began; only 24 percent of voters declared themselves satisfied with her.[23] Table 1.1 plots the descent of government, party, and prime minister into the electoral abyss. All three, as the table shows, recovered slightly, but only slightly, in the early months of 1982.

The reasons for the government's unpopularity are not far to seek. The most important are implicit in table 1.2. The government was elected to combat inflation. After it had been in office for one year, the rate of inflation had nearly doubled. After it had been in office for two years, the rate had fallen but was still no lower than when Labour was in power. At the end of 1981, inflation was, if anything, beginning to rise again. From the government's point of view, the trends in unemployment were even worse. The Conservatives had been careful not to commit themselves to restoring full employment. On the contrary, unlike Reagan in the United States, they had been at pains to warn the country that it might have to go through a hard transitional period, as resources were shifted from unprofitable to profitable sectors and as wasteful public expenditure was cut back. Even so, neither the Conservatives nor anyone else had prepared the British people for anything like the steep rise in unemployment that took place. When the Conservatives came to power in May 1979, 1,161,000 people, 4.9 percent of the labor force, were out of work. Thirty-one months later, in December 1981, 2,663,000 people, 11.6 percent of the labor force, were out of work. Britain, traditionally a country with little unemployment, now had one of the highest rates of unemployment in the industrial world. Worse, there seemed no end to it. As table 1.2 shows, unemployment rose inexorably. It was to go on rising for many months to come.

Inflation induced anger. Unemployment induced anger but also fear: who could be certain that his or her job might not be the next to go? Industrial production fell sharply between 1979 and 1981, and so, beginning in the third quarter of 1980, did people's real disposable incomes.[24] The political effects of all this might have been mitigated if the government had succeeded in meeting its own economic targets, if the sufferings of the present had seemed to form part of some realistic plan for the future. But something seemed to go wrong with everything the government touched. Taxes were supposed to come down; instead they went up, from just under 34 percent of gross domestic product (GDP) in 1978–79 to just under 40 percent in 1982–83. Public spending was also supposed to come down, but it also went up, from roughly 41 percent of GDP in 1978–79 to roughly 44 percent in 1982–83. Interest rates, too, were supposed to come down, but they, too, soared to record levels. Until 1982–83, the government could not even meet its own targets for reducing the rate of growth of money supply. In 1980–81, for example, Sir Geoffrey Howe announced that money supply would grow by between 7 and 11 percent; it actually grew by 19 percent. The government succeeded only in reducing the budget deficit; the "public sector borrowing requirement"—roughly, the gap that needs to be filled between total public spending and total tax receipts—fell sharply as a proportion of GDP, further than in any other industrial country.[25]

Economists and politicians still argue about how much the Thatcher government should be blamed for the depths of the post-1979 recession. The view is widely though not universally held that, by rigidly applying in government policies that had been worked out in the very different circumstances of opposition, Thatcher and her colleagues gave a sharp downward twist to an economic situation that was already deteriorating. In other words, the effects of the world recession were compounded by Thatcher and Howe's errors of timing and judgment.[26] Whether or not this assessment is correct, the government's loss of support among voters was undoubtedly compounded by the fact that, while public expenditure as a whole was going up, largely thanks to increased spending on the police and defense and also to the mounting costs of social security resulting from the recession, the amount spent on a number of services with widespread support among the public was actually declining—in real not just money terms. Real spending on education and science declined by 1.2 percent between 1978–79 and 1982–83, on the arts and libraries by 3.4 percent, on environmental services by 7.7 percent, on public housing by a massive 56.2 percent.[27] Spending on the National Health Service increased, but higher wages in the service and the growing demands made on it, together with the government's attempts to redistribute resources among the regions on a more equitable basis, inevitably meant the imposition of cuts in specific places and specific services, each cut attracting volumes of unfavorable publicity. The Conservatives, once thought of as a national party, a caring party, increasingly appeared in the public's eyes to be harsh, unconcerned, uncaring, and insensitive.[28]

Predictably, the cuts in social service spending, the government's rigid fiscal and monetary policies, the rising tide of unemployment, and the precipitous decline in the government's fortunes in by-elections and the opinion polls led to divisions in the Tory ranks and to something approaching a crisis of confidence in Margaret Thatcher's leadership. Once dubbed the Iron Lady, she was now more commonly known as Attila the Hen. In the cabinet and on the Tory back benches, battle lines were drawn between the "wets," those ministers and MPs whose skepticism about Thatcher's policies had seemingly been confirmed by events and who therefore wanted to see those policies changed, and the "drys," who remained steadfastly loyal to Thatcher and Howe and who wanted, if anything, to see the policies applied with even greater rigor.[29] On both sides, philosophical disagreements were reinforced by personal animosities. Calculated leaks to the press, hitherto a Labour prerogative, now became endemic in the Tory ranks too. Moreover, with both public spending and interest rates running at record levels, with the rising value of the pound increasingly pricing British goods out of world markets, and with bankruptcies in the private sector multiplying, a rift started to open up between the government and the ranks of its natural supporters in the business community. Sir Michael Edwardes, the managing director of British Leyland and Britain's best-known industrialist, declared at the Confederation of British Industry (CBI) conference in 1980 that the pound was overvalued, that high interest rates were leading to business penury, and that the situation was being aggravated by North Sea oil's effects on the exchange value of sterling. "If the cabinet," he went on, "do not have the wit and imagination to reconcile our industrial needs with the fact of North Sea oil, they would do better to leave the bloody stuff in the ground."[30] Sir Terence Beckett, the CBI's director-general, warned that there might have to be a "bare-knuckles fight" between the government and industry if interest rates and public spending did not begin to come down.[31] An unnamed northern industrialist was even cruder: "The trouble is with this lot, they believe that if you chop off industry's balls they'll grow again."[32]

Had the prime minister in the two and a half years after the 1979 election been anyone other than Thatcher, the government's policies might well have been changed. Certainly, of her chief rivals for the party leadership in 1975, James Prior and William Whitelaw, one, Prior, was an acknowledged wet, while the other, Whitelaw, was well known to have considerable sympathy with the wets. And pressure for change from outside the government remained intense. But Thatcher refused to be moved. She believed in her policies; she was adamant that there was no alternative to them. At the Conservatives' 1980 conference, she said flatly, "The lady's not for turning."[33] Likewise, at a CBI dinner in the summer of 1981, she quoted the First World War American general who, asked whether his troops were going to retreat in the face of an enemy onslaught, replied, "Retreat? Hell no, we've only just got here."[34] At the 1981 Conservative conference, at the nadir of her own and her party's fortunes, she reiterated her determination:

> I will not change just to court popularity. . . . If ever a Conservative government starts to do what they know to be wrong because they are afraid to do what they are sure is right, then is the time for Tories to cry "Stop." But you will never need to do that while I am prime minister.[35]

Statements like these were, in effect, invitations to the wets in the cabinet either to resign en bloc or else acquiesce in her economic policies. In the event, they did not resign either en bloc or singly. They preferred to fight a rearguard action inside the government, and in any case most of them had tacitly to acknowledge that, while they were unhappy about the general thrust of Thatcher's policies, they did not really know any better than they thought she knew how to effect a permanent recovery in Britain's economic fortunes. She had a theory. They had none. As a result, they were at an intellectual disadvantage, even though they were convinced that her theory was incorrect.[36] Their position was weakened further by the fact that, although none of them resigned, Thatcher began, gradually, in ones and twos, to push them out. She was determined not only to stick to her policies but, as far as she could, to make over the cabinet in her own image, to diminish the number of her critics, and to strengthen the position of ministers loyal to her and her ideas. In January 1981, Norman St. John-Stevas was dismissed (his sins, it was alleged, included having dubbed the prime minister "the Immaculate Misconception"). In

September of the same year, he was followed by Lord Soames, Mark Carlisle, and Sir Ian Gilmour (the latter one of Thatcher's most trenchant and outspoken critics, even while he was still a member of the government).[37] Also in September 1981, she moved Prior from his position as secretary of state for employment, where he could influence economic policy, to the position of secretary of state for Northern Ireland, where he could not. By the autumn of 1981, although her critics and potential critics still outnumbered her in the cabinet, she was now in charge for most purposes. In particular, all of the economic posts were now occupied by Thatcherites.

Nevertheless, the outlook for both the economy and the Conservative government from the winter of 1980-81 onward remained bleak. An article in the *Times* asked, "Can the Tories hope to win again?"[38] A profile of Thatcher in the *Economist* was headed "Portrait of a prime minister at bay."[39] Despite the slight upturn in the Tories' fortunes in the early months of 1982, this was still broadly the position when, on 2 April 1982, Argentina invaded the Falklands.

Labour Moves Left — and Down

The principal beneficiary of the Conservatives' difficulties between 1979 and early 1982 should have been the Labour party, especially since the Conservatives were most unpopular in fields such as employment, education, and the social services where Labour had historically been strong. In the past, Labour had reckoned to pick up support almost automatically whenever unemployment increased under a Tory government. And indeed, Labour did lead the Conservatives in the Gallup Poll, often by large margins, during the whole of the period from the May 1979 election until well into 1981. James Callaghan, the party's leader until November 1980, was a widely respected figure, and although Labour had in the end lost the 1979 election it was evident that the party could still draw on substantial reservoirs of goodwill and loyalty among the electorate. Fundamental changes were, however, taking place inside the party, and all of these changes were shortly to work to Labour's detriment.

The British Labour party has always consisted of three main elements. One is the parliamentary Labour party or PLP, the body of Labour members in the House of Commons. The second consists of trade unions affiliated to the party; they cast just under 90 percent of the vote at Labour's annual conference and contribute just under 80 percent of the party's central income. The third is made up of constituency Labour parties (CLPs), the organizations of rank-and-file party members in the constituencies, who undertake the routine work of the party and whose main political function is to select the party's parliamentary candidates. The political relationship among these three elements was reasonably straightforward during most of the postwar period. The parliamentary party was largely moderate, with right-wingers outnumbering left-wingers by about two to one. The trade unions were also largely moderate; they usually supported the parliamentary leadership, and it was an event of major significance when they did not. Only the constituency parties were largely in left-wing hands; most of the CLPs backed left-wing resolutions at the annual party conference and supported left-wing candidates for the constituency section of the National Executive Committee.[40]

Beginning in the late 1960s, however, this traditional relationship among the Labour party's constituent elements was, at first slowly but then at an accelerating rate, transformed. The PLP remained for the time being in moderate hands, but the majority of unions moved to the left, and the majority of constituency parties, already on the left, moved still further in that direction. Not only did the unions and the CLPs become far more left-wing; equally important, they became far more assertive than in the past, far more determined to claim what they saw as their legitimate rights under Labour's constitution. These changes were partly a response to the failures of the moderate-led Wilson and Callaghan Labour governments. Labour in office between 1964 and 1970, and again between 1974 and 1979, had neither "built socialism" nor solved the country's economic problems nor even been particularly successful electorally (both had given way to Tory administrations after only a few years). But they were also a response to what left-wingers saw as a lack of commitment on the part of Labour ministers and MPs. Following the disappointments of the early Wilson years, the party between 1970 and 1974 had adopted a new and very radical program, committing any future Labour government to bringing about "a fundamental and irreversible shift of power and wealth in favour of working people and their families."[41] A Labour government had duly come to power in 1974, but the desired "fundamental and irreversible shift" had not taken place or ever looked like taking place. Far from it: the economic policies pursued by the post-1974 government had been, by and large, orthodox, and many of the more radical commitments in the party's 1974 manifesto had either been explicitly abandoned or else allowed to slip quietly down toward the bottom—or even off the bottom—of the government's agenda.[42]

The result, not surprisingly, was a sense of outrage among many trade union leaders and, even more, among many party activists in the constituencies. They felt that they had been badly let down—worse than that, cheated—by the party's parliamentary leaders who, they believed, had never had any intention of carrying out the wishes of the party in the country, even though those wishes had been formally embodied in party policy. They drew the conclusion from this experience that it was not enough to adopt left-wing policies: they must devise means whereby the party's leaders in the House of Commons could be made more accountable to the party conference and the rank and file. As early as June 1973, a Campaign for Labour Party Democracy (CLPD) was launched with the express aim of achieving this greater degree of accountability. The great majority of those who supported CLPD were democrats, both in the sense that they believed in British-style parliamentary democracy and in the sense that they were prepared to function openly, in strict accordance with the Labour party's rules, in the furtherance of their objectives. They were not conspirators, and anyone who took the trouble could easily find out what they were up to.[43]

At the same time, however, as the perfectly aboveboard CLPD was gaining rank-and-file support, the party was also being joined—their enemies said "infiltrated"—by leftist elements of an altogether less benign character, by people, mainly Trotskyists, who were not democrats in anything like the generally accepted sense, who advocated, in many cases, the violent overthrow of the capitalist order and who, again in many cases, were quite ready, in their struggle to gain control of CLPs, to resort to tactics of verbal abuse, harassment, and intimidation. In practice, since both the constitutionalists and the Trotskyists inside the party wanted to turn Labour MPs into little more than parliamentary spokesmen for the party outside Parliament, and since the left-socialist policy aims of the two groups were often almost identical, it was not surprising that those outside CLPD and the various ultraleft factions often failed to distinguish between them. It was also the case that, since the two groups shared so many aims, and since they believed that they had a common enemy in the form of the existing parliamentary leadership, they increasingly collaborated with one another, forging a wide range of single-purpose and ad hoc alliances. More and more was heard of the most important Trotskyist group, the Militant Tendency, and also of bodies like the Rank and File Mobilizing Committee, which brought together Trotskyists and leaders of CLPD. Nevertheless, the central point remains that the Trotskyists, however unpleasant, were at every stage more nuisance than menace. The main impetus for change within the Labour party came from ordinary party members.[44]

The shift to the left and the rank and file's new assertiveness manifested themselves in four main ways. First, successive annual conferences moved the party's policies further and further in a leftward direction. In 1973, toward the end of Labour's last period in opposition, the conference had adopted *Labour's Programme for Britain*, widely described at the time as the most radical policy statement in the whole of the party's history.[45] A decade later, in March 1983, the party published *Labour's Plan: The New Hope for Britain*, based on four years of policy work initiated by the National Executive Committee and approved by the party conference.[46] It is instructive to compare the two documents. In 1973, the party talked vaguely of reducing the Atlantic alliance's reliance on nuclear weapons and of reviewing the position of Britain's independent nuclear deterrent, based on Polaris missiles. In 1983, the party committed itself to unilateral nuclear disarmament, to abandoning Britain's existing Polaris weapons, to canceling the Conservative government's plans for the purchase of Trident, to refusing to accept the deployment of American Cruise missiles on British soil, and to requiring that the United States withdraw all of its nuclear weapons already based in Britain. In 1973, *Labour's Programme* spoke of the desirability of renegotiating the terms of Britain's entry into the Common Market, with the results of any renegotiation to be put to the British people either in a referendum on the issue or at a new general election. In 1983, *New Hope for Britain* pledged that the next Labour government would, without a referendum, take Britain out of the Common Market forthwith. The 1973 document promised to repeal the anti-trade-union legislation passed by the Heath government and it spoke, in general terms, of the need for closer cooperation between a new Labour government and the trade union movement. The 1983 document not only promised to repeal the Tories' 1980 and 1982 Employment Acts but promised a whole series of measures—on economic planning, on prices and incomes, on industrial democracy—that would have the effect of making the trade unions, formally as well as informally, an integral part of the country's entire structure for the making of economic policy. Labour's program in 1973 contained roughly a dozen proposals for the extension of public ownership (and one of the most important of these was subsequently dropped from the party's 1974 election manifesto). Labour's program in 1983 contained nearly thirty proposals for the extension of public ownership (none of which was dropped from the manifesto).[47] And so it went. In its declared policies, Labour by the early 1980s was scarcely recognizable as the party of Clement Attlee and Hugh Gaitskell (or even, as they themselves conceded privately, that of Harold Wilson and James Callaghan).

Second, changes in the party's policies were accompanied by important changes in its constitution. The left and its allies wanted to remove responsibility for drawing up the party's election manifesto from a joint meeting of the National Executive and the cabinet (or shadow cabinet) and place it in the sole hands of the National Executive. The aim was to prevent the moderates in the cabinet or shadow cabinet from vetoing proposals emanating from the National Executive, a body that was much more likely to have a left-wing majority. In this, the CLPD and its allies failed, losing by a narrow margin in a vote at the 1980 party conference. They succeeded, however, in achieving all of their other main objectives. Power to elect the party's leader had been, since the turn of the century, in the hands of Labour MPs, but at the party's regular conference at Blackpool in October 1980 the decision was taken in principle to transfer the election of the leader and deputy leader from the PLP to a more broadly based electoral college, and at a specially convened conference at Wembley in January 1981 it was decided that 40 percent of the votes in the electoral college should be cast by trade unions and another 30 percent by CLPs, leaving only the remaining 30 percent for the hitherto dominant MPs. This decision had, as we shall see, momentous consequences.

The 1980 Blackpool conference also confirmed a decision made a year earlier to require the "mandatory reselection" of Labour MPs. Under the previous arrangements, a sitting Labour MP could be ousted as the Labour candidate for his constituency only if his local party supporters took positive steps to oust him; he had personally to be repudiated. Now, under the new arrangements, every Labour MP had, in the course of every four- or five-year Parliament, to submit himself to reselection under a procedure that made it relatively easy for rival candidates to be put up against him. The left, operating on the principle that "you can't beat somebody with nobody," hoped and expected that mandatory reselection would make it easier for left-wing constituency parties to deselect right-wing sitting MPs and, by the same token, that fear of deselection would encourage right-wing MPs to move, or seem to move, to the left.[48] In a further step in the direction of increasing accountability, the January 1981 special conference also decided that, in future elections for the leadership and deputy leadership, the votes of every individual and organization would be recorded. It would no longer be possible for moderate Labour MPs (or trade union leaders or constituency delegates) to cast their ballots in secret for moderate candidates. From now on everyone in the party was to know what everyone else in the party was doing.

The third manifestation of Labour's shift to the left—and of the rank and file's increased assertiveness—related, like one of the constitutional changes just described, to the selection and reselection (or, alternatively, deselection) of Labour's parliamentary candidates. Although left-wingers had long been preponderant in the majority of constituency parties, they had never, rather oddly from their point of view, shown much interest in selecting left-wing candidates. Like others in the party, they had tended at constituency selection conferences to vote for "the best man" (or, more rarely, the best woman) and, if the best man turned out, as frequently happened, to hold right-wing opinions, those on the left still appeared to be content.[49] From the late 1960s onward, however, more and more left-dominated constituency parties showed themselves determined to ascertain the political views of the aspiring MPs who appeared before them and, having ascertained them, to select only those they considered sufficiently left-wing. One result was that, as each new cohort of Labour MPs entered the House of Commons, it was seen to contain a higher ratio of left-wingers to right-wingers than the one before. After the 1979 election, in particular, the Labour candidates selected for winnable seats were overwhelmingly on the left of the party (the majority of them on what was known by that time as the "hard left").[50] In addition, constituency Labour parties increasingly refused to readopt right-wing sitting MPs. In the whole of the period from 1950 to 1974, only three sitting Labour MPs were denied readoption on mainly political grounds. In the much shorter period from 1974 to 1979, three more suffered this fate. In the still shorter period from 1979 to 1981, eight more were denied reselection. All but one of the eight was a right-winger, and even the one left-winger deselected was replaced by someone who was even further to the left than he was.[51] The moderates' traditional hold on the PLP was thus progressively weakened, partly because of changes in its membership and partly because more and more of the remaining moderates (still a majority in the PLP in the 1979–83 period) became hesitant about expressing their moderate views.

Finally, the party's shift to the left was one of the factors that led in November 1980 to the election of Michael Foot to succeed James Callaghan as party leader. Callaghan had soldiered on for a time after the 1979 election, apparently hoping that he could use his influence, if not to stem completely the left-wing tide that threatened to engulf the party, then at least to direct it into reasonably safe channels. But he was getting on in years (he was 68 in 1980); the constitutional changes made at the 1980 party conference, notably the change in the method of electing the party's leader, probably convinced him that, in the short term at least, the moderates' cause was hopeless; and he probably also wished to resign before the institution of the new electoral college in January 1981 so that Labour MPs should, on this one last occasion, have the opportunity to choose their own leader.[52] Whatever his precise motives, Callaghan announced in mid-October 1980 that he would soon be giving up his post.

Four senior Labour members stood in the ensuing election: Denis Healey, a tough former defense minister and chancellor of the exchequer, the acknowledged candidate of the right; John Silkin, a relatively unknown centrist who declared himself to be the candidate of party unity; Peter Shore, another centrist who had originally hoped to be acceptable as the candidate of the left; and Michael Foot, who, although relatively inexperienced as a minister and only a year younger than Callaghan, allowed himself at the last minute to be talked into standing with the backing of more or less the whole of the party's left wing. (Foot later told the press that, if he had not stood, his wife, a former actress, might have divorced him.) In the first ballot, on November 4, Healey obtained 112 votes, Foot 83, Silkin 38, Shore 32. Silkin and Shore then dropped out, both announcing that they now intended to support Foot. In the second ballot, on November 11, the majority of Silkin's and Shore's supporters duly voted for Foot, who was declared the winner by 139 votes to Healey's 129. Appearing with his wife on television that night, Foot was almost tearful in his elation and surprise.[53]

The election of Michael Foot was not necessarily the most important development in the Labour party between 1979 and 1983, but it was certainly the most bizarre. In the previous *Britain at the Polls* volume, attention was drawn to the fact that British MPs, in choosing party leaders, often show a remarkable lack of interest in electoral considerations. In 1975, the general public wanted Whitelaw as leader of the Tory party; it got Thatcher. A year later, the public wanted Callaghan as Labour leader and prime minister; it did get him in the end, but only after he had been runner-up to Foot in the first ballot.[54] This pattern was repeated in November 1980, but on an even grander scale than before. Shortly before the first ballot in 1980, the Gallup Poll asked a sample of the general public, "Do you think _____ would or would not be a good leader of the Labour party?" Nearly two-thirds of Gallup's respondents, 64 percent, thought that Healey would be a good leader, only 21 percent that he would not. If the latter figure is subtracted from the former, Healey's overall approval rating works out at +43. By contrast, only 30 percent of Gallup's sample thought that Foot would make a good leader, compared with 55 percent who thought that he would not, yielding an overall approval (or, rather, disapproval) rating for Foot of −25.[55] The two men could hardly have been further apart. Yet Foot won. The left, now far larger in the parliamentary party than ever before, voted for him solidly, but it seems that what put him over the top was a minority of MPs on the right and in the center of the party who believed that Foot, unlike Healey, could maintain some semblance of party unity.[56] If they did believe this, they were soon to be rudely undeceived.

In fact, Foot turned out to be, with the possible exception of George Lansbury, who functioned briefly as Labour leader in the 1930s, the worst leader of any major political party since Britain became a democracy. He failed to preserve the unity of his party. He was held in utter contempt by a large minority of his own followers, including many members of the shadow cabinet. He was never taken seriously by the press. He was at no time regarded by the majority of the electorate either as a good leader of the Labour party or as someone who would make a good prime minister. British readers of this book, having seen Foot on television, will be familiar with his thick spectacles, his disheveled clothes, his jerky puppetlike walk, strongly reminiscent of Charlie Chaplin's, his rambling speeches, and his complete inability ever to offer straightforward, well-informed answers to questions asked by television interviewers; they may recall that he was dubbed "Worzel Gummidge" after a character in children's fiction who resembled an amiable but demented scarecrow. But American readers can perhaps gain some idea of the impression he made on the general public from the opening two paragraphs of a sketch of Foot attending a trade union conference that appeared in the *Times* in the summer of 1981:

> Simply to look at, he was like any other old age pensioner from the traditional public service class enjoying Bournemouth this week: white-haired, courtly, still with his wits about him though occasionally a little forgetful, and perhaps rather out of place while the resort was taken over for the annual delegate conference of the Iron and Steel Trades Confederation. Yet this was no ordinary leader of the Labour party. This was Michael Foot.
>
> In these days of rapid change, he tends to be forgotten. But he still takes a lively interest in what is going on. For example, they tell him that

the country now has a woman prime minister. Bless my soul! And from what he has heard, he didn't like the sound of her. "I repeat, the economic policy of this government is a CATASTROPHE," he bawled at the steelmen.[57]

The writer went on to note that Foot, having been elected by the left wing of the Labour party, increasingly found himself under attack by the left as he tried, in vain, to maintain some kind of balance between the party's two wings.

Labour's shift to the left, culminating in the election of Foot, was observed with growing distaste by substantial majorities of ordinary voters. In response to a Gallup survey in October 1980, considerable numbers of voters gave the strength of the left as one reason for disliking the party. In early 1981 another polling organization found that 69 percent of its respondents agreed with the proposition that "the Labour party is moving too much to the left for my liking."[58] Labour's electoral decline from early 1981 until the eve of the Falklands war is documented in table 1.3, which also records the sharp drop in the proportion of voters believing that Foot (in italics) as compared with Callaghan (in roman type) was proving a good party leader. Foot in February 1981 became the least well regarded leader of the opposition since the Second World War, but he was to break his own record many times during the coming months.[59]

Both Labour's shift to the left and the party's growing disunity (in October 1980, fully 83 percent of Gallup's monthly sample thought that Labour was disunited) were underlined during the first nine months of 1981 by a contest for the deputy leadership, the first to be held under the new rules, between Denis Healey and the champion of the hard left, Tony Benn.[60] Day after day, week after week, practically everything about the Labour party that appeared on television or in the press concerned the deputy leadership contest, which was bitter and acrimonious and from which it looked as though the left-winger Benn might emerge victorious. In the end, Healey, who had previously been elected deputy leader by the PLP, was confirmed in his post, but by the tiniest of margins: 0.85 percent of the electoral college.[61] The Healey–Benn fight was terribly damaging. It was not nearly as damaging, however, as the other development that made 1981 Labour's *annus horrendus*—the formation of the new Social Democratic party.

Breakaway and Alliance

Labour's electoral fortunes were in decline in 1981–82. So were the Conservatives'. If the British party system had still been a two-party system, this could not have happened; one party's loss would have been the other's gain. But from the early spring of 1981 the British party system was no longer a two-party system. A third force, with greater potential than any since the 1920s,

Table 1.3 Public standings of Labour party,
Callaghan, Foot (quarterly averages, 1979–82)

	Percent intending to vote Labour	Percent believing Callaghan, then Foot proving good leader of Labour party[a]
1979		
June–September	45	59
October–December	44	55
1980		
January–March	46	52
April–June	45	51
July–October	44	49
November–December	48	*34*
1981		
January–March	39	*24*
April–June	36	*25*
July–September	39	*25*
October–December	27	*21*
1982		
January–March	32	*19*

Source: Gallup Political Index.
Note: For the details of the voting-intention question, see the note to table 1.1. The question of the Labour leader was worded, "Do you think Mr. Callaghan/Mr. Foot is or is not proving a good leader of the Labour party?"
[a] Callaghan was leader of the Labour party until November 1980. Foot succeeded him in that month. Accordingly, Callaghan's last four months as leader are reported in the table, Foot's first two months. Callaghan's standing as Labour leader is given in roman type, Foot's in italic.

had arrived on the scene. Its sources lay partly in the Liberal party, partly in the increasingly left-inclined and divided Labour party.

The Liberals, formerly the proud party of Gladstone, Asquith, and Lloyd George, had effectively been outsiders in British politics for the previous half-century. By the early 1980s, no Liberal leader or MP had ever been in government, the party lacked a stable electoral base, and it showed no real signs of being able to overcome the obstacle posed by Britain's first-past-the-post electoral system. However many votes they got, the Liberals won very few seats in the House of Commons.[62] Nevertheless, the Liberals' standing with the voters gradually improved over the 1960s and 1970s, largely as the result of the growing unpopularity of the other two parties. Whereas in the five general elections of the 1950s the Liberals' average share of the vote was a mere 5.1 percent, in the two elections of the 1960s it was 9.9 percent, and in the four elections of the 1970s 14.7 percent.[63] In the general election of February 1974, the last in which an unpopular Conservative government had faced a divided Labour opposition, the Liberals had won the support of nearly one voter in five, 19.3 percent. But despite this gradual improvement and despite the fact that their leader, David Steel, was one of the most popular politicians in the country, the Liberals in the year and a half after the 1979 election did not fare especially well. They won no seats in by-elections and their standing in the Gallup Poll edged up only slightly. In December 1980, for example, 14.5 percent of voters told Gallup they would vote Liberal at an early election—less than 1 percent more than had actually done so eighteen months before. The Liberals clearly needed some additional stimulus if they were to persuade voters that they were a serious political proposition and that a Liberal vote was not necessarily a wasted vote. That stimulus was provided, early in 1981, by the Social Democrats.

From what has been said already, the dismay with which many Labour moderates viewed the developments inside their own party can be imagined. They were anti-Soviet and pro-NATO; the party was increasingly anti-American, anti-NATO, and neutralist. Most on the right of the party were pro-European; the party was now committed to pulling Britain out of Europe. The moderates were increasingly critical of the trade unions; the party was tying itself to the unions more and more firmly. The moderates' whole political approach was gradualist and reformist; the party was increasingly radical and revolutionary. To a man and woman the moderates were liberals and democrats, but they saw some trade unions, and many more constituency parties, being taken over by what they termed the "illegitimate left"—totalitarians and revolutionary Marxists whose doctrines and tactics they found deeply abhorrent.[64] Some of the more prominent right-wingers also found themselves in an increasingly uncomfortable moral position. The party had moved left. They had not moved left with it. Yet the frontbench spokesmen among them were expected in the interests of party unity to advocate—or at least not publicly repudiate—policies that they did not believe in, indeed that in some cases they strongly objected to. The situation was even worse for those right-wingers, a small but significant minority, who not only had failed to move left with the party but had, on the contrary, come to have grave doubts about the intellectual basis of democratic socialism. Most of those who were unhappy said of the Labour party, "It is no longer the party I joined." A few said, in effect, "Even if it were still the party I joined, I am no longer really sure that it would have the answers to the country's problems."

A gulf had opened up between the Labour party's policies and the personal convictions of many of its MPs and supporters in the country and, inevitably, some people began to contemplate the idea of quitting Labour and forming a new political party that would be somewhere on the center-left of British politics.[65] Some took up the idea readily, others very reluctantly, but, either way, they did so in increasing numbers, especially after the October 1980 conference at which most of the major constitutional changes described earlier were either instituted or confirmed and at which British withdrawal from the Common Market was formally written into the party program. One of the first to conclude that there was no alternative to the formation of a new party was Roy Jenkins, former Labour chancellor of the exchequer, former deputy leader of the Labour party, twice home secretary in Labour administrations. Jenkins in 1980, however, was absent in Brussels as president of the European Commission and, although he was due to return to Britain at the beginning of 1981, there was little he could do in the meantime except make occasional speeches (his televised Dimbleby Lecture in November 1979 caused a considerable stir) and keep in touch with his friends.[66] The initiative was increasingly taken by three former cabinet ministers still in Britain and still in the party, the so-called gang of three: David Owen, who had been foreign secretary in the Callaghan government; William Rodgers, who had been Callaghan's transport minister and, more important, had a considerable personal following on the Labour back benches; and Shirley Williams, another former minister who was the most popular of the three inside the party (she had been for nearly a decade a member of Labour's National Executive) and also in the country generally.[67]

For them and for others similarly placed, the issue of whether or not to quit Labour and form a new party raised more than just abstract questions of political philosophy. It involved the likelihood of destroying old friendships and the certainty of breaking emotional ties that had lasted a lifetime. It also involved taking enormous risks. A few of those thinking of setting up a new party were so fed up with Labour that they were not in the business of making fine political calculations, but the great majority of potential defectors, perhaps more emotionally tied to the party, possibly with more at stake personally, had to ask themselves a series of practical political questions. One was whether the moderates' cause in the party was indeed hopeless, as it increasingly appeared, or whether some turn of the political wheel might not restore the right to its previously dominant position. Another was whether Labour in anything like its present condition could—as distinct from should—win a future general election. If the answer to this question was no, that a divided Labour party with left-wing policies and leaders had no chance of winning a future election, then to remain loyal to Labour might be merely quixotic; but if the answer was yes, that Labour did have some chance of winning despite its current policies and leadership, then perhaps the moderates ought to stay on, in the hope that Labour in government might, as had happened in the past, turn out to be more sensible and worthwhile than Labour in opposition.[68] Potential defectors had also to decide whether a new party, presumably in alliance with the Liberals, had any real chance of attracting support in the country. Could it win votes? If not, then the obvious course for any disaffected Labour politician would be to leave politics completely. No one could avoid thinking sooner or later about his or her own political future. There might seem no way forward in the Labour party, but the precedent of the Liberals—with a fair number of votes, but precious few seats in the House of Commons—was not exactly encouraging.

Most of the potential defectors agonized for months, and in the end a number of them decided that they could not bring themselves to desert Labour. The issues were finely balanced; the deepest emotions and loyalties were engaged; everyone in the end had to decide for himself. Even so, a handful of Labour MPs decided to leave the party even before the disastrous 1980 conference, and several more concluded soon after the conference that the game was up. Another group decided to leave when, to their dismay and astonishment, Foot rather than Healey was elected Labour leader in November. Still, even after Foot's election, a substantial number of the moderates—notably William Rodgers and Shirley Williams—went on hoping against hope that somehow or other Foot would show signs of wanting to, and being able to, stem the left-wing tide. For this last group, the moment of final decision came at the special party conference at Wembley in January 1981. The special conference rejected decisively the right's plea that the new electoral college should be founded on the principle of one member, one vote and opted instead, as we saw earlier, for a 40:30:30 arrangement, with the trade unions having the largest say. That was it. The day after the Wembley conference the gang of three, together with Roy Jenkins, met at David Owen's house in east London to sign the Limehouse Declaration and to announce the formation of an interim Council for Social Democracy. During the next few weeks, they and eleven other Labour MPs (in addition to Owen and Rodgers) severed their remaining links with Labour, and on 26 March 1981 the new party was launched in a whirlwind of publicity.[69] The name Social Democratic all but chose itself. Television and the newspapers needed to call the new grouping something. They began to use the phrase Social Democratic. People seemed to know what it referred to. The name stuck.

The short-term success of the new party was phenomenal. The Social Democrats (SDP) were "box office." Here was a brand-new political party, the first with any real political pretensions since the early 1930s, quite possibly since 1900; yet, although new, the party was led, unlike any of its predecessors, by familiar, popular politicians, capable of holding their own in television debates, able to attract vast audiences to public meetings.[70] More than enough money was raised to make the party viable; members were recruited at the rate of more than a thousand each week; the comings and goings of Jenkins, Owen, Rodgers, and Williams—the gang of three had, inevitably, become the gang of four—were reported avidly; and the SDP's red, white, and blue logo was to be seen everywhere. The new party's enemies maintained, sometimes dismissively, sometimes fearfully, that the SDP was "a media creation." In one sense, they were wrong: the media could hardly have ignored one of the great political events of the decade, and much of the comment in the press was in fact hostile, even contemptuous. But, in another sense, they were right: the SDP's initial success owed much to the fact that, for nearly a year, the party was seldom off the nation's television screens, seldom far from the front pages of its newspapers.

The SDP in its early days was featured in the news so often largely because it and its leaders were at the center of developments that the media deemed newsworthy (developments that were bound to be contrasted favorably with mounting unemployment and the endless bickering between wets and drys on the Tory side and with the acrimonious Healey–Benn deputy leadership contest in the Labour party). One such development, helpful to the new party, damaging to Labour, was the slow but steady procession of Labour backbench MPs out of the Labour party and into the SDP. Thirteen Labour MPs and a maverick Tory were members of the SDP at the time of the launch in March 1981. Another Labour member joined in July, another in September, seven more in October, another in November, two more in December, yet another in March 1982.[71] The process seemed inexorable; no one could see an end to it. The great majority of the Labour MPs who defected were political unknowns and some were accused of jumping before they were pushed.[72] All the same, the total body of defectors, numbering thirty at the end, included, apart from the gang of four itself, four ex-ministers, all of them young, and the man who had been chief political adviser to James Callaghan in Downing Street.[73]

Another development that attracted publicity and was important in itself was the gradual piecing together of an alliance between the Social Democrats and the Liberals. A few in each party dissented, but the overwhelming majority of both were overjoyed at the prospect of at last achieving a breakthrough by the political center and of breaking the long Labour and Conservative monopoly of power. Roy Jenkins and Shirley Williams were rapturously received at the September 1981 Liberal assembly, amid scenes of near-religious fervor; and David Steel's peroration at the end of that assembly captured the optimism of the time:

> Now at last we have the reality in our grasp. We must have the nerve and courage not to let it slip. I have the good fortune to be the first Liberal leader for over half a century who is able to say to you at the end of our annual assembly: go back to your constituencies and prepare for government.[74]

The Liberals insisted that any pact between the two parties must not be for purely electoral purposes, that there must be a substantial measure of agreement on policy. In the event, few policy disagreements between the two parties arose. They were, after all, at one in being libertarian, in being committed to the welfare state (unlike the post-1979 Conservatives), in being committed to free enterprise and the market economy (unlike the post-1979 Labour party), and also in being committed to both the European Community and the Atlantic alliance (again unlike post-1979 Labour). Both parties were keen on electoral reform (though most of the Social Democrats, it must be said, were recent converts to the cause). They tended to differ only to the extent that Social Democrats were still more centralist and state-socialist in their views than the majority of Liberals, while most Liberals were "greener"—more concerned with ecology and the environment—and more devolutionist than most Social Democrats.[75] The two parties also had no difficulty in agreeing that, in the next general election, they should each fight roughly half of the parliamentary constituencies in the country. The other parties took a predictably sardonic view of all this matiness: "Take the politics out of politics," read a lapel badge on sale at the 1981 Labour conference, "join the SDP." Nevertheless, the Liberals and Social Democrats undoubtedly succeeded at this stage in creating an impression of niceness, of friendliness, of two parties prepared to work together in the national interest.

The new Alliance's niceness, its novelty, its middle-of-the-road image, the volume of favorable publicity it received, and the popularity of its leaders at once combined with the widespread popular alienation from the other two parties to produce a surge of electoral support for the Liberals and Social Democrats unprecedented in British history. Someone remarked that the launch of the Alliance reminded him of one of those giant rockets lifting off from Cape Kennedy. A widely reprinted cartoon from February 1981 showed the gang of four in a small boat borne aloft by a seal labeled "opinion polls seal of approval." The four in the boat looked amazed and a little apprehensive, and William Rodgers was depicted as saying, "What do you mean, can't we slow down a bit? We haven't even started the motor yet!"[76] The Liberals' 14.5 percent in the Gallup Poll in December 1980 had more than doubled to 32 percent for the Liberals and Social Democrats together by the time of the new party's launch in March 1981. The Alliance vied with the Conservatives for second place to Labour during most of that spring and summer. Then, in October, the Alliance overtook both the Conservatives and Labour, 40 percent of the electorate saying they would vote for it in an early election. That figure became 50.5 percent in December 1981—the highest figure recorded by Gallup for any party during the whole of the 1979 Parliament. Table 1.4 charts, on the same basis as tables 1.1 and 1.3, the Liberals' and then the Alliance's progress from the time of the 1979 general election until the spring of 1982.

Even greater shock waves emanated from the four by-elections held during this period. In July 1981, Roy Jenkins became the first SDP parliamentary can-

Table 1.4 Public standings of Liberal party,
Liberal-SDP Alliance (quarterly averages, 1979–82)

	Percent intending to vote Liberal, then for Liberal-SDP Alliance[a]
1979	
June–September	12
October–December	16
1980	
January–March	15
April–June	14
July–September	15
October–December	15
1981	
January–March	*24*
April–June	*31*
July–September	*26*
October–December	*44*
1982	
January–March	*36*

Source: Gallup Political Index.
Note: For the details of the voting-intention question, see the note to table 1.1.
[a] The Social Democratic party was not launched officially until March 1981, but the Gallup Poll began to pick up considerable numbers of voters saying that they would vote for the SDP from January 1981 onward. The figure for the quarter January-March 1981 includes these prelaunch SDP supporters. The figures from the beginning of 1981 onward include all those who, asked for their voting intention, replied Liberal or SDP or Alliance. These figures are given in italics.

didate, contesting the northern industrial seat of Warrington where the Liberal stood down. Warrington had always been a safe Labour seat and everyone thought that Jenkins was running an enormous personal risk in fighting it. Jenkins agreed. Yet at the by-election he raised the Liberal's 1979 share of the vote, 9 percent, to 42.4 percent and, although Labour held the seat, its share of the general election vote dropped by more than one-fifth. The Tories, finishing third, lost three-quarters of their 1979 vote.[77] Three months later, in October 1981, an unknown Liberal gained the London suburban seat of Croydon North West from the Conservatives. In November 1981, Shirley Williams took the Merseyside seat of Crosby, also from the Conservatives, winning 49.1 percent of the vote. She managed to lop nearly one-third off the Tories' 1979 share of the vote and nearly two-thirds off Labour's. Finally, in March of the following year Roy Jenkins was returned to Parliament for the Glasgow seat of Hillhead. His share of the vote, 33.4 percent, was lower than the others', but he faced Scottish National as well as Conservative and Labour opposition.

A pace like this could not be maintained and by the spring of 1982, as table 1.4 shows, the Alliance's standing in the Gallup Poll had fallen back considerably. The government began to pull itself together, the destructive contest between Healey and Benn in the Labour party was over, and a public row within the Alliance over the allocation of seats between the two Alliance partners inevitably caused damage. Nevertheless, the Liberals and Social Democrats, even if they had ceased to be euphoric, remained tolerably confident. The Alliance led both the Conservatives and the Labour party in the Gallup Poll in two of the first three months of 1982 and was tied with Labour, just ahead of the Tories, in the third. Hillhead had been harder going than either Croydon or Crosby, but it had been won. Anyone in the spring of 1982 told that the Alliance partners would shortly fall into third place in the opinion polls, and would remain there for the rest of the Parliament, would have been disposed to attribute such an abrupt and total reversal of political fortune to an act of God.

The Falklands and After

Argentina invaded the Falkland Islands at the beginning of April 1982. The British government was taken completely unaware. It announced the next day, under intense pressure from its own backbench supporters in the House of Commons, that it was assembling a naval task force for immediate dispatch to the South Atlantic. The islands would be retaken by force if British efforts to recover them by diplomatic means proved unsuccessful. The task force arrived in the waters off the Falklands on 22 April. British troops landed at San Carlos Bay on 21 May, captured Port Darwin and Goose Green on 28 May, and then set off across the rugged terrain of East Falkland toward the capital, Port Stanley. British marines and soldiers captured the high ground around Port Stanley in early June and, on 14 June, as the British prepared for their final assault on the town, the Argentinian garrison surrendered. Major-General Jeremy Moore, commander of the British land forces, cabled to the government in London:

> In Port Stanley at 9 PM Falkland Islands time tonight, 14 June 1982, Major-General Menendez surrendered to me all the Argentine armed forces in East and West Falkland, together with their impediments. Arrangements are in hand to assemble the men for return to Argentina, to gather in their arms and equipment, and to mark and make safe their munitions. The Falkland Islands are once more under the government desired by their inhabitants. God save the Queen.[78]

Britain had lost 255 men killed, 777 wounded. Argentinian casualties were far higher.[79]

The Falklands war—and, more to the point, Britain's victory in that war—transformed British politics. In the last Gallup Poll taken before the Argentinian invasion, that of March 1982, the electorate was divided into three more or less equal parts: 31.5 percent said they would vote Conservative in an early election, 33 percent Labour, and 33 percent Alliance. The percentage satisfied with Margaret Thatcher as prime minister was 34. The first Gallup survey conducted after the surrender of Port Stanley, that of June 1982, showed that the political landscape had changed almost beyond recognition. The Conservatives, narrowly in third place in March, were now far out in the lead, 16.5 percentage points ahead of the Alliance, 20 ahead of Labour. The proportion of voters saying they would back the Tories in an early election had shot up from 31.5 percent in March to 45 percent in June; the Alliance and Labour, both with 33 percent in March, had fallen by June to 28.5 percent and 25 percent, respectively. The prime minister's own standing was likewise transformed; the 34 percent satisfied with her in March had become 51 percent by June.[80] A few short weeks before, many inside her own party had regarded her as an electoral liability. Now she was indubitably an asset. Her authority as prime minister was never challenged again.

Even better evidence of the changes in public opinion wrought by the Falklands war is to be found in a series of panel surveys carried out for the *Economist* magazine by Market and Opinion Research International (MORI).[81] Members of the panel were interviewed as many as five times in the course of the Falklands conflict. The proportion of them satisfied with the government's handling of the invasion and the war gradually increased from 60 percent to 84 percent. When the war was over, 7 percent of MORI's respondents said that their opinion of Thatcher had gone down because of it; 45 percent said that their opinion of her was more favorable than before. Like Gallup, MORI found a strong surge of support for the Conservative party. Asked, "How would you vote if there was a general election tomorrow?" 34 percent of MORI's panel said they would vote Conservative after the Argentinian invasion but before the British task force arrived in the Falklands. That figure had risen to 51 percent by the time the war was over. Never again after the Falklands war did the Conservatives surrender their lead over all the other parties. Never again did their support in the polls fall below 40 percent.

The Falklands war was a relatively minor affair. It never engaged Britain's national interests, though it did engage its pride. Why did it have such an immediate and profound impact? In particular, why did it give such a fillip—and such a long-lasting fillip—to the Thatcher government's fortunes?[82]

Unfortunately, hard data bearing directly on these questions are lacking, but a complete and satisfactory answer to them would probably contain at least four elements. In the first place, and most obviously, any government that had defied a foreign enemy, engaged it, and succeeded in defeating it would be bound to have reaped a considerable reward in terms of public esteem. Second, and less obviously, the size of the reward to any Conservative government would probably have been greater than that to any Labour government, since the Conservatives have always been more closely associated in the British people's minds with the symbols of British nationhood. The Conservatives at their annual conference sing "Land of Hope and Glory" and drape the platform with the Union Jack; Labour delegates at their conference sing "The Red Flag," and the Union Jack is never anywhere to be seen. Third, many people in Britain must have responded favorably to the spectacle of a British government, at last, after so many years of disappointment and national humiliation, acting decisively and taking a lead, especially in foreign affairs. Talk of the Dunkirk spirit was a drug on the market; it was nice to see some of that spirit in action for a change.[83]

But these factors, even if taken together, cannot account for the fact that the government not only recovered its position in the eyes of the electorate but remained in a commanding position for the whole of the rest of the Parliament (and indeed for many months after that). It was probably the fourth element in what became known as "the Falklands factor" that was crucial. The Thatcher government had come to power in 1979 committed to a set of substantive policies, but also to a new style of government: unswerving, dogged, determined. The national interest required that tough decisions be taken. The government would take them. The government would, moreover, stick to them, even if they became unpopular. It would persevere. And, because the government had such courage and determination, and because the decisions were the right decisions, it would win in the end. There would, under a Thatcher government, be no hesitations, no turnings back. In the short term, as we saw earlier in the chapter, this approach made Margaret Thatcher's government one of the most unpopular in British history. The Falklands war, however, and Britain's victory in it, seemed a vindication, a triumphant vindication, of this particular style. Tough decisions had been taken. They had been followed through. Britain had won. People, including many people who did not become Conservatives overnight, were impressed. In other words, the government benefited so much from the Falklands war, and for such a long time, in large part because its conduct of the war could so easily be seen as a grand metaphor of its conduct of affairs generally. A style that before the war had seemed blundering and inept suddenly, during and after the war, seemed heroic and farsighted. To repeat, this view of the Falklands factor is impossible to prove; but any alternative view is hard to square with the scale and the long-lasting quality of the public's response.

No one will ever know how British party politics would have developed if

Table 1.5 Public standing of government, parties, and leaders, inflation and unemployment (quarterly averages, 1982–83)

	Percent approving of government's record to date	Voting intention			Leaders		Percentage increase in retail price index during previous twelve months	Percent of labor force unemployed
		Con.	Lab.	All.	Thatcher	Foot		
1982								
January–March	26	29	32	36	32	19	11	12
April–June	41	40	27	32	43	18	9	12
July–September	43	45	29	25	50	16	8	12
October–December	39	41	33	24	45	21	6	13
1983								
January–March	41	43	31	25	45	18	5	13
April–May	42	45	34	21	47	20	4	13

Note: For the wordings of the questions and sources, see the notes and sources to the previous tables in this chapter.

the war in the Falklands had not taken place. The political scientist looking at the figures finds it hard to resist the conclusion that the war was decisive and that, but for the war, the Conservatives would probably not have been returned with an overall parliamentary majority at the next election. Be that as it may, the Falklands war was not the only factor influencing voters' evaluations of the government and, even without the war, it seems likely that there would have been some improvement in the Conservatives' position, some deterioration in that of the Alliance.

The main factors working in the Conservatives' favor, apart from the Falklands, were a gradual but steady reduction in the rate of inflation and a similar reduction, not in the absolute number of men and women out of work, but at least in the rate at which the number of people out of work was increasing. Both trends are evident from table 1.5, which sets out the parties' standings as well as the inflation and unemployment rates for the period from January 1982 until the general election of June 1983, and which should be read in conjunction with the four previous tables in this chapter. As can be seen, the rate of inflation, having peaked in the spring of 1980, fell gradually during the rest of 1980 and most of 1981, increased very slightly toward the end of 1981, then continued to fall during the whole of the rest of the government's first term. The Conservatives said they would combat inflation and they did. The annual rate of inflation was 11 percent in June 1979, their first full month in office; it was 4 percent, less than half of that, in May 1983, their last full month before the election. At the same time, the rate of increase in unemployment slowed considerably. Having doubled between June 1979 and the spring of 1981, the proportion of those without work increased by only two percentage points during the remainder of 1981 and then increased by only one percentage point during the whole of the rest of Thatcher's first term. This slowing down in the rate of increase may have been cold comfort to the three million or more who were still on the dole, but it reassured those who were still at work that they were likely to remain so. Britain was a less fearful country in 1983 than it had been two years earlier.

The principal casualty of the Conservatives' advance after the Falklands was the Liberal-SDP Alliance. Support for the Alliance remained higher after the Falklands than support for the Liberals ever had been before the formation of the new party; but, as table 1.5 shows, the Alliance after the second quarter of 1982 never again obtained the support of as many as 30 percent of voters in the Gallup Poll. In the seven parliamentary by-elections held after Hillhead, although the Alliance in every case improved on the Liberals' 1979 showing, it captured as much as 30 percent of the vote only twice.[84] The Alliance was not rooted in any region or section of society, and those who voted for it tended to hold a mixture of Conservative and Labour views rather than views that were distinctively "Liberal" or "Social Democratic." Substantially fewer Alliance voters than Conservative or Labour voters told the polls that they felt "very close" or "fairly close" to their party and, asked to say which was stronger, their like of their own party or their dislike of the other parties, Alliance supporters were far more likely than Conservative or Labour supporters to opt for "dislike of the other parties."[85] Alliance support was thus especially vulnerable to the pattern of external events and to voters' evaluations of the other parties. Following the Falklands war, it was mainly the Conservatives who benefited at the Alliance's expense.

The Alliance also suffered from not being nearly as newsworthy as it had been at the beginning. The media were inevitably intrigued by a brand-new party. They were considerably less intrigued by that same party when it was a year old, then eighteen months old, then two years old. When the SDP held its first "rolling conference" in the autumn of 1981, with the party's leaders traveling in a chartered train from city to city, the media were amused; when the party held another rolling conference a year later, the media were faintly bored (on top of which the chartered train broke down). Moreover, one running news story that had undoubtedly helped the Alliance gain political momentum in 1981 gradually ceased to run, then stopped altogether: the defection to the SDP of Labour MPs. Twenty-five defected in the course of 1981. One more did so in March 1982, another in June 1982. But then the process stopped and, as the flow of defectors dried up, so did newspaper speculation about the names of possible future defectors. The Labour party thereby appeared more solid than it had in recent months, the SDP less attractive.[86]

The Alliance was thus to some extent a victim of bad luck and the whims of the media, but the parties to the Alliance also inflicted a good deal of damage on themselves. The Alliance had undoubtedly gained support at first by being friendly and nice, by appearing to be "not like the other parties." It now proceeded to forfeit a good deal of whatever support it had gained on that basis. One source of difficulty was the allocation of parliamentary seats between the Liberals and the Social Democrats. The two parties had not had much trouble agreeing to the general principle that each should fight roughly half the seats at the next election; but in many cases they had a great deal of trouble deciding which particular seats should be fought by which party. The Liberals, characteristically, wanted negotiations between the parties conducted mainly at the local level. The Social Democrats, equally characteristically, wanted a considerable degree of central control. The Liberals, naturally, wanted to fight most of what were, from the Alliance's point of view, the best seats, since these were precisely the seats where the Liberals had done well in the past and where they had already adopted strong candidates. The SDP, equally naturally, having brought (as they saw it) an important access of strength to the Alliance, did not want to find that Liberal MPs vastly outnumbered Social Democratic MPs in the new House of Commons. In the end, the two parties succeeded in striking deals covering virtually the whole of the country: out of the 633 constituencies in Great Britain, only three were contested by both the Liberals and the SDP in June 1983. But the process of arriving at deals on such a large scale was protracted and sometimes acrimonious and it involved, as it was bound to do, a good deal of old-fashioned, un-nice, unedifying horsetrading. The Liberals and Social Democrats were not so very different from the other parties after all.

The other development that seemed to reduce the Alliance to the other parties' level was a hard-fought contest for the leadership of the SDP. Many Social Democrats thought that Roy Jenkins should be accepted as SDP leader without an election. He was much the most senior person in the party. No one had played a larger part in founding the party than he had. He had much closer relations with the Liberals, and in particular with David Steel, than any of the others. Other party activists, however, regarded him as too conservative a figure and believed, moreover, that Jenkins was not the appropriate person to project the image of a party that wanted to be regarded as young (Jenkins was over 60), fresh (he had first been elected to Parliament in 1948), and dynamic (Jenkins's public demeanor tended to be that of a measured elder statesman). Some of Jenkins's followers also caused resentment by giving the impression that Jenkins had somehow acquired a God-given right to lead the party. Few in the SDP were passionately hostile to Jenkins becoming its leader, but a substantial number wanted someone different, and a minority believed (probably wrongly as it turned out) that a serious and good-humored election campaign would attract favorable publicity to the party, irrespective of who won. Shirley Williams was the obvious alternative contender, but when she proved unavailable, David Owen, the former Labour foreign secretary, stood instead with Williams's support. The election was, as both sides hoped it would be, serious and reasonably good-humored, but it is doubtful whether the holding of an election, especially in the mood of national unity prevailing after the Falklands, did much to enhance the SDP's reputation for niceness and selflessness. Jenkins won by 26,256 members' votes to Owen's 20,864.[87]

As many Social Democrats had feared, Jenkins's leadership turned out to be lackluster. The former chancellor of the exchequer and home secretary seemed to find it hard to adjust to being leader of a new, struggling opposition party. Back in the House of Commons after Hillhead, he had considerable trouble commanding the attention of an assembly that he had once dominated with ease. He was solemn and portentous on television, appearing uncomfortable, and often giving long, orotund answers to interviewers' questions when short, pithy ones were what the situation required. His long experience and grasp of detail seemed to weigh on him rather than propel him forward, and at times he appeared more as an international civil servant than as a "hungry" British politician. Although there were no mutinies in the Social Democrats' ranks, there was little enthusiasm for Jenkins either, and many of those who had voted for him clearly wondered whether they had done the right thing. His standing with the general public gradually declined. In the first month of his leadership, July 1982, 50 percent of Gallup's monthly sample thought he would do a good job as SDP leader. At the end of the year, in December 1982, only 34 percent thought that he was actually doing a good job as leader and by the eve of the general election, in May 1983, that figure had fallen to 30 percent. Symptomatic of Jenkins's difficulties in communicating himself and his views was the fact that, even after he had been SDP leader for nearly a year (and after he had been in public life for thirty-five years), a quarter of the electorate, sometimes more, was still replying "don't know" to Gallup's standard leadership question. It was with considerable trepidation that the Liberals (and some people in the SDP) agreed that, on the grounds of his far greater governmental experience, Jenkins rather than Steel should lead the Alliance, with the title "prime minister-designate," in the coming election.[88]

Figure 1.1   Party voting support, 1979–82

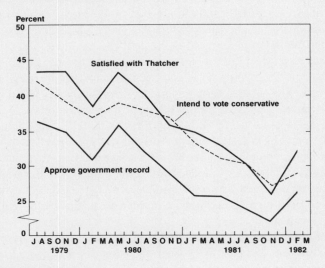

Source: Gallup Political Index.

The Labour party's position, as a glance back at table 1.5 will show, scarcely changed between the time of the Falklands war and the 1983 campaign. In the month before the war, Labour stood at 33 percent in the Gallup Poll. In the month before the election, it stood at 31.5 percent. While the war was going on, Labour was deeply divided: some MPs gave wholehearted support to the government and its policies while others, led by Tony Benn, fulminated against the absurdity of expending British blood and treasure protecting some eighteen hundred Falkland Islanders (equivalent to the population of a medium-sized English village), who lived eight thousand miles from Britain, whose economy was unviable, most of whose land was owned by absentee landlords, and who, far from being enamored of something called "the Falklands way of life," showed a disconcerting tendency to want to emigrate. Michael Foot dithered, claiming to support the government while constantly maintaining that a diplomatic solution should be found, ideally through the United Nations; his Gallup approval rating dropped in a mere eight weeks from an appalling 23 percent to an abysmal 14 percent. Labour nevertheless recovered the allegiance of many of its traditional supporters in the ensuing months, largely because, in the absence of the Healey–Benn controversy and with some movement back toward the right on the National Executive Committee, the party succeeded in assuming an air of near-normality.

Figure 1.1 charts the fortunes of all three parties over the course of the 1979

Parliament. The stability of the Conservatives' position from the spring of 1982 onward, and the size of the gap between the Conservatives and the other parties, inevitably led early in 1983 to pressure on the prime minister to call an early election. On the one hand, the Parliament still had more than a year to run; on the other, the Tories' lead in the polls was formidable, and there was always the danger that, if inflation accelerated again or if the rate of increase in unemployment began to go up again, the Alliance might recover and politics might revert to its pre-Falklands pattern. Conservative worry about a possible Alliance recovery was intensified in February 1983 when, to everyone's astonishment, the Liberals succeeded in capturing the hitherto impregnable Labour seat of Bermondsey in south London. But Bermondsey turned out to be a fluke —the Labour candidate was not only a left-winger, but an Australian, a draft-dodger, and a homosexual—and in March Labour held onto the marginal seat of Darlington, driving the SDP into third place. With the Conservatives' lead in the opinion polls tending, if anything, to increase, the pressure on the prime minister mounted.

The remaining chapters in this book deal with how Thatcher responded to that pressure, with the short 1983 general election campaign, and with the results of the election and their significance. The year before the election had been one of political stasis, with little change in the parties' standings, apart from a long, slow decline in the position of the Liberal-SDP Alliance. Two questions were thus in politicians' minds at the beginning of the 1983 campaign: Was there any way in which the Conservatives' huge lead in the polls could be overcome by either of the opposition parties? If the Tories' lead could not be overcome, who would finish second, the Conservatives' traditional opposition, the Labour party, or the new and completely untried Liberal-SDP Alliance?

The Conservative Campaign
MICHAEL PINTO-DUSCHINSKY

———— The 1983 election created new challenges and uncertainties for the Conservative Central Office. Despite the strong Tory lead in the opinion polls in May and June 1983, the party managers remained worried about the outcome throughout the campaign. Not since the 1930s had Britain faced such high levels of unemployment, of which the political consequences remained unknown. The emergence of a serious third party meant that fresh tactics needed to be considered. The Conservative strategists had constantly to review which party posed the main threat: the Labour party or the Liberal–Social Democratic Alliance. Above all, public opinion had shown itself to be so changeable in the years since the election of 1979 that there was always the risk of a sudden loss of electoral support.

This chapter examines the problems of Conservative organization during the run-up to the election and party strategy during the campaign. It concludes with an assessment and a note on Conservative party finances.

Election Preparations

When a British party is in government, it can expect to suffer a serious loss of support during the middle of its term of office and to recover as the general election approaches. However, by 1981 the unpopularity of the Tories and of Prime Minister Margaret Thatcher personally had broken all records. The combination of rising inflation, falling industrial output, rocketing unemployment, urban riots, by-election disasters, and unprecedentedly low poll ratings made Conservative reelection prospects bleak. In December 1981, a Gallup Poll showed the Conservative share of popular support down to 23 percent, the lowest ever for a party in government. The Labour party's internal divsions made it incapable of benefiting from Tory distress and the recently created Alliance found itself in the lead with 50.5 percent. Market and Opinion Research International (MORI) polls were only a trifle less gloomy for the government. In their worst month, November 1981, the Conservatives were in third place, with 27 percent (compared with 44 percent for the Alliance and 29 percent for Labour). Even if the Alliance failed to maintain this overwhelming level of support, it still threatened to ruin the prospects of a Conservative majority in a future Parliament. Virtually all the constituencies in which Liberal candidates had gained second place in the 1979 campaign had been Conservative-held seats. It was these seats that Alliance candidates stood the best chance of scooping up at the next election.

As if these troubles were not enough, the Conservatives faced a variety of internal problems. The 1979 campaign left the central party organization with serious financial losses. During the two accounting years covered by the election (April 1978–March 1979 and April 1979–March 1980) Central Office had a deficit of nearly £2 million (a loss corresponding to the cost of its advertising in the 1979 campaign).[1] There followed a controversy about the control of the headquarters budget that interrupted the fund-raising process. The task of raising central funds, which came largely from companies and small business people, was in any case difficult because of the recession. In 1980–1981, central party income was 42 percent below expenditure—the loss amounted to £2.3 million. Economies made in the summer of 1980 proved insufficient. Further cuts were announced in March 1981, with 10 percent of the staff being made redundant and vacancies being left unfilled. The Community Affairs Department was disbanded and its functions were assigned, on a reduced scale, to the Organization Department.[2] The Community Affairs Department had been responsible for encouraging Conservative activities among trade unionists, youth, ethnic minority groups, and small business people. The cuts also bit deeply into the Communications Department, the Conservative Research Department, and the area offices of Central Office. Other financial measures included the raising of emergency loans totaling about £0.5 million from a number of local Conservative associations and sustaining an overdraft of some £1.5 million.[3]

A side effect of these economies (which had a demoralizing effect on the Central Office) was the dismissal of senior staff in the Community Affairs Department, who had been among the most "wet" members of the central organization.[4] Another controversial change, motivated partly by a desire for economy and partly by political considerations, was the removal of the Conservative Research Department from its elegant, separate quarters in Old Queen Street to the main headquarters building at 32 Smith Square. The physical separation of the Research Department had symbolized its special, semi-independent status. The department had not been directly responsible to the party chairman but to a chairman of its own, a prominent politician appointed by the party leader. For many years R. A. Butler (Lord Butler) had been the department's chairman and, even after his departure, it continued to follow his tradition of moderate Toryism. During Thatcher's first four years as party leader, the director of the Research Department was a forthright "wet," Chris Patten, who became MP for Bath in the 1979 election. After that election, the department was made directly accountable to the party chairman and its status and independence were checked.

At the constituency level, the gradual, long-term decline in membership and organization appear to have continued, though the declines do not seem to have been as severe as might have been expected in view of the government's low political standing. According to one Central Office estimate, constituency membership had declined by 1982 to 1.2 million (compared with 1.5 million in 1973, and 1.5–1.75 million in the late 1960s, and a temporary peak of 2.8 million in 1952). Agents noted a growing reluctance of party workers to undertake door-to-door canvassing, especially in urban areas in the evenings. (This may have resulted as much from the increasing fear of mugging as from political inhibitions.) In order to encourage local enthusiasm and to recruit new activists, the party introduced Impact 80s. The object was to train constituency workers to produce local news sheets, to make use of local radio (a new and important medium), and to take up and develop neighborhood issues. This method had been exploited successfully by some local Liberal parties. The other priority of the Organization Department was to recruit and train full-time constituency agents so that the decline in their numbers could be arrested.

During the first two years of her ministry, Mrs. Thatcher was probably less concerned with matters of party organization than with her authority in the cabinet and parliamentary party. While there were no dramatic revolts during the 1979–83 Parliament, there were undercurrents of dissatisfaction about her economic policy, considered by the wets too deflationary. There were also divisions over immigration policy, proposed restrictions on local authorities, and the European Economic Community. Thatcherites and other Conservatives differed in their social backgrounds and styles as much as in their policies. Some of the prime minister's principal critics had traditional, privileged backgrounds, while her associates tended to be self-made and identified themselves with the struggles of the small business owner.

The new rules introduced after the October 1974 election under which Thatcher had been elected Conservative party leader meant that her reelection could be challenged each year. In 1981, there were rumors that a former cabinet minister, Geoffrey Rippon, was to stand against her. This move failed to materialize and, in 1982, Thatcher's handling of the Falklands crisis put her position beyond dispute. Nevertheless, she remained sensitive to potential disloyalty. "Is he one of us?" was her frequent question to close colleagues. The Thatcherites knew that if she failed to win the next election, her leadership would be threatened.

In September 1981, Thatcher reshuffled the cabinet to consolidate her position. Three of the wets were dropped from the government (Sir Ian Gilmour, Mark Carlisle, and Lord Soames) and another, James Prior, was moved from the Department of Employment to the Northern Ireland office, limiting his influence over economic policy. Thatcher took the opportunity to install a new party chairman, Cecil Parkinson, who, unlike his predecessor, would have a seat in the cabinet.

The previous Conservative chairman, Lord Thorneycroft, was a senior politician in his early seventies, who could not be expected to remain in charge of the party machine at the next election. The change was therefore not unexpected, though the choice of Parkinson, a little-known, middle-ranking minister, was a surprise. Alongside his friend, Norman Tebbit, who became the employment minister, Parkinson soon established himself as one of the prime minister's most trusted advisers and as a major public figure. During the Falklands crisis of April–June 1982, Parkinson was appointed to the five-person "war cabinet" responsible for the conduct of the conflict. As the election approached, he and Sir Geoffrey Howe, the chancellor of the exchequer, met regularly with Thatcher to discuss political strategy. Sir Geoffrey was chiefly responsible for the coordination of policy planning and Parkinson for political advice. The two ministers were in constant attendance, together with a changing cast of advisers and ministers, at informal tactical meetings regularly held at 10 Downing Street on Mondays.

Parkinson was the first party chairman to have served, before his election to the House of Commons, as chairman of a Conservative constituency association. Nevertheless, his professional background as an accountant and company director made him impatient with some of the traditional methods of British doorstep politics. His priority was to promote modern campaign technologies such as the direct mail techniques employed by the Republican party and its associated organizations in the United States. Two of his key appointments reflected his aims. As vice-chairman (and effectively chief of staff) he chose his parliamentary private secretary, Michael Spicer, an expert in systems analysis and computers. He also recruited Chris Lawson to the newly created post of director of marketing. Lawson, a marketing specialist and managing director of one of the Mars companies in the U.S.A., had been friendly with the party chairman since they had been active together in the Hemel Hempstead Conservative Association. He was to be responsible for the party's advertising strategy, party political broadcasts, private opinion polls, and the development of direct mail strategies.

By the end of 1982, a large computer had been installed at Conservative headquarters. Its eventual purpose was to store and process lists of party supporters and contributors. In the short run, direct mail had to be limited to a few dozen "critical" constituencies where local party organizations had provided lists of members. Over eighty thousand letters were mailed in December

1982 and there were additional mailings in February and May 1983. Conservative party members were asked to return questionnaires about policy issues and to contribute money. About 10 percent responded and 3 percent enclosed contributions. These, however, did not meet the full costs of the mailings. The exercise was considered successful as a pilot scheme but, due to the early general election date, direct mail made little impact on the outcome.

Marketing developments included the introduction of a meticulously researched logo: a short Olympic flame symbolizing leadership, striving to win, dedication, and a sense of community. Arrangements were made to ensure closer control over the party's advertising agency than in the previous general election. It was decided that the agency, Saatchi and Saatchi Garland Compton, should advise on the style of communication alone; they should not influence strategy or the content of the party's messages to the electors. The agency's representatives were not to have regular access to the main decision-making committees at Central Office but were to work through the Marketing Department and the chairman. At the same time, the chairman insisted that advertising style should not be discussed by the Central Office departments that were not directly involved with marketing.

Advertising in the 1983 campaign departed from established patterns in two ways. First, the director of marketing decided that the party should not use its full allocation of free television time for party election broadcasts. As usual the Conservatives were allotted five slots of ten minutes each on all television channels during the campaign period. (Labour had the same allocation and the Alliance received four slots of ten minutes.) Lawson felt that a ten-minute commercial was too long and that the party's message would be conveyed more effectively if it used five minutes. Only in the final broadcast, which included a four-minute talk by Thatcher, was the full ten minutes used. A second novel feature was the late timing of the national party's press advertisements and posters. In past elections, these were spread over the months (even years) before the announcement of the election date. This was partly because of existing interpretations of election law. It was thought that paid advertising by national party organizations during election campaigns (but not in the period before the announcement of the election date) risked contravening the spending limits for parliamentary candidates. Since 1974 the law has been interpreted more liberally. Central party organizations now can purchase unlimited press space and poster sites provided that the advertisements boost the party, not individual candidates, and provided that the poster sites are not obviously concentrated in particular target constituencies. In 1983, the Conservatives took advantage of the new legal interpretation to concentrate their advertising effort on the campaign period. They considered that the impact of advertising was short-term and that publicity during the run-up to an election was wasteful. Apart from an advertising campaign costing £120,000 in the days before the local government elections of 5 May 1983, the entire budget for election advertising was spent in the four weeks before the poll.

The drive for modernization and efficiency affected the method of screening parliamentary candidates. Central Office has a limited influence on the selection of candidates, which is the responsibility of the constituency associations. A Central Office vice-chairman (normally a senior backbencher) is responsible for maintaining a list of centrally approved contenders, whose names and particulars are circulated to constituencies about to make a selection. A more rigorous method for screening applicants for the central party's list of candidates was adopted after the 1979 election. Groups of aspirants were evaluated on the basis of two days of written work, discussions, debates, and problem-solving exercises. The effect of this procedure on the quality and background of candidates is uncertain. Whether as a result of the new procedures or for other reasons, the 101 Conservative MPs elected for the first time in 1983 differed markedly from the established pattern. Only 23 percent had been educated at public schools (that is, high prestige private schools) and 38 percent had attended Oxford or Cambridge.[5] Between 1910 and 1979, the proportion of Conservative MPs from public schools never had fallen below 72 percent.[6]

Party Chairman Parkinson's combination of informality and drive and his determination to encourage new campaigning initiatives reinvigorated the party machine, but some of its difficulties persisted. By the 1983 campaign, Central Office's long-term financial problems remained unresolved. They stemmed from the gradual decline in the level of corporate donations. Some of the short-term difficulties were eased in 1982 when the party treasurer and deputy chairman, Alistair McAlpine, arranged for the sale and leaseback of the headquarters building. The party had purchased the freehold two years before, with the aid of a bridging loan. According to press reports, the sale and leaseback arrangement was calculated to produce a profit of £1 million. The long-run price to be paid for the deal was that the party subsequently would have to pay rent for its offices.

In 1981–82 and 1982–83 Central Office income barely matched spending. In 1983, the treasurers faced the daunting task of raising £3.5 to 4 million for the election campaign, £5 million for routine central spending, and, if possible, a surplus for the year after the election, when funds are hard to collect. McAlpine took the bold view that his first function was to provide whatever sums the party strategists felt were required to win the campaign. If deficits were incurred in the process, the problem of meeting the routine needs of the headquarters could be tackled later.

The local problem of falling constituency membership remained unresolved. The task of the director of organization at Central Office, Anthony Garner, was complicated by the far-reaching changes in parliamentary constituency boundaries, which were under review by a set of Boundary Commissions. Not until November 1982 were the commissions' proposals clear, and they did not become law until March 1983. Since the boundaries of Conservative constituency associations correspond with those of parliamentary constituencies, the changes made it necessary to disband the old associations, to form new ones, and to make arrangements for the transfer of MPs, candidates, agents, and financial assets (or debts) from the old to the new organizations.

In the event, the changes were achieved rapidly and relatively smoothly. This was no mean feat. There were, however, bitter fights in a handful of seats where the reselection of sitting MPs was disputed. Boundary alterations made the political complexion of some of the new seats unclear and this, together with the uncertainties created by the Alliance surge in popularity, made it hard to draw up the list of "critical seats" on which the headquarters would focus its attentions. Ideally, the central organization and its area offices try to ensure that all critical seats have full-time agents, are visited by prominent political speakers, receive financial aid (if necessary), and receive help with canvassing from party workers in adjoining safe constituencies ("mutual aid").

Since the aim of the national campaign was to ensure the retention of a Conservative government, most of the constituencies on the critical-seats list were Conservative-held marginals, which the party needed to win if it was to keep its majority. Based on the *BBC/INT Guide to the New Parliamentary Constituencies* (published after the critical seats list was drawn up),[7] 80 out of 102 critical seats were constituencies that would have been won by the Conservatives had the 1979 election been fought on the new boundaries. Labour was the main challenger in sixty-seven of these seats, the Alliance in ten, and the Scottish Nationalist party in three. The list included three seats won by the SDP at by-elections and nineteen seats the Conservatives could hope to win, sixteen of them from Labour and three from the Alliance.

Despite the priority given to the recruitment of constituency agents and the temporary return of some retired agents during the campaign, the number of constituencies with full-time agents was lower in 1983 than in previous campaigns. Even critical seats were short of agents. Of 102 criticals, 54 had full-time agents, 15 shared agents with other constituencies, and 33 had no professional agent. Throughout Britain, 294 agents served 333 constituencies.[8] This compares with 324 agents in 1977, 386 in 1970, and 446 in 1966.

While the headquarters was making its routine preparations for the next general election, the Conservatives benefited from a dramatic improvement in the political climate. From December 1981, the popularity of the Alliance started to fall steeply, though it still remained a formidable force. Between November 1981 and March 1982, popular support for the Alliance, according to MORI, dropped from 44 percent to 30 percent. The three main parties were now neck and neck (Conservative: 34 percent, Labour: 34 percent, Alliance: 30 percent). The Falklands crisis then propelled the Conservatives into the lead.

By June 1982, they had a commanding 48 percent, compared with 28 percent for Labour and 23 percent for the Alliance.

The Tory ascendancy continued after the completion of military operations in the Falklands. Yet it was too early in the parliamentary cycle for Thatcher to take advantage of the situation by calling an early election, even if she had wished to do so. Her popularity had been won precisely because she had acted as a determined, national leader. These positive feelings could evaporate if she appeared to be taking political advantage of events in the South Atlantic. Nevertheless, the improvement in Conservative fortunes opened the option of a reasonably early appeal to the voters. The latest legal date for the next election was 1 June 1984. Any time from spring 1983 on would be within the bounds of acceptability. By autumn 1982, contingency plans were being prepared at Central Office for an election in the late spring of 1983, though October 1983 still was considered the most likely month and a late election in spring 1984 was another possibility.

On 5 January 1983, some of Thatcher's ministerial colleagues met with senior party officials and advisers at her official country residence, Chequers, to discuss electoral strategy and dates. At the same time, detailed campaign arrangements (the "warbook") were formulated at Central Office. By this time, Parkinson was becoming attracted to the idea of an election in June. The Public Spending White Paper, published at the beginning of February, embodied a set of political commitments that formed the core of a future Conservative government's programs. During February cabinet ministers were asked to draw up proposals relating to their departments that they wished to be included in a draft election manifesto. The ministers most actively involved in the manifesto preparations were Sir Geoffrey Howe and Cecil Parkinson. It was to these two that nine policy committees of MPs and advisers, organized in conjunction with the Conservative Research Department, were due to report by the end of March. Besides taking an active personal interest, Sir Geoffrey was assisted by one of his political advisers, Adam Ridley, who had formerly been a senior official of the Conservative Research Department. Ridley worked with the director of the Research Department, Peter Cropper, a previous political adviser to Sir Geoffrey. These arrangements meant that, despite the apparent downgrading of the Research Department, the 1983 manifesto bore many of the marks of the cautious, Butlerite tradition of Conservatism with which the department had been associated.

A barrier to an early election was removed in February 1983, when the Law Lords refused to prolong the Labour party's legal action against the Boundary Commissioners. This decision opened the way for the rapid introduction of the new parliamentary boundaries, which had been ready since the previous November. The new boundaries took account of population movements, mainly from the inner cities to the suburbs. City constituencies with small electorates, most of them Labour strongholds, were amalgamated; oversized suburban constituencies, mainly Conservative, were broken up. The boundary changes thereby ended Labour's previous advantages and meant that the Conservatives were likely to win between fifteen and twenty more seats than under the old boundaries. This provided a major incentive to Labour to block the Boundary Commissioners' proposals and for the Conservatives to wait until they could be introduced.

As the problem over parliamentary boundaries was solved, another arose. For a few weeks in February and March, the Alliance emerged once more as a serious threat. On 24 February, the Liberal-Alliance candidate, Simon Hughes, swept to victory in the Bermondsey by-election and the Conservative performance was derisory. Bermondsey was an inner London Labour stronghold. The by-election had been called because of the resignation of the sitting Labour MP following bitter divisions between moderates and left-wingers within the constituency Labour party. Michael Foot originally had refused to ignore the candidate selected by the local Labour party, Peter Tatchell, because of his extreme views. Labour moderates, supporters of the previous MP, split the party's vote by putting forward a rival "Real Bermondsey Labour" candidate. Thus it was Labour, not the Conservatives, who were the real losers. Nevertheless, the result caused intense worry at Conservative Central Office. The Alliance candidate, starting as an outsider, had managed to create an impressive bandwagon of support, aided by an opinion poll a week before the vote that had shown him in second place. The poll had won him the votes of many Conservatives and Labour moderates who wished to see the official Labour candidate defeated. Was there not a danger that Alliance bandwagons could be created in other constituencies?

It also was feared that the Bermondsey result could lead to a national resurgence of Alliance support. Polls carried out after Bermondsey showed this was a well-founded anxiety. On 27 February, a MORI poll, published in the *Sunday Times*, showed national support for the Alliance at 34 percent, the Tories only five points ahead at 39 percent, and Labour in third place with 26 percent. A similar poll a month earlier had given the Conservatives 44 percent, Labour 36 percent, and the Alliance 19 percent.

A few days after the election at Bermondsey, the Labour party moved the writ for another by-election at Darlington, a Labour-held seat in the north of England. It was to be held on 24 March. The Conservative nightmare was that the Bermondsey pattern would be repeated: if any poll showed the Alliance candidate in second place to Labour, the Conservative vote would disintegrate since Conservatives would turn to the Alliance as the best way of defeating Labour. To the intense relief of Central Office, the Conservatives beat the Alliance into third place, the seat being retained by Labour. The result was considered a personal triumph for the Conservative candidate, who had easily outshone the Alliance candidate in a televised debate conducted before an audience of schoolchildren. Following the Darlington result, the Alliance standing in the opinion polls slumped almost to its level at the end of January. However, the meteoric Alliance performance during February demonstrated to the Conservative strategists the potential for a sudden, rapid movement in favor of the new party.

On 15 March, nine days before the poll at Darlington, Sir Geoffrey Howe introduced a cautiously reflationary budget. It was more generous than his previous budgets, though it gave away far less than the opposition parties wished. Scope for modest tax relief had been provided by the discovery that public spending, particularly on capital projects, was lower than expected.

By Easter, the decks were clear for a June campaign. On 7 April, Thatcher held another meeting at Chequers with selected ministers, party officials, personal staff, and (as at the January meeting and the subsequent meeting in May) a representative of the advertising agency, Saatchi and Saatchi. Arguments for different election dates were considered in detail. A display board had been prepared at Central Office showing detailed schedules of economic announcements, domestic and world events in May and June; a second board gave similar information for October.

According to later accounts, supporters of the June option included the party chairman, Parkinson, Tebbit, and Sir Geoffrey. William Whitelaw, the home secretary, and John Biffen, leader of the House of Commons, favored delay. The arguments for June were: (1) there was no guarantee that the existing Conservative lead in the opinion polls would be maintained; (2) the retail price index would be at its lowest in May (the statistics would be announced on 17 June) and then would start to rise; (3) the unemployment figures to be announced on 3 June would show a substantial fall but they would rise again over the summer as unemployed students and new graduates came onto the register; and (4) the opposition parties, particularly the Liberals and the SDP, would be boosted by the wide coverage of their party conferences in September. Other reasons for an early poll were that the prospect, however remote, of a Labour government committed to devaluing the currency was depressing sterling and harming the economy; British economic recovery was endangered by international economic uncertainties (a possible rise in United States interest rates over the summer might lead to higher British interest rates); the government's popularity stemming from the "Falklands factor" was likely to wane; and election fever was leading to a paralysis of public policy and administration.

Some political and economic arguments pointed to delay. The Alliance was still a dangerous force but its popularity could wane by the autumn as the "Bermondsey effect" faded. By autumn, the recovery in industrial production would be more pronounced. At the parliamentary level, an October election would permit the completion of bills such as the Telecommunications Bill and the Police and Criminal Evidence Bill. The most compelling argument against an early dissolution of the House of Commons was that it might appear opportunistic, thereby damaging the prime minister's strongest asset—a reputation for resolution.

Thatcher did not reveal her own thoughts and left some with the feeling that she would wait until 1984. She did, however, agree to hold another meeting at Chequers on 8 May, immediately after the local government elections due to be held on 5 May. This procedure suggested that, barring danger signals from the opinion polls or from the local election results, a June election was likely. Campaign preparations intensified. Ridley and Ferdinand Mount, the prime minister's political adviser, drafted an election manifesto to which some sections were added by Sir Geoffrey Howe. The text was refined at a further meeting at Chequers. The director of the Research Department worked to ensure that the *Campaign Guide*, a 548-page reference document originally scheduled for completion in July, was finished in April. At the public level, a well-advertised speech by Thatcher to 150 Conservative parliamentary candidates and various statements and press leaks led to intense media speculation and prepared the ground for public acceptance of an early dissolution of Parliament.

On Sunday, 8 May, the circle of advisers gathered at Chequers once again. The meeting was a major media event. The party chairman brought some reasonably optimistic reports about the state of public opinion. Most polls published during April and early May had shown a Conservative lead of at least 10 percent over Labour. Support for the Alliance remained about 22 percent, its normal post-Falklands level. The local election results (always difficult to translate into national terms) broadly confirmed this picture, though the Conservatives had not been quite as successful as hoped. According to David Butler in the *Times* of 7 May, the results had indicated a Conservative lead over Labour of only 5 percent. An analysis carried out at Central Office with the aid of the new computer concluded that the local election results showed that Conservative candidates and Independents (whose support was reckoned to come from Conservatives) led Labour by 13 percent. A breakdown of the results in each parliamentary constituency also gave grounds for satisfaction. In addition, Central Office had commissioned two exceptionally large private polls to be carried out immediately before the Chequers meeting, one from the Harris Research Centre, the party's regular pollsters (sample size 2,307), the other from Gallup (sample size 2,103). The Harris poll showed a Conservative lead of 10 percent (Conservative: 44 percent, Labour: 34 percent, Alliance: 20 percent) and Gallup showed a 15 percent Conservative lead (Conservative: 46 percent, Labour: 31 percent, Alliance: 20 percent). The polls also showed that only a minority of voters now felt that a June election would not be in the national interest. This undermined the main argument for delay. By now some ministerial supporters of a later election, such as Whitelaw, had come to accept the idea of June. Soundings among Conservative MPs revealed a preference for October but, above all, the desire for an end to the uncertainty.[9]

The meeting discussed which day in June would be most advantageous. Thursday, 23 June would allow the party to benefit from the favorable retail price figures to be announced on 17 June. Thursday, 2 June, apparently was excluded because of the bank holiday earlier in the week. The next Thursday, 9 June, would make it possible to avoid television coverage of the fashionable Ascot races, due to be held in mid-June (this social event, which would be prominently reported, would highlight the contrast between the rich and the unemployed). A disadvantage of 9 June was that it would come soon after the planned mass rally of the unemployed organized by the Trade Union Congress for 4 June. Other considerations were the premier's scheduled visit to the economic summit meeting at Williamsburg, Virginia, and the imminence of a by-election at Cardiff North West, which the party managers were keen to avoid. The decisive reason for an early date — 9 June — was that it allowed little time for a recovery by the opposition parties.

The choice of election date is the sole prerogative of the prime minister. She announced no verdict at the meeting. By the next morning her mind was set and she lost no time in announcing that the election would be on 9 June.

The Campaign

The Conservative lead at the start of the campaign was enviable but it was not secure. Previous campaigns had witnessed considerable movements of opinion against the governing party. In 1970 the Labour premier, Harold Wilson, had been ousted from office following a sudden movement of opinion to the Conservatives in the final days of the campaign. Edward Heath, the Tory premier, had lost the February 1974 election due to a Liberal surge. This time, the emergence of a three-party battle heightened the possibilities of swings of opinion, as the polls had shown at the time of the Bermondsey by-election, when the national standing of the Alliance had risen 15 percent within four weeks.

A primary Conservative aim was Safety First. The choice of election date itself had been influenced by the desire to give Labour and — more important — the Alliance as little time as possible to gain ground. The pacing and style of the campaign, as well as the manifesto, were designed with caution in mind. Parkinson decided on a late start and a slow pace. The manifesto would not be issued until Wednesday, 18 May, and the daily press conferences would commence only on 20 May, leaving just two complete weeks of active campaigning. Television appearances by the Tory "big guns" (Tebbit, Heseltine, and Parkinson) were to be delayed as well. Thatcher's appearances were limited and her tours tightly controlled. She was to address merely six ticket-only meetings. The venues for her daily regional tours were kept secret and were not determined far in advance so that hecklers could not gather. The prime minister could be at her best when confronting hostile questioners, but the party organizers were determined to avoid agitators (the "rent-a-mob crowd") who played to the television cameras accompanying the prime minister. The result was a series of ceremonial visits to factories, a farm, and a lifeboat. The demands of security made a close control over Thatcher's movements essential. Twice in 1983, bombs had been sent to places where she was due to make political appearances. During the election itself, there were reports of an IRA (Irish Republican Army) threat against her and an explosive device was delivered to Parkinson's office at 32 Smith Square. Nevertheless, tactical considerations also affected the decision to shield Thatcher from the hurly-burly of the stump.

The manifesto surprised those who expected a series of radical commitments. Apart from the pledge to abolish the metropolitan councils and the Greater London Council (reportedly included at a late stage by the prime minister herself), the manifesto was a résumé of earlier ministerial pronouncements and commitments. This reflected partly the fact that the early election date had not permitted time for proposals of the Research Department's policy committees to be evaluated, and partly that a governing party has less room for maneuver in its manifesto than an opposition party. The main reason for the manifesto's blandness was the desire to avoid giving unnecessary targets to the Labour party or to the Alliance.

All campaign planners fear unexpected gaffes and "banana skins"—stray remarks or minor errors that receive disproportionate media attention. To guard against this, the day-to-day operational structure of the headquarters had been meticulously thought out and responsibilities carefully demarcated.[10] One wall of the chairman's office was covered by a chart (usually concealed and locked) showing the main plans for each day of the campaign: a schedule of press conference topics and which ministers were to appear with the premier, party election broadcasts, and other landmarks.

A tight schedule of daily briefings and strategy meetings had been arranged, according to Central Office precedent. The first series of meetings was designed to prepare for the press conferences (held at 9:30 A.M. following the Alliance press conference at 8:30 and Labour's at 9:00). Each Conservative press conference featured the premier (who was only rarely absent), the party chairman, and one or more ministers. At 7:30, a small chairman's briefing considered an abstract of press reports and a draft press release prepared by the Publicity and Public Relations Department, a list of possible press conference topics prepared by Stephen Sherbourne, a former member of the Research Department and a political adviser at the Department of the Environment, and a résumé of the state of public opinion presented by the director of marketing, who frequently brought charts to the meeting. Members of the prime minister's personal staff sat in on the meetings. At 8:30, there was a larger briefing for

Thatcher and the ministers who were to appear at the press conference. Answers to likely questions were rehearsed and the director of the Research Department could depute members of his staff to find additional factual material.

The chairman's main strategy meetings, attended by the directors of Central Office departments and a small number of senior staff and advisers, were held every weekday at 11 A.M. and 7 P.M. and on Sundays at 7 P.M. A daily "tactical lunch" was held in a room at the Research Department at which about two dozen staff and advisers could keep in touch with developments.[11] The chairman did not normally attend.

Information about public opinion came from several sources. Before the evening strategy meetings, the director of organization and his deputy, Angela Hooper, spoke by telephone to each Central Office area agent. Each morning, the director of marketing reported to the chairman's briefing the result of Fast Feedback reports organized by an outside marketing company, AGB. They were drawn up on the basis of telephone calls made the previous evening by a panel of thirty-nine participants. The aim was to tap the opinions of a group of 180 businessmen who were undecided how they would vote. Though unscientific, the reports were pithy and gave useful ideas about points that needed to be answered at the morning press conferences. Finally, public and private polls were analyzed constantly. Each week, Harris carried out a 2,000-respondent poll (the State of the Battle survey) that was delivered early on Sunday morning and analyzed in time for the Sunday evening strategy meeting. Brief "quickie" polls were carried out on Tuesdays and Thursdays and the results were produced for the chairman's briefing meetings on Wednesdays and Fridays. For Parkinson, the private polls were to provide an early warning of an impending Alliance advance. As it was anticipated that Alliance gains would first be apparent in strongly Tory regions, such as the south of England, regional breakdowns were prepared of each week's State of the Battle survey.

Well-planned staff work produced valuable dividends. For example, Thatcher's unhurried schedule avoided the fatigue that plagued Foot and enabled her to prepare for vital television interviews, press conferences, and speeches. The close working relationship between the prime minister and the party chairman meant that the conflicts that tend to occur between the premier's staff at Downing Street and the party headquarters were usually avoided. The careful organization of committees meant that the main tactics (such as the attack on Labour's manifesto, described below) were executed effectively. In general, the Tory campaign had a coherence that the opposition parties lacked. However, some decisions emerged informally and not at committee meetings. Sometimes Parkinson personally acted as coordinator.

Conservative strategy needed to address several questions: Could the "Falklands factor" be deployed? How important was the issue of unemployment? How could the party deal with the accusation that it was uncaring about pensioners and the National Health Service? How grave a danger was the Alliance and how could it be tackled?

The first question posed no problem. It was taken for granted that no direct use could be made of the Falklands operation. As one departmental director noted, jingoism and nationalism were to be avoided. The party's private opinion research did not even ask questions about the Falklands factor. Yet it was evident that the voters' perception of Thatcher as resolute owed much to her handling of the South Atlantic crisis. Her steadiness of purpose was seen to offer hope for the country's economic problems, especially when juxtaposed to Labour's seemingly frantic and shortsighted reflationary proposals.

There was general confidence at Central Office about the unemployment issue. Though it was by far the most important issue for voters, several of the party's polls indicted that the government was not widely held responsible. Joblessness was blamed on the world recession or on other factors outside the government's control. These findings appeared to be substantiated by other "qualitative" research. This form of opinion research, in which small groups of men and women were videotaped while engaging in discussions, was becoming increasingly influential. There was encouraging evidence that about half of the electorate felt that the economy was about to improve. It was decided to deal with the issue by stressing repeatedly in party election broadcasts that "every Labour government in history has increased unemployment."[12]

Different opinions were expressed about "caring." Some felt that it would appear unduly defensive and unconvincing for the Conservatives to declare concern for the disadvantaged. The party's positive appeal was in its willingness to make the hard choices required to secure long-term prosperity. Another view was that the party could not afford to let accusations on such issues as the National Health Service go unanswered. In practice, a compromise was reached. "Caring" was featured in some press conferences but some advertising materials on the National Health Service went unused.

For some strategists, the Alliance posed the true threat. They feared that Liberal and SDP support could "take off." Any significant increase in the Alliance's poll rating could lead to gains as millions of voters might vote for the new party if they felt it had a chance of making a breakthrough. To attack the Alliance directly was inadvisable: it could stoke up the fire, that is, have a backlash effect. The plan was to ignore David Steel and Roy Jenkins but to keep anti-Alliance publicity material in reserve in case of need. In the meantime, the main target was to be the Labour party. By stressing the danger of left-wing extremism, the Conservatives could not only tackle Labour, they could, indirectly, deal with the third-party threat by convincing waverers that the only reliable way to avoid a Labour government was to vote Conservative. For at least one adviser, the danger of an Alliance surge was so real that he felt attacks on Labour should be moderated. If Labour were knocked out of serious reckoning too early, Labour votes would flow to the Alliance, thus starting a bandwagon.

The central strategic decision, possibly influenced by an analysis provided by Saatchi and Saatchi, was that the campaign should not focus on the government's own record but on the opposition. Labour had published at the end of March its campaign document *New Hope for Britain*. This gave a detailed indication of the proposals to be included in the party's manifesto and enabled the Conservatives to prepare their attack. The strategy was unusual and not without risk. British elections are usually in the public mind a judgment on the government of the day, not on its opponents. Central Office reckoned that Labour's bitter public divisions and the unpopularity of its far-reaching socialist program made it a vulnerable target. However, *New Hope for Britain* had been published with the aim of reconciling the policy differences between warring Labour factions.

The Conservative scheme was to lie low in the first week after the announcement of the election date, to launch a strong attack on Labour's manifesto in the second week (16 to 22 May), to continue attacks on Labour in the following week, combined if necessary with attacks on the Alliance, and in the final phase of the election to stress positive Conservative achievements and that "Britain's on the right track. Don't turn back."

The opening phases of the battle went according to plan. The first Conservative party election broadcast, carried on all television channels, was screened on Tuesday evening, 17 May, the day after the launch of Labour's manifesto. It showed scenes of chaos caused by strikes during Labour's final winter in office before the 1979 election. The attack on the manifesto continued on 18 May, when a two-page advertisement was placed in the national press. It took the form of a fifteen-point "contract" that voters would be signing if they voted Labour—a contract that would remove their rights and threaten their savings. Thatcher, interviewed on ITN's *News at Ten*, called the manifesto "the most extreme that has ever been put before an electorate."[13] The Conservative Research Department contributed to the onslaught by producing a daunting list of the cost of Labour's proposals to illustrate their irresponsibility. In another well-publicized move to emphasize the horrors of Labour's program, the Conservative party purchased several thousand copies of the Labour manifesto to circulate to Conservative candidates and party workers.

The launch of the Conservatives' own manifesto on 18 May was shakier than the attack on Labour's. Thatcher and the collection of ministers who formed the platform party at the press conference for the manifesto were more accustomed to meeting each other in the cabinet room at 10 Downing Street. Thatcher was accused of being "headmistressy" for interrupting the foreign secretary, Francis Pym, when he implied that there could be negotiations over the Falklands if Argentina accepted an end to the hostilities. The talks, the prime minister stressed, would be on "commercial links." [14] Party advisers suggested that in later press conferences ministers should refer to each other by first names and that they should avoid civil service language. The phrase "in real terms" should be abandoned and ministers should refer instead to raises that were "ahead of inflation."

As the campaign moved into full swing, there were a number of potentially disastrous developments for the Tories. On Monday, 23 May, Labour leaked the confidential minutes of a meeting held two months previously of the national executive committee of the National Economic Development Council, an official advisory body including representatives of unions and employers. The document revealed the private economic assessment of the president of the Confederation of British Industries, Sir Campbell Fraser. His off-the-record views appeared to differ markedly from his buoyant public declarations about economic recovery. On 24 May, Labour leaders produced another document, a draft of a report of a House of Commons committee on international monetary arrangements. What made it damaging was that it had appeared under the name of Edward du Cann, chairman of the 1922 Committee of backbench Conservative MPs, and that it cast doubt on the government's claim that the world recession was the principal cause of unemployment. Three days later, the Conservatives were confronted, in the words of the *Sunday Times*, by "one of the worst sets of trade figures this century." For the first time since the industrial revolution of the eighteenth century, Britain had become a net importer of manufactured goods.

There were problems on other fronts. A Conservative advertisement prepared for ethnic newspapers led to controversy. "Labour Say's He's Black. Tories Say He's British" was the slogan. Some immigrant leaders protested that they regarded themselves as black and British too. A more embarrassing episode occurred when it was revealed that the Conservative candidate for the marginal constituency of Stockton South, Thomas Finnegan, had stood previously as a candidate for the National Front, an extreme right-wing organization that was openly anti-immigrant and, some suspected, covertly anti-Semitic. Central Office had not known of Finnegan's background when he was adopted. Thatcher was subjected to some of the most persistent questioning of the campaign at the press conference of Friday, 26 May. Two Jewish cabinet ministers, Nigel Lawson and Sir Keith Joseph, went out of their way to distance themselves from Finnegan when they fulfilled speaking commitments in his constituency and at least one prime ministerial adviser urged that he should be disowned altogether. Central Office was reluctant to take this step since the final date for nominations had passed and no other candidate could be put forward. Finnegan, summoned to meet Parkinson at Smith Square, explained that he had left the National Front in 1975 and now admitted that "their policies were repugnant to all decent people." After this assurance he was allowed to continue as candidate, though no senior Conservatives were to speak in his support. To general relief he lost the seat. However, the affair undermined the Conservative attack on extremists within Labour's ranks by suggesting that the Conservatives were not entirely untouched by extremist infiltration.[15]

Prime Minister Thatcher's authoritative handling of the daily press conferences and her effective use of briefing materials enabled her to explain and dismiss the leaked economic documents. Fortunately for the Conservatives, the press was distracted by a blazing row within the Labour party. By the beginning of the week of 23–27 May, there were already signs that the shaky truce between Foot and Healey over the issue of nuclear disarmament was about to break down. Their differences over the future of the Polaris missile emerged at Labour's press conference on Monday, 23 May. By the following day, the quarrel was the main campaign issue. On Wednesday, 25 May, the former Labour premier James Callaghan entered the fray, and on Thursday, 26 May, the Labour party's general secretary felt it necessary to reaffirm that "Michael Foot is the leader of the party," which served to underline the depth of the rift.

Labour's quarrel was a godsend to the Conservatives. Although the public did not approve of the installation of cruise missiles, there was an overwhelming opposition to unilateral nuclear disarmament. A poll in the *Observer* of 22 May recorded that only 20 percent of voters wished to get rid of all nuclear weapons (including Polaris), while 74 percent favored an independent British deterrent. On the broad issue of defense, 61 percent thought that the Conservatives were the best party to handle it compared with 21 percent for Labour and 7 percent for the Alliance.[16] The rift within the Labour party served to bring to the forefront an issue on which the public decisively favored the Conservatives. Equally important, it made it impossible for Labour to develop its case on unemployment. The trade figures and Labour's leaks of documents on the economy were relegated to the inside pages or bottom columns of the newspapers. Equally important, the defense controversy aided the Conservative strategic plan of focusing the election on extremism within the Labour party.

On Saturday, 28 May, Thatcher flew to the United States for a brief appearance at the Williamsburg economic summit meeting of leaders of the world's seven largest industrialized nations. The election was twelve days away and the opinion polls were indicating that the Labour party had committed political suicide. Surveys published in the Sunday newspapers of 29 May showed a growing Conservative lead over Labour of between 16 and 17.5 percent.

Inside Central Office, satisfaction about Labour's misfortunes was outweighed by an alarm about a possible Alliance breakthrough. In the first half of the campaign, support for the Alliance had slumped. From about 22 percent at the time of the local government elections of 5 May, it had dropped to 14–18 percent by 23–26 May.[17] Now the polls showed the Alliance at about 20 percent and regional breakdowns of the Conservatives' private State of the Battle survey, delivered to Central Office on Sunday morning, showed that there were signs of Alliance improvement in certain parts of the country such as East Anglia and the South East. Though the changes over the previous week were modest, the Harris Research Centre warned there was still vulnerability to an Alliance bandwagon. Another Harris survey, this time of opinion in marginal seats, was even more worrying. The poll, commissioned by London Weekend Television's *Weekend World* revealed that in twenty of the seats where the Alliance was thought to have its best chances of winning (and where Liberal candidates had been first or second in 1979), Liberal-Alliance candidates had increased their support by 8 percent over the previous week while the Tories had dropped by 5 percent and Labour by 4 percent. The findings struck a raw nerve and it was tentatively decided to commission an extra private poll of marginal Conservative versus Alliance seats. On Monday, 30 May, a bank holiday, the idea of the extra survey was abandoned, partly for technical reasons. On Tuesday, tension grew inside the headquarters as the result of a poll by Audience Selection for the new breakfast television show *TV-AM*. This showed Alliance support at 24 percent, 9 percent higher than some polls of the previous week and only 6 percent behind Labour. For some time the party's advisers had expressed their reservations about the validity of the telephone poll technique used by Audience Selection. Telephone ownership is not as widespread in Britain as in the U.S.A., where telephone polls are well established. Moreover, Audience Selection was known to be the pollster for the Alliance, leading to speculation that the Alliance was deliberately manipulating the results to create a bandwagon.

Other polls, however, also were showing Alliance gains. A MORI poll published in the *Daily Star* on Tuesday, 31 May, showed Alliance support at 21 percent, a six-point improvement over the same poll the previous week. Disagreeable confirmation of the trend came in the Conservative private "quickie" poll, the results of which arrived early Wednesday morning. Because of the speed at which such midweek surveys were carried out and the relatively small number of sample points used, they were not considered reliable as indicators of voting intention, and John Hanvey, the managing director of Harris, had a policy of eliminating the voting intention figures from his reports on them. On this occasion, the full findings were passed to the morning briefing meetings: Conservative: 47 percent, Labour: 28 percent, Alliance: 24 percent. Hanvey warned that the rate of Alliance advance made it probable that some polls would be showing the Alliance ahead of Labour before the end of the week. This could release to the Alliance from Labour the votes of millions of anti-Conservatives. In the minds of some Central Office staff, an even more nightmarish scenario presented itself: once the Alliance was well ahead of Labour, it was likely to pick up support from dissatisfied Conservatives as well. The party's private polls indicated that one-third of those intending to vote Labour and nearly a quarter of those intending to vote Conservative said that they would be more likely to vote for the Alliance if they considered it had an opportunity to hold the balance of power or to form a government. If these potential switchers joined those already intending to vote for the Alliance, then it could emerge as the winning party. Whether this could become reality depended upon the speed of the Alliance advance. If Labour managed to stay in second place until the weekend, then the Tories were safe.

At the press conference held on Wednesday morning, 1 June, Parkinson could not conceal the sense of alarm: "I repeat the statistic that the eighty seats where the Alliance think they have a chance are all Conservative. Therefore Alliance activities are still good news for the Labour Party."

Tense debates continued within Central Office through the day. There were at least two areas of disagreement. Some felt that the situation called for extra spending on anti-Alliance advertising—even £1 million—while others considered this ruinously extravagant and probably counterproductive. Apart from money, there were differences of opinion as to whether the Alliance was actually the principal threat and, if so, how it could be countered. Some proposed to continue the attack on Labour, some favored attacking the Alliance, and others favored stressing the positive achievements of the government. A decision emerged to insert three pages of advertising in the Sunday newspapers, one page setting out reasons for voting Conservative, one page for reasons for not voting Labour, and an almost blank page for the Alliance, implying it had no policies.

As these deliberations were taking place at Conservative Central Office, Healey, the deputy Labour leader, again helped the Conservative cause by accusing Thatcher of "glorying in slaughter" during the Falklands operation, a remark he withdrew the following day. This attack and a similar one by Neil Kinnock, who was to become Foot's successor as Labour leader, raised an issue on which the public sympathized with Thatcher. It also impeded Labour's attempts to revive their case on unemployment.

At this point, the debate on issues was almost dead. The polls had become the main influence on the conduct of the election. On Wednesday night came news of the Audience Selection poll due to appear in the next morning's issue of the *Sun*. Based on a small telephone sample of 504, it put the Alliance at 25 percent, four points behind Labour. During Thursday, the poll news improved. It was learned that Friday's poll in the *Guardian* by Marplan would show the Alliance at only 22 percent and Labour at 30 percent. Two other polls gave the Alliance 24 percent and 23 percent. The next set of poll results was not due until Saturday night (when surveys for the Sunday newspapers were to be released). It was not clear that the end of the week was about to be reached with the Labour party still ahead of the Alliance. The private Conservative quickie poll carried out by Harris Research Centre during Thursday confirmed the general picture with the Alliance at 24 percent and Labour at 29 percent.

The apparent slowing of the Alliance bandwagon led Parkinson and his vice-chairman, Spicer, to have second thoughts about the advertisements planned for the Sunday newspapers. Quite apart from the high costs involved (a major factor in the discussions at Central Office), it could be unwise to attack the Alliance unnecessarily. In the early hours of Friday morning, the Conservative chairman contacted Mr. Bell of Saatchi and Saatchi and cancelled the projected advertisement. In place of the three pages of copy that already had been delivered to the newspapers, it was decided to rerun the two-page advertisement of 18 May. There was a growing feeling at party headquarters that it was better to keep calm and cool than to ridicule the Alliance. When electors defected to the Alliance, it usually was not because of a positive attachment to specific Alliance policies but because of a diffuse sense of unease with Labour and the Conservatives. If this analysis was correct, a frontal attack on the Alliance would intensify voters' distaste for the "two-party slanging match."

The results of the opinion polls appearing on Sunday, 5 June, as well as the final State of the Battle private poll, confirmed that the danger had passed. All but one showed Labour still in the lead. The Alliance had made little headway over the previous five days and time was running out. On Monday night there was a brief alarm at reports of another Audience Selection poll, for Tuesday morning's *Sun*, showing the Alliance 4 percent ahead of Labour. By this time the discrepancy between Audience Selection's results and those of the other polling organizations had been widely noted. In any case, another survey, by Marplan for Tuesday's *Guardian*, showed Labour still ahead. The Conservative lead over Labour was a mighty 21 percent.

Several events in the final week of the election would have caused interest under more exciting circumstances. A set of unemployment statistics was released on Friday, 3 June. The total of registered unemployed had fallen by 121,000. But when seasonal and other factors were taken into account, the adjusted figure showed an increase of 23,000. On Saturday, 4 June, the rally organized by the Trade Union Congress to coincide with the end of the People's March for Jobs was held in London. The disappointing attendance showed the demoralization of the Labour movement. Neither the unemployment figures nor the rally about jobs made much impact. The campaign effectively was over.

Assessment

Tools do not exist to permit a scientific assessment of the effectiveness of political campaigns. The comments that follow are impressionistic. They focus on three aspects of the election: the unemployment issue, the impact of Conservative advertising, and the choice of the election date.

It used to be accepted as gospel that a British government that permitted unemployment to rise was sure to be punished by the electors.[18] Recently, a variety of reasons have been adduced to explain why unemployment has become politically tolerable: state benefits have decreased the material hardships of joblessness; the unemployed are isolated, unorganized, and thus unable to make an impact (as shown by the poor turnout for the People's March for Jobs); despite high rates of unemployment, the vast majority are working and they care little about those who are not; and governments have succeeded in educating the public to lower their economic expectations.

What light does the 1983 election throw on this discussion? Survey evidence gives no clear answer.[19] There appears to have been a measure of acceptance of unemployment and disposition to blame international factors beyond the government's control.[20] There were also signs of serious dissatisfaction that could have been damaging to the Conservatives had Labour exploited them. The election of 1983 demonstrated the incompetence and disunity of the Labour party. It did not put the importance of the unemployment issue to the test.

Not only was unemployment seen by an overwhelming majority to be among the most important issues facing the country,[21] over a third of voters had personal experience of the problem, either through being jobless themselves or having a close family member or friend out of work. A majority felt that the government needed to spend more on the unemployed. The Conservatives were seen to be far more complacent and out of touch with the problem than Labour. A majority accepted such pessimistic statements as "many school leavers will never get a job at all," "unemployment inevitably leads to increased crime," "Britain is in such a state at the moment that things cannot go on much longer like this." What seems to have prevented these negative feelings from being translated into votes for Labour was a degree of trust in the capacity of the Thatcher administration combined with a low rating of Labour's practicability and competence, a feeling that grew steadily during the campaign.

To what extent was this lack of confidence in Labour a consequence of Conservative party advertising and party election broadcasts? In 1983, as in other recent elections, journalists were fascinated by the techniques of political persuasion employed by the party machines and, in particular, by the Conservative party's advertising agency, Saatchi and Saatchi. The assumption behind this interest was that advertising and "image making" can and do have a decisive impact on voting. While advertising was one significant part of the Conservative campaign, its importance can be exaggerated. Moreover, it is unclear whether the Conservative publicity won votes or lost them.

Within Central Office, verdicts on the party's election publicity were mixed. The creative flair shown by the agency was highly praised. The press advertisements were thought to have been more successful than the posters. The opening press advertisement attacking Labour's manifesto was especially admired. One strength of the publicity, particularly in the opening phases of the campaign, was its coordination and persistence. The general secretary of the Labour party was later to envy "the repetitive Conservative emphasis on the statement that 'every Labour Government in history has increased unemployment.' "

A few senior party officials were unhappy about the style of some of the advertisements, which they considered unduly negative and extreme. No detailed surveys on the effects of party publicity appear to have been carried out at Central Office during the election, though the responses to a question in one private poll yielded the information that a larger number of those questioned felt less likely rather than more likely to vote Conservative as a result of seeing party publicity. In any case, the press advertising for which a party pays occupies far less space than the coverage by newspaper reporters. Party election broadcasts on television and radio receive less air time than news broadcasts or interviews of party leaders by professional broadcasters. It is likely that the way in which a party plans its press conferences or briefs its leaders for speeches and interviews is at least as important as its advertising program.

Had the Labour party been able to take the initiative and to exploit the underlying dissatisfactions of the public, particularly concerning unemployment, or had the Conservative campaign been undermined by outside events or unexpected incidents, the government easily could have found itself in trouble. It walked a tightrope between unresponsiveness and overreaction. The cautious Conservative manifesto, the slow pace set by Central Office, and the concerted attacks on Labour in speeches and party publicity easily could have seemed evasive and negative. In the 1970 general election, the incumbent Labour prime minister, Wilson (later created Lord Wilson), was accused of complacency, negative Tory-bashing, and lack of vision for his campaign, which was in some ways similar to the Conservative campaign of 1983. Wilson lost the election.

The style of the Conservative campaign was based on the calculation, which was to prove amply justified, that Labour's internal divisions made it susceptible to attack and that it would be caught off guard and unable to present a coherent, credible economic alternative. The key to the success of the Conservative strategy was arguably the skillful timing and short duration of the election. The advocacy of June 1983 by Parkinson and some of his Central Office advisers was their critical contribution to Thatcher's reelection.

A Note on Conservative Party Finances, 1979–83

This note presents statistics on Conservative finances in the 1983 campaign and during the previous parliamentary cycle. It has been drawn up on the same basis as the figures for earlier years presented in the author's *British Political*

Table 2.1   Conservative party central income and
expenditure, 1979–83 (in thousands of pounds)

| Year | Income | | | | Expenditure | | |
	Donations (net)	Constituency quotas	Interest (net)	Total	Routine	General election	Total
1979–80*	4,263	907	118	5,302	4,586	1,299	5,895
1980–81	2,241	926	70	3,237	5,541	—	5,541
1981–82	2,934	953	21	4,098	4,201	—	4,201
1982–83	3,738	1,046	30	4,814	4,623	150	4,773

Source: Conservative Central Office.
Notes: *denotes general election year. The table has been drawn up on the same basis as table 28
of *British Political Finance*, p. 138. Virtually all of the costs of the 1983 general election will fall
into the accounting year 1983–84.

Finance 1830–1980 (Washington, D.C.: American Enterprise Institute, 1981)
and "Financing the British General Election of 1979," in Howard R. Penniman,
ed., *Britain at the Polls, 1979: A Study of the General Election* (Washington,
D.C.: American Enterprise Institute, 1981). Technical problems involved in
distinguishing routine and campaign finances are discussed in "Financing the
British General Election of 1979," pp. 213–14.

Routine central finance   Conservative central income and expenditure in the
period between the general elections of 1979 and 1983 is shown in table 2.1.
Expenditure for 1979–80 includes a portion of the party's central spending for
the general election of 1979 and the relatively high income for that year reflects
extra donations for the campaign. The statistics are a continuation of those
given in table 28 of *British Political Finance*. During the time between the
general elections of 1979 and 1983 inflation was over 50 percent. In real terms,
routine central spending was 40 percent lower in 1982–83 than in 1979–80.

Routine constituency finance   The routine finances of the 633 constituency
associations in Britain seem to have declined slightly in real terms since 1979.
Total routine constituency income and expenditure is probably about £7–9
million per annum. As shown in table 2.1, the constituency associations contributed about £1 million per annum (including quota credits). These constituency contributions failed to keep pace with inflation.

Central campaign finance   The central cost of the 1983 election was marginally higher in real terms than that of 1979. The 1983 campaign cost £3.9
million while that of 1979 cost £3.7 million at 1983 values. In 1983, the early
election date meant that spending was concentrated in the short campaign
period (9 May–9 June) whereas in the 1979 election much of the expenditure

Table 2.2 Conservative party central precampaign and
campaign expenditures (in thousands of pounds)

| | 1978–79 | | | 1983 | | |
Item	Pre-campaign	Campaign	Total	Pre-campaign	Campaign	Total
Grants to constituencies	0	42	42	0	62	62
Advertising						
Posters	(380)	(211)	(591)	(40)	843	(883)
Press	(267)	(499)	(766)	(80)	1,725	(1,805)
Cinema	(111)	(33)	(144)	0	0	0
Total	758	743	1,501	120	2,568	2,688
Political broadcasts (production costs)	276	149	425	200	306	506
Opinion research	0	70	70	0	96	96
Party publications (net)	0	113	113	0	212	212
Leaders' tours and meetings[a]	0	13	13	0	52	52
Staff and adminis-tration costs[b]	0	169	169	0	262	262
Total	1,034	1,299	2,333	320	3,588	3,908

Source: Conservative Central Office.
[a] Thatcher's tour cost an estimated £26,000 net of receipts from journalists for seats on the campaign airplane.
[b] Cost of additional staff and overtime payments for routine staff.

was for pre-election publicity. In 1983, as in 1979, press advertisements, renting poster sites, and production costs for party political broadcasts were the most important items of expenditure.

Constituency campaign finance   Legal limits on spending by parliamentary candidates were raised in line with inflation since the last election. The inflation-linking of spending limits had been enacted in 1978. Candidates in county constituencies were permitted to spend £2,700 plus 3.1 pence per elector and in borough constituencies £2,700 plus 2.3 pence per elector. This worked out to be £4,700 for an average county constituency (at an exchange rate of $1.50, this was equivalent to $7,050) and £4,200 for an average borough ($6,400). Conservative candidates spent an average of £3,320 or 72 percent of the legal maximum. In total, Conservative candidates spent £2.1 million, slightly less in real terms than in 1979. In almost all winnable constituencies, Conservative candidates spent almost to the legal limit. The pattern of local campaign expenditure was similar to that for 1979, the most important item being printing costs.

Summary   Total Conservative central party spending in the 1983 election and in the preceding financial year amounted to approximately £8 million (nearly £4 million for the campaign and the rest for routine headquarters spending). Local party spending amounted to some £8.5–10.5 million, of which £2.1 million represented campaign spending. This makes a grand total of £16.5–18.5 million, £6 million of which was for the election and the rest for one year's routine operating costs of the party organization. These figures are net of transfers of money from the constituencies to Central Office and vice versa.

The Labour Campaign

PETER KELLNER

———— Almost nothing went right for Labour in the 1983 general election. The party entered the election with unpopular policies, an unpopular leader, and a vivid public image of a party at war with itself. The month-long campaign, instead of erasing those impressions, intensified them. In virtually every respect—personal, political, tactical, organizational—the campaign was a disaster. At the start of the campaign Labour commanded the support of 34 percent of the electorate—four points lower than its support in the 1979 general election, despite the sharp rise in unemployment that had occurred since Margaret Thatcher came to power four years earlier. During the campaign Labour's support fell another six points to 28 percent, to give the party its lowest share of the national vote since 1918.[1] To explain why Labour lost the 1983 election as heavily as it did, we must therefore analyze two things: why Labour failed to recover from its already low level of support between 1979 and the start of the 1983 campaign; and why Labour lost further ground during that campaign.

Labour's Internal Divisions

When Labour lost power in 1979 it had been in government for eleven of the previous fifteen years. Under first Harold Wilson and then James Callaghan, Labour had assumed the air of Britain's natural party of government. It was a false assumption that provoked on the one hand fatal complacency in the party leadership, and on the other hand destructive frustration among many local activists. In government, Labour ministers had gone to considerable lengths to distance themselves from the more radical aspects of the party's program in order to maintain Labour's appeal to "moderate" electors whose votes were believed to determine the outcome of British general elections. The 1974–79 Labour government, for example, had not withdrawn Britain from the European Economic Community (a referendum was held in 1975 to enable Wilson to retreat gracefully from this obligation); there was no great expansion of public spending or public ownership of industry; and a specific 1974 election promise to end some of the financial privileges of private schools was not implemented.

The performance of Labour in those five years precipitated many of the troubles that culminated in the disaster of 1983. For while James Callaghan, in particular, was willing to risk alienating left-wing activists after becoming prime minister in 1976, he failed to reap sufficient electoral support for his political strategy. When he lost the 1979 election, not only did Labour achieve its lowest share of the vote for more than 40 years, its support fell most sharply among the group of electors whose votes Labour always needs if it is to win power: the votes of skilled manual workers and their families. The subsequent battles that afflicted the party can, to a large extent, be reduced to the bitterly conflicting approaches to this question: how should Labour seek to win back the missing voters—by developing a better "moderate" strategy, or by reasserting the party's socialist principles? In the event it was the noise of those battles rather than their outcome that made the greatest impact on the public mind, with the result that Labour lost yet more support.

First, the party's annual conference at Blackpool in October 1980 voted to change the method of electing the party leader, removing the power from MPs alone and giving a greater say to activists (who are generally left-wing) in local constituency parties and in the trade unions. A rearguard action led by the former foreign secretary, David Owen, to minimize the power of the activists failed when a special conference was held at Wembley in January 1981 to settle the details of the new electoral college.[2] This event precipitated the final departure of Owen, together with former cabinet ministers William Rodgers and Shirley Williams from the Labour party; two months later, together with Roy Jenkins, they set up the new Social Democratic party.

With the new system for electing the leader and deputy leader in place, the left's most prominent figure, Tony Benn, challenged the party's deputy leader, Denis Healey, for his job. In the six-month campaign that followed, Labour was portrayed as a party at war with itself. The deputy leadership is itself a post with little power, but the contest symbolized the bitter division between Labour's left and right wings. Healey won by the narrowest of margins—less than 1 percent—a result that illuminated the party's plight. For while Healey had majority support in the unions, and a two-to-one lead over Benn among MPs, Benn secured 80 percent of the support of local constituency parties.

Over the following eighteen months other disputes kept the left-right division in the public eye, with each division putting greater stress on the party leader, Michael Foot, who was desperately trying to generate at least the appearance, if not the reality, of party unity. The most stormy of these issues was the fate of the editorial board of a Trotskyist weekly newspaper, *Militant*. The charge against *Militant* was that it was a cover for a secret organization—a "party within a party"—attempting by unconstitutional means gradually to take over the Labour party. A year-long wrangle, involving a halfhearted official party inquiry, an inept resolution at the 1982 annual conference that was wrongly thought would give the party leadership the power to expel *Militant* members, and an embarrassing trudge through the courts as the editors of *Militant* sought to block any expulsions: all these events helped to reinforce the impression of a party incapable of putting its own house in order.

Labour's essential problem at the beginning of the 1983 campaign was that most electors simply did not believe the party was able to act as an effective government. Foot consistently was found by the opinion polls to be the most unpopular party leader since polling began. In April 1983 Market and Opinion Research International (MORI) found that only 20 percent of the electorate were "satisfied" with Foot's performance.[3] A Gallup survey in the same month found that just 19 percent considered Labour to be a "united" party, while 73 percent thought it "divided."[4]

Foot and his colleagues hoped and expected that Thatcher would delay calling an election until the autumn of 1983 or the spring of 1984. This would have given the party more time to recover from the disasters of the previous three years, which had culminated in the heavy defeat of Peter Tatchell, a controversial left-wing Labour candidate in February 1983 in Bermondsey—a rundown inner London constituency and previously one of Labour's safest seats anywhere in Britain. Following the Bermondsey by-election there was widespread press speculation that the 69-year-old Foot would resign as party leader and make way for Healey. In fact Foot had no intention of stepping down: the press reports had stemmed mainly from right-wing Labour MPs disgruntled with Foot's performance.

Had Labour lost the following by-election, held in a Labour marginal in the northern town of Darlington, Foot might have been compelled to resign. Aware of the danger, Labour's national organization put an unparalleled effort into holding the seat. The party commissioned a private poll to guide its strategy, a fact that would not normally merit attention. It was, however, the first quantitative poll of any kind anywhere that the party had commissioned since 1979. Late in the day—too late—the party was beginning to apply some degree of professionalism to its task. In Darlington Labour also benefited from having an outstanding local candidate, Ossie O'Brien, who achieved a rapport both with voters and the media, in sharp contrast with Tatchell in Bermondsey.

In the event, Labour held Darlington with an increased majority. The swing to Labour was insufficient to indicate a nationwide Labour victory, but it finally scotched talk of Foot's resignation. The Darlington result, however, was double-edged for the Labour leader. While it confirmed his personal position, it also offered encouragement to the Conservatives, whose candidate had climbed from third place at the beginning of the campaign to a good second at the end. The result suggested that Foot might not have the time he needed to improve Labour's public image, as Thatcher might be tempted to call a June 1983 election after all. Nationwide elections for local councils were held on 5 May, and confirmed opinion poll evidence of a comfortable Conservative lead nationally. Four days later came the announcement Foot was dreading: the election would be held on 9 June.

Labour's Manifesto: All Things to All Socialists

Labour's 1983 general election manifesto, *New Hope for Britain*, was the longest produced by an major party in modern times. Its twenty thousand words embraced promises on everything from full employment to fox hunting. It contained fatal ambiguities on both defense and economic policy—ambiguities which, under the intense spotlight of a four-week campaign, exploded in Labour's face. In a list of "seven major failings" drawn up by Geoff Bish, the party's head of research, two weeks after the election, the manifesto came out on top. Bish criticized "our failure to prepare a manifesto, and a policy programme, which accurately reflected the concerns and needs of ordinary voters."[5]

Labour's election manifestos are traditionally a source of much friction and maneuvering between the parliamentary leadership and the National Executive Committee. Under Clause V of the party's constitution they have a joint responsibility for drawing up the manifesto. This generates an almost automatic conflict because, for the past quarter-century, the parliamentary leadership has been consistently to the right of the National Executive, whose membership is determined overwhelmingly by the trade unions and the constituency parties. In practice the conflict traditionally has been resolved by the party leader. Both Wilson and Callaghan were ruthless in discarding policies they disliked, even when those policies had won clear support at annual conferences. Although it was theoretically possible to outvote even the most determined party leader on the manifesto contents, both Wilson and Callaghan invariably had their way. In 1979, for example, Labour's manifesto was written by Callaghan's personal staff at 10 Downing Street and effectively imposed on the party's national machine.

In 1983 the manifesto was drawn up differently. For one thing Foot, though by no means as left-wing as many in the party, still retained many of his left-wing views. (He was, for example, a long-standing opponent of the possession by Britain of nuclear weapons.) For another thing, while the left was making advances on a number of constitutional matters, such as the method of electing the party leader, it also was securing a succession of policy victories at annual conferences. In 1982, for the first time, the conference approved by a two-thirds majority an unambiguous resolution demanding the scrapping of Britain's nuclear weapons and the expulsion of American nuclear bases, and requiring a future Labour government to prevent the stationing of cruise or Pershing missiles in Britain.[6]

According to Labour's constitution, any resolution that obtains a two-thirds majority becomes part of Labour's "programme": an evolving catalog of policies from which the contents of each election manifesto are supposed to be selected. The issue in each manifesto is the nature of that selection. What happened in 1983 was that barely any selection was done; everything went into the manifesto.

The manifesto itself was simply a reprint of Labour's campaign document, agreed in March 1983; only Foot's introduction was new. The decision to reissue this document was made on 11 May, two days after the election was called. With Foot unwilling to exert his authority to insist on a shorter, clearer, more popular manifesto, none of his parliamentary colleagues in the shadow cabinet were able to argue for one with any success; only Peter Shore, the shadow chancellor of the exchequer, even tried. The decision to reissue the March campaign document was made in under one hour—by far the shortest manifesto meeting in living memory.

The central defect of the manifesto was that it was not, in reality, a policy program at all: It was, rather, a document spelling out the terms of a policy truce between left and right. This was most noticeable, and became acutely embarrassing, in the areas of defense and economic policy.

Defense   The party leadership was, by early 1983, united on a number of defense issues: continuing membership in NATO, but rejecting the stationing of cruise or Pershing missiles, or the purchasing of Trident missiles to modernize Britain's nuclear arsenal. Where the leadership was divided was over the future of Britain's Polaris force. The left wing, having won its two-thirds majority at the previous autumn's annual conference, wanted a commitment to scrap Polaris unconditionally within the lifetime (five years) of the next Labour government. The right wing led by Healey—who in the 1960s had been defense secretary in the first Wilson government, and was now shadow foreign secretary —wanted Polaris to be included in multilateral arms reduction talks with the Soviet Union, and its phasing out to be negotiated in those talks. The logic of this position was that if those talks failed, Polaris would not be phased out.

This is how that particular square was circled in the campaign document-cum-manifesto:

> We will propose that Britain's Polaris force be included in the nuclear disarmament negotiations in which Britain must take part. We will, after

consultation, carry through in the lifetime of the next parliament our non-nuclear defense policy.[7]

The first sentence gave the right what it wanted, while the second sentence upheld the views of the left. But together the two sentences failed to confront the central question: what if the negotiations should fail? The left argued that the second sentence still would apply, and that a Labour government should relinquish Polaris regardless. The right argued that this was nonsense: there is no point in negotiating with the Russians about something you intend to do anyway. If the negotiations failed, all bets would be off. To the left, Labour's unilateralist posture was a commitment to be implemented regardless; to the right it was an objective whose attainment would be conditional on the success of negotiations with the Soviet Union. As the election campaign developed, this issue came to haunt Labour, and defense, which Foot believed would be a big vote-winner for Labour, turned out to be a major vote-loser.

An incomes policy?   On the economy, Labour was united on the need for a major increase in public spending to reduce unemployment. Labour proposed to employ basically Keynesian techniques to stimulate demand, including a considerable increase of government borrowing in the early years. By these means Labour hoped to reduce unemployment from three million to less than one million in five years. To opponents of Keynesian economics, Labour's economic strategy was doomed to fail; but many economists who maintained their Keynesian beliefs detected a more specific weakness in Labour's plans: the absence of any effective mechanism to prevent a rapid rise in money wages that in turn would provoke explosive inflation.

Labour's problem was spelled out vividly in the *Guardian* by Christopher Huhne in April 1982. Huhne had taken the ingredients of an "alternative" budget prepared that spring by Shore and tested them on the treasury's model of the British economy. Huhne wrote:

> Without an incomes policy, the economy can grow quickly and unemployment can be cut. . . . But those benefits come only at the cost of a wage explosion in the first and second years, which does cause inflationary horrors. . . . The conclusion must be that another Labour government will need a firm incomes policy if it is to stand any chance of meeting its unemployment target.[8]

Labour's campaign, however, ducked the issue. It referred to "the national economic assessment, to be agreed each year with the trade unions. The assessment will . . . *take into account* the impact of cost increases on the future rate of inflation."[9] (Emphasis added.)

The "national economic assessment" was to be an annual agreement on economic and social policy between a new Labour government and the trade unions. What never was made explicit, however, was exactly what the unions would be expected to deliver in terms of pay restraint in return for the government delivering lower unemployment, improved public services, higher pensions, and so on. Labour's parliamentary leadership, including (privately) Foot himself, believed a firm incomes policy would be essential, but this course had been rejected both at Labour party conferences and by the annual "parliament" of the trade union movement, the Trades Union Congress. For the purposes of the election manifesto, "take into account" was the best that could be managed.

Common Market There was one other issue where the manifesto was clear, but which Healey and another prominent right-winger, Roy Hattersley, attempted to qualify during the course of the election campaign: withdrawal from the European Economic Community (EEC). The manifesto stated:

> British withdrawal from the Community is the right policy for Britain—to be completed well within the lifetime of the parliament. That is our commitment. But we are also committed to bring about our withdrawal in an amicable and orderly way, so that we do not prejudice employment or the prospect of increased political and economic co-operation with the whole of Europe.[10]

In previous elections the more fervent pro-EEC members of the Labour party had fought to prevent an outright commitment to withdrawal, but the most prominent of those people left Labour in 1981 to form the SDP. There was, therefore, little resistance in principle to the 1983 manifesto taking an anti-EEC line. However, some right-wingers felt the commitment was too absolute. They were not convinced that withdrawal could be negotiated in a way that would keep jobs safe. One week before polling day, Healey appeared to make withdrawal conditional on successful negotiations with other EEC members. Appearing on BBC television he said Labour would pull out of the EEC "providing—and we promise to do this in our manifesto—we negotiate a trade agreement with the countries which stay in the Common Market." The same day Hattersley told a press conference, "I support the manifesto which clearly states we should leave the EEC subject only to it not having an adverse effect on the economy."[11]

By this time it was probably too late for Healey's or Hattersley's words to have much impact—positive or negative—on Labour's campaign. Perhaps surprisingly, the EEC never became a major election issue. Had it done so, it undoubtedly would have become an addition to the list of Labour's policy embarrassments.

Foot's Campaign

Labour's Campaign Committee Only one senior Labour official held the same post in 1983 that he had in 1979: Geoff Bish, the head of research. Otherwise Labour's campaign committee was built around people some of whom had little experience organizing a general election campaign, and others who had previously done so in a more junior capacity. The party had a new leader (Foot), a new general secretary (James Mortimer, whose career had previously been as a trade union official and subsequently industrial relations conciliator), and a new national agent (David Hughes, who had been a regional organizer in Newcastle upon Tyne in 1979). Foot's political adviser, Richard Clements, previously had edited the small left-wing weekly paper *Tribune*, and the party's head of publicity, Nick Grant, recently had come from a trade union to work for the party. Foot's own press officer, Sir Tom McCaffrey, had been Callaghan's press officer four years earlier; but then, as a civil servant working for a prime minister, he carefully avoided involving himself with the party campaign. To this lack of experience, and partly because of it, the party machine added two mistakes of its own at the start of the campaign, according to Bish:

> 1. The Office Campaigns Committee, the only body which was able to give some sort of coherence and follow-through to the work of the Campaign Committee *prior* to the election, disappeared.
> 2. Joyce Gould,[12] who was directly responsible for pulling the strands together prior to the campaign, also "disappeared" into the job of arranging the Leader's tours, etc.[13]

The campaign committee itself epitomized Labour's problems in the 1983 election. In previous elections it had contained a core of just ten or twelve members working for the party leader. In 1983 typically twenty to twenty-five people attended. As Bish subsequently wrote, "Even before the campaign started, we knew we had a serious problem with the campaign committee. It was far too large; attendance fluctuated between, and even during, meetings; and it quickly became, for the participants, another chore."[14] Sam McCluskie, Labour party chairman for 1982–83, agreed. The campaign committee, he said, a week after Labour's defeat, was a "rag, tag and bobtail" affair. "People I had never seen before just seemed to wander in and out giving advice, and then vanishing. There was no structured approach and very few members of the shadow cabinet were present."[15]

Formally the campaign committee was supposed to run Labour's election campaign. It met each morning at 8 A.M., was briefed by Robert Worcester, managing director of MORI, on the results of Labour's private poll conducted the day before,[16] and discussed tactics for the day ahead, starting with the morning press conference, held each day in London at 9 A.M. For any campaign committee to operate effectively it needs to be able to make clear decisions, to communicate them, and to secure acceptance of them. Labour's 1983 campaign committee failed in all three functions. In a detailed report in the *Guardian* on 30 June 1983, Martin Linton wrote:

> The committee was rather too large to take decisions or, when it did, to impose those decisions or to check that they had been carried out. Some people paid scant attention to it. "I was conscious of a number of highly individualistic people who would encounter strong opposition to what they were intending to do in the campaign committee, but would then go ahead and do it anyway," said one regular attender. There often appeared to be a vacuum at the centre of the campaign. "It was never clear who made the decisions. You could never work out who was in charge because no one really was," said one adviser. There was no adequate chain of command when Jim Mortimer was out of the office. Instructions took a long time to be passed on. A decision taken by the campaign committee at 8 in the morning might not be conveyed to the person charged with the task until 5 in the evening.

Press Conferences The round of morning press conferences is one of the journalistic rituals of British election campaigning. In 1983 they started earlier than ever before. Reporters who were so inclined—and there were quite a number—would take an early breakfast in the imposing Victorian grandeur of the National Liberal Club, near the north end of Whitehall, before proceeding up the majestically wide circular stairs to the 8:30 press conference held jointly each morning by the Liberals and Social Democrats. By 8:50 the press conference would be over and a special bus then carried reporters for the one-mile journey down Whitehall, past the Houses of Parliament, to Smith Square. In one corner of the square resides Transport House, the headquarters of the Transport Workers Union; in another the Conservative Central Office. Labour's press conferences began at 9 A.M. and finished in time for reporters to cross Smith Square for the Conservatives' 9:30 press conferences.

The Transport Workers Union used to lease part of its building to the Labour party. In 1980, however, Labour acquired its own building two miles farther south, across the River Thames. But Labour's new premises did not have a hall large enough to accommodate election press conferences; in any case the tight schedule of the conferences required them all to be held near to each other. So the main hall of Transport House was employed, as in previous elections, for Labour's press conferences. One immediate problem this posed for the party was that of having a geographically split base. On more than one occasion artwork being prepared at the party's headquarters in south London to illustrate the theme of a morning press conference was delayed by heavy traffic, and failed to reach Transport House in time.

From the outset Labour realized it had to overcome the problem of Foot's unpopularity. One way it tried to do this was to use the morning press conferences to project Labour's other leading spokespeople — Healey, Shore, and Hattersley in particular. Whereas Thatcher chaired most of the Conservative press conferences, and dominated the ones she took, Mortimer chaired all of Labour's. Foot took part in some press conferences, but he was the dominant figure in only a few.

At first the strategy seemed to have some success. The main purpose of the morning press conferences was to obtain favorable coverage in television news bulletins between lunchtime and the early evening. During the first week of the campaign, when Shore usually had the lead role, Labour achieved its highest poll ratings of the election campaign.[17] As the campaign progressed, however, Labour's press conferences became ordeals to be endured with minimum harm, rather than opportunities to gain support.

Labour's first disadvantage, compared with the Conservative press conferences, was the physical setting. The Conservatives had gutted and re-equipped their conference hall to provide the best possible setting and lighting for television cameras, with the aim that the extracts shown on television screens should portray Thatcher and her team in a confident, reassuring mood. Labour, on the other hand, decorated the hall at Transport House as if the party were mounting a rally for the faithful. The platform, raised some three feet above the body of the hall, made the speakers appear aloof and remote. The platform table and backcloth were decked out in bright red, which came across garishly, even threateningly, on television screens. (Not until mid-campaign was this image problem noticed; then the backcloth had a wide strip containing a softer pink-and-orange Labour party motif added at the height most regularly recorded by the TV cameras.)

Another contrast between the Conservative and Labour press conferences was in the way they were chaired. Thatcher controlled the Tory conferences with the air of an effective teacher marshaling a group of schoolchildren on a day outing, while Mortimer ran the Labour conferences like a union official trying to control members he did not like and whose loyalty he doubted. At first he tried to block questions about any subject other than the one chosen by the party for that day's conference; this raised a number of reporters' hackles. Thatcher, in contrast, would say, "Could we first have any further questions there may be on . . ." (health, education, or whatever) "If you don't mind? Would that be all right?" It always was. Only after Mortimer was made aware that he was handling the problem badly did he, too, change the procedure to allow general questions at the end of each press conference.

Mortimer's worst moment came on 26 May, after stories of dissension within the Labour campaign, and especially about Foot's performance, had leaked to the press. He announced at the start of that morning's press conference that the campaign committee had expressed its unanimous support for Foot's leadership. Mortimer intended to end press speculation; instead he merely increased it. If the campaign committee felt it necessary to pass a vote of confidence in the party leader, so the argument ran, then things must be really bad. Someone with more experience of party politics and election campaigns would not have made that mistake.

Foot's travels   The centerpieces of all modern British election campaigns are the tours, speeches, and television interviews of the party leaders. While the morning press conferences were used to maximize the exposure of other members of Labour's team, it was still inevitable that Foot himself would dominate television coverage of the Labour campaign, especially in the evening bulletins.

Part of the point of a leader's tour is to rally the faithful and enthuse party activists, especially in marginal constituencies. But by far the most important point of a leader's tour is to generate favorable coverage on television and radio and in the newspapers. One of the most routine ways of doing this is to insert in each major speech an original, self-contained, two-to-three-minute section that can be used in news bulletins. This requires careful crafting and execution; Harold Wilson, for example, used to rehearse and time the "TV excerpt" part of each speech, and ensure that he presented the most favorable image for the cameras by not looking down at his text, and modulating his voice to avoid sounding like a demagogue.

Foot's very skill as a public orator let him down in the 1983 campaign. Foot, who suffers from poor eyesight, had been making effective, impassioned public speeches without notes for four decades. But during the 1983 campaign he was unable to master the precise demands of public speaking for a TV audience. On 17 May, in one of his first big speeches, Foot electrified an audience of fifteen hundred people in Liverpool with his attack on the Conservative record. He received an ecstatic ovation. However, as the party faithful were cheering, Foot's political adviser, Richard Clements, was sunk deep in gloom; he knew that in media terms the speech had been a disaster. The episode was described by Peter Gillman in the *Sunday Times*:

> Clements's problem was that Foot had just dismembered his plans to ensure that the speech received maximum media coverage.
>
> The scheme had been devised on the train carrying Foot's entourage and the accompanying press corps from Glasgow to Liverpool that morning. In order to ensure that the reporters had a strong passage from Foot's speech ahead of delivery so they could file it for their first editions, Clements drafted a crisp 500 words for the Labour leader on the ravages of

youth unemployment. He typed it out on the train and distributed it that afternoon.

But that night Foot spoiled everything. Apparently carried away by his own exuberance he omitted to utter the crucial words.

"What happened?" a reporter asked Clements as the applause for Foot's speech died away. Clements raised his eyes to the ceiling and said weakly: "It's up to him what he says." [18]

The effect was, first, that television coverage concentrated on the climax to Foot's speech—which came across far less well on a small screen than in a large auditorium—and, second, that the episode soured relations between Foot and the press. The *Times*, for example, removed the 500-word extract from its later editions and lodged an official complaint with the Labour party about its election arrangements. It was one further addition to the media's difficulties of following Foote's campaign. For £1,000, reporters were given a complete transport package for following Thatcher's campaign; as a part of the deal, reporters always were taken ahead of the prime minister to each whistle-stop destination so they could report her arrival. No such arrangements were made for reporters with Foot. They were told where he would be and when, and left to their own devices to keep up with him.

It was not only in relations with the press that Foot's tour went wrong. By a spectacular misjudgment, Foot's itinerary was drawn up to include an appearance on 28 May in Bradford, where one of Labour's local candidates was Pat Wall, a leading member of *Militant*. At one point during the *Militant* controversy, Foot had spoken of his wish to prevent known *Militant* members from standing as Labour candidates. He had lost that battle, but now found himself apparently choosing to share a platform with one of them. When Foot's plans were disclosed in the *Observer* on 22 May, they caused the kind of row that make unwitting politicians wish they could disappear into a hole in the ground. Foot refused to change his plans—to do so might have looked worse than keeping to them—but it was neither surprising nor helpful to Labour when the only part of his Bradford speech that received wide publicity was his instruction to Wall to behave himself if he were elected to the House of Commons.[19]

Foot's television interviews went only slightly better. The main television channels broadcast more programs consisting of interviews with the party leaders than ever before: sixteen in less than three weeks, or roughly one every weekday on average. Although it would be wrong to overstate the influence a party leader has on his or her party's performance, the qualities of the different party leaders were more important in 1983 than in any other recent election. Foot's task was to overcome the fact that only 21 percent rated him a "capable leader" and a mere 9 percent thought he was good in a crisis, while Thatcher's rating on both points was 62 percent.[20]

Foot failed to close the gap. At the start of the campaign Gallup found that 49 percent of the electorate thought the Conservatives had the best leaders, compared with 16 percent who named Labour. By the end of the campaign the figures were 56 percent Conservative, 10 percent Labour.[21] His television interviews did not help. On 29 May, eleven days before polling day, he faced independent television's most penetrating interviewer, Brian Walden, for an hour-long interview on *Weekend World*. By this time differences of opinion among senior Labour politicians on defense policy had become a dominant election issue. Far from deflecting Walden on to other areas of policy where he might be able to project Labour in a favorable light, Foot allowed more than half the interview to be taken up by a tortuous discussion of just where Labour stood on nuclear weapons. Walden asked Foot seven times whether a Labour government would give up Polaris regardless of any response by the Soviet Union. Each time Foot gave a qualified response that did nothing to dispel the public impression of uncertainty and ambiguity in the party leadership.[22] Foot's inability to give straight answers (or, if one is trying to be generous, his refusal to make glib, oversimple statements on a complex issue merely to satisfy the demands of "good television") made him appear uncertain and confused.

As the campaign progressed, the gap between Foot's perception of the campaign, and the public's perception of Foot grew ever wider. Foot was, indeed, receiving enthusiastic receptions wherever he went; his audiences loved his meetings. But in the final two-and-a-half weeks of the campaign, Labour's national support, as measured by the opinion polls, declined almost without break. On the Sunday before the election Foot said, "There must be two elections going on at the same time. I have been attending a different one from the one reflected in the polls."[23] He was, of course, right, but not in the sense he meant.

The defense and Falklands disasters   On 29 May the main feature in the *Sunday Times* was headed: "How Labour shot itself." It was a harsh, but not unfair, way to introduce an account of how, in the second week of the campaign, Labour suffered a self-inflicted wound over the party's policy toward nuclear weapons. As we already have seen, Labour's manifesto fudged the issue of whether the achievement of a non-nuclear defense policy within five years was to be an unqualified commitment, or an objective that might have to be modified. Anthony Bevins, the political correspondent of the *Times*, had asked Foot a number of times to clarify the position. On 23 May Bevins asked again: would Foot scrap Polaris "willy-nilly?" Foot did not offer a straight answer; he said Labour headquarters would be "happy to supply you" with further details of the party's nuclear policy. Later that day, however, the press office told Bevins that no further details were available.[24]

Meanwhile Healey, in a phone-in program at a local radio station in the east midlands town of Leicester, was acknowledging the difficulties of negotiating Polaris away. As soon as Healey's words were reported by the wire services, the media had its election story of the day: Labour was "split" on defense. Attempts to clarify the party's policy only made things worse. During the following forty-eight hours Healey said that if negotiations with the Russians failed, Labour would *not* scrap Polaris; then Foot, asked whether he agreed with Healey, said, "Read the manifesto very carefully and I think clarity will descend in all quarters." The following day Foot said he was in "full agreement" with Healey. Finally, a few hours later, John Silkin, Labour's defense spokesman, said in contrast that Labour would scrap Polaris *whatever* the Russians did. When Callaghan, speaking at a meeting in his own constituency in Cardiff, said the same week that it would be disastrous for Labour to pursue a unilateralist policy, the public image of a party in chaos was complete.

Labour's other major self-inflicted wound occurred in the final week of the campaign. Ever since the Falklands war in the spring of 1982, Labour leaders had been careful to avoid attacking the government for its handling of the war. Some backbench MPs, such as Benn, had consistently criticized government policy from the beginning, but as Labour had officially backed the sending of the task force (even though Foot at the time criticized Thatcher for not working hard enough to secure a diplomatic settlement of the crisis), and as the war had been not only successful but highly popular, Labour's best election strategy was manifestly to keep quiet about it.

Nevertheless, on 1 June, in a speech in Birmingham, Healey raised the Falklands issue. He said that Thatcher

> wraps herself in the Union Jack and exploits the sacrifices of our soldiers, sailors and airmen in the Falkland Islands for purely party advantage— and hopes to get away with it. It wasn't a very credible approach from the word "go" because this Prime Minister, who glories in slaughter, who has taken advantage of superb professionalism of our armed forces, is at this very moment lending the military dictatorship in Buenos Aires millions of pounds to buy weapons—including weapons made in Britain—to kill British servicemen.[25]

In the view of this writer, Healey's view of Thatcher and the Falklands has considerable justice; however it cannot be denied that his remarks were politically inept. His phrase "glories in slaughter" was condemned immediately by much of the press and by the Conservative party chairman, who said, "This must win the prize for the most contemptible statement of the election campaign." At the following morning's meeting of Labour's campaign committee Healey apologized to his colleagues for what he had said. Later in the day he told a television studio audience, "I do regret using the word 'slaughter.' I think

I should have used the word 'conflict.' When I used the word 'slaughter,' it was not a prepared remark."[26]

The following Monday, 6 June, remarks made by Neil Kinnock also caused a considerable stir. He was a member of a panel taking part in a local south of England television program, *The South Decides*. When one of the audience asked a question about Thatcher's handling of the Falklands crisis, another member of the audience stood up and shouted, "At least Mrs. Thatcher has got guts." Kinnock replied, "And it's a pity that people had to leave theirs on the ground at Goose Green in order to prove it."[27] The Conservatives, scarcely able to believe their luck at yet another Falklands own-goal by Labour, lost no time in pressing home their advantage. The same evening Michael Heseltine, the Conservatives' defense secretary, won considerable publicity for his description of Kinnock as "the self-appointed king of the gutter of politics."

As the election campaign entered its final seventy-two hours, almost everyone in the Labour leadership knew that the campaign had been a disaster, and the party was heading for catastrophic defeat.

Aftermath

On Sunday, 12 June, three days after the election, Foot declined nomination to serve as leader of the Labour party beyond its autumn 1983 annual conference. Healey also declined to stand again for the deputy leadership.

Four men stood for the leadership: Kinnock, Shore, Hattersley, and Eric Heffer. Broadly speaking, both Shore and Hattersley were on the right of the party, Heffer on the left, and Kinnock on the "inside left": he supported many of the left policy positions, for example on defense, but distanced himself from the far left on internal party matters. He refused to support Benn in the 1981 deputy leadership election and supported moves to expel the leading members of *Militant*. Kinnock quickly attracted the support of enough MPs, trade unions, and constituency parties to make his victory certain. On 2 October 1983, Kinnock was elected leader of the Labour party with 71 percent of the electoral college votes on the first ballot. He obtained a plurality of votes from his fellow MPs and large majorities from the trade union and constituency sections.

Hattersley was elected Kinnock's deputy, also on the first ballot. He obtained 67 percent of electoral college votes, 40 points ahead of his nearest rival, the left-winger Michael Meacher. The decisiveness of both the leadership and deputy leadership ballots came as something of a surprise. Until just a few days before the vote, Hattersley was believed to hold only a slim lead over Meacher. In the end two factors prevailed. First, individual ballots of party and trade union members were held on a far wider scale than before. Overwhelmingly those ballots showed a clear preference for the Kinnock-Hattersley "dream ticket" (a reference to the fact that both men have favorable public—especially television

—images, as well as to the fact that between them they span most of the ideological positions adopted by mainstream members of the party). The second factor that, in particular, gave Hattersley his large majority was the decision of Britain's largest union, the transport workers, to change its mind on the day of the ballots and to cast its 8 percent of the electoral college vote for Hattersley rather than Meacher.

The party that Kinnock and Hattersley inherited in October 1983 had to regain five million lost votes if it were to win power at the next general election. In one sense the party had reason to be hopeful. Unless some remarkable event like the Falklands war should recur, and if the British economy continued to be depressed, there was every reason to expect support for the Conservatives to decline to below 40 percent. That would leave at least 60 percent to be divided among the opposition parties. If Labour could regain its former public image as *the* alternative government to the Conservatives, it would stand some chance of taking the major share of that 60 percent and once more winning power.

At the party conference that immediately followed the leadership ballots the party presented a far more favorable and united face to the public than it had for at least a decade. The shock of defeat, combined with genuine enthusiasm for the new leadership, seemed to persuade all but a minority of left-wingers to seek common ground across the party. Immediate public reaction was encouraging. Two opinion polls conducted during the week of the conference showed Labour just three to five points behind the Conservatives—the narrowest gap since the start of the Falklands war eighteen months earlier.[28] Most of Labour's newly won support had come at the expense of the Liberal-SDP Alliance.

It will take some time to tell whether this represented a new beginning or a false dawn for the Labour party. Its appearance of new unity has been bought at the expense of sidetracking continuing policy problems and ambiguities: on defense, the Common Market, and incomes policy. There is no guarantee that they will not return to haunt and, once more, divide Labour. Moreover, the long-term social trends that have deprived Labour of so much support among trade union members and among the more affluent blue- and white-collar workers—especially the growing number of homeowners—might continue. In that case the anti-Conservative vote might be drawn increasingly to the Liberal-SDP Alliance. Labour then will face the prospect of irreversible decline. In order to challenge for first place in 1987 or 1988, the party will have to start by making sure that does not happen. It is a measure of the catastrophe that befell Labour in the 1983 general election that this issue should even be in doubt.

The Alliance Campaign, Watersheds, and Landslides: Was 1983 a Fault Line in British Politics?

JORGEN RASMUSSEN

———— By-election triumphs "do occur and help to put the troops in good heart, but they don't happen frequently enough to alter the fundamental realities of political power in Britain."[1] My closing words in the chapter on the Liberals in the previous book in this series had come to look extremely unprescient only two-and-a-half years after the 1979 general election. By the close of 1981 a couple of dozen moderate MPs had broken away from the Labour party to form the Social Democratic party that, in turn, had agreed to form an electoral alliance with the Liberals. Not only had that alliance won two incredible by-election victories, but an astounding Gallup poll found that 51 percent of the electorate intended to vote for candidates offered by this alliance at the next general election. In the cliché of the hour, the "mold" (in the sense of template but, to some extent, also in the sense of fungus) of British politics appeared to have been broken.

By the time the 1983 election campaign started, however, my verdict on the Liberals following the 1979 election had come to seem quite applicable to the Liberal-Social Democratic Alliance (or the Alliance, as it came to be called). So before examining the role of the Alliance in the election, it is necessary to summarize how its skyrocket zoomed into public consciousness and burst into a dazzling display of pyrotechnics, only to shimmer into darkness thereafter.

Party System Dealignment and Electoral Volatility

The 1970s were a decade in which the foundations of the traditional British two-party system, which had prevailed for a quarter of a century after World War II, were shaken. The electorate's partisan preferences, long frozen in the ice of class cleavage, began to thaw. Voting, which to a considerable extent had been an automatic statement of personal status, became more an act of deliberate choice.[2] In the eyes of parties and of scholars, this new behavior appeared not so much rational as volatile. While the old alignment that had committed firmly those of one social class to one party and those of another to the other had crumbled, no new alignment had solidified to provide coherence and consistency to electoral behavior.[3] No better example of the electorate's unpredictability can be found than the rapidly shifting fortunes of the Alliance at the start of the 1980s.

The Alliance rockets ahead   Internal conflict in the Labour party finally reached a crisis point in January 1981 when three prominent MPs, Shirley Williams, David Owen, and William Rodgers, broke with the party. They were joined immediately by Roy Jenkins who, in effect, had been exiled to Brussels at the start of 1977 to be president of the European Economic Community (EEC) Commission. The "Gang of Four," as they were promptly dubbed, issued a short statement of principles, widely referred to as the Limehouse Declaration. This included the two policies of fundamental importance to the four leaders: continued British membership in the EEC, in contrast to Labour's policy of withdrawal, and multilateral nuclear disarmament, rather than Labour's unilateralism.

Also alluded to in the Limehouse Declaration were procedural changes in the Labour party. Labour had abandoned its practice of permitting only MPs to select the party leader. The new procedure gave MPs only a 30 percent voice, with local constituency Labour parties also having 30 percent of the votes, and trade unions having 40 percent. Labour also had decided that during every Parliament the constituency party of every Labour MP *must* provide an opportunity for anyone wishing to do so to challenge the MP for the nomination as that constituency's Labour candidate at the next election.

Making these procedural changes crucial and, for that matter, helping to account for Labour's shift in policy on the EEC and disarmament, was the party's declining membership. As the number of local activists declined, the proportion among them with rather far left political views increased. Moderate Labour MPs increasingly found that they either had to accept policies abhorrent to them or have their political careers terminated.

With the issuance of the Limehouse Declaration the "Gang of Four" founded the Council for Social Democracy. The very next day nine Labour MPs joined the council. Ads appeared in the national newspapers with the names of a hundred prominent people, many of them active Labour party members, supporting the declaration and asking for financial support for the council. In March, when the council was transformed into the Social Democratic party (SDP), its strength in the House of Commons was fourteen—three greater than the Liberals. Eventually it rose to thirty-one—nearly two-and-a-half times the Liberals' strength.[4]

As for the Liberals, their support in 1980 had stabilized at the level obtained

Figure 4.1 Alliance support in polls, 1981–83

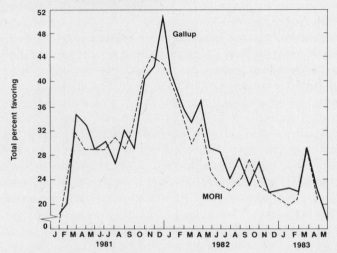

Notes: In those cases in which a polling organization conducted two surveys in a single month, the results have been averaged. *Source: Gallup Political Index* (provided by Robert Nybrow of Social Surveys Gallup Poll Ltd.) and *Public Opinion in Great Britain* (provided by Robert Worcester of Market and Opinion Research International).

in the 1979 election. With the party becalmed, the desire of its leader, David Steel, to negotiate an arrangement with the Social Democrats was understandable. The two parties' policies were similar in most cases and they were likely to appeal to the same voters. For both to offer candidates in the same constituency would be mutually destructive. Finally, the strengths of the two parties complemented each other. While the quality of Liberal local party organization varied, it still was better than that of a party newly created at the national elite level rather than from the grassroots up. Liberal grassroots strength had failed to produce an electoral breakthrough, however, largely because the Liberals simply were not credible to the voters; their leaders had no executive experience at the national level. The SDP, with Jenkins, who had been home secretary and chancellor of the exchequer, and Owen, who had been foreign secretary, as well as other MPs who had held positions in Labour governments, could provide this credibility. Largely in response to Steel's badgering, the two parties agreed in principle by October 1981 on an electoral alliance.

Meanwhile, the Alliance appeared to have caught the public's fancy, as figure 4.1 shows. Not only did a substantial number of people indicate that they would vote SDP, but the Liberals improved their support. Thus in the first half of 1981, 30 percent or more of the electorate favored the Alliance. The Warrington by-election in mid-July provided the first significant test of this apparent popularity. Although Jenkins failed to win, he cut a Labour majority of more than ten thousand to only seventeen hundred. This strong showing had no impact on total support for the Alliance, but did tend to shift support from the Liberals to the SDP.

Nonetheless, the Liberals produced the first breakthrough for the Alliance. In the Croydon North West by-election, the same Liberal candidate who in 1979 had polled little more than four thousand votes received nearly fourteen thousand, gaining the seat from the Conservatives by a margin of almost thirty-three hundred. Interestingly, this remarkable success also did nothing for the Liberals' standing in the polls, but sharply increased support for the SDP and the Alliance as a whole. This shift was reinforced by the Crosby by-election, where Shirley Williams won by more than five thousand votes a seat that the Conservatives had held in 1979 with a majority over Labour of more than nineteen thousand. Thus in the last quarter of 1981 the Alliance was by far the most popular political group in Britain. Its 40 percent or more support in the polls far surpassed that of both Labour and the Conservatives.

The Alliance declines   Anyone even slightly familiar with British politics will explain the Alliance plummet with three words: the Falklands factor. This assessment oversimplifies the reason for loss of support. As can be seen from Figure 4.1, in January the Alliance already had begun to decline and by March was down to a third of the electorate or less. Argentina's invasion of the Falklands on 2 April may well have prevented Jenkins's by-election victory in Glasgow, Hillhead, only a week earlier from helping the Alliance fortunes as much as it otherwise would have done.

With the outbreak of fighting in the South Atlantic and the sinking of both British and Argentine ships at the start of May, support for the Alliance was dealt a serious blow, declining and then stagnating at little more than a fifth of the electorate. The Falklands, however, did not initiate but rather accelerated a decline in support that already was under way. Both Liberal and SDP headquarters agree on the source of the trouble: negotiations over the allocation of constituencies between the two parties.

Although the two parties had agreed on an alliance, detailed negotiations were necessary to determine which party would contest which seats. In some areas agreements were prompt; in others the negotiations made little progress. Rodgers, who was in charge of negotiations for the SDP, suspended all discussions in January 1982, more as a tactical ploy than in frustration, and publicly denounced the Liberals for their unreasonableness.

A source at SDP headquarters acknowledged after the election that this maneuver had been a mistake. The SDP "initially had gained support with the image that we are all nice people and don't have disagreements. The voters found that attractive." The squabble over the sharing of constituencies made the Alliance seem just like the other parties, rather than being a fresh alternative to the confrontational mold of British politics. The two headquarters differed on the ultimate impact of Rodger's maneuver. The SDP view was that it made little difference because the Falklands factor would have cut support for the Alliance significantly in any event. The Liberals were less willing to exculpate him. Eventually negotiations did resume, but the damage to the Alliance's image had been done.

The need to look beyond the Falklands to explain fluctuating Alliance support can be seen in the impact of two by-elections early in 1983. Labour had held Bermondsey, a working-class constituency in the London docks area, for sixty years, winning in 1979 by nearly twelve thousand votes. Bermondsey's aging MP had resigned from Labour in disgust at its leftward shift, especially in his constituency, and then in his pique resigned from Parliament as well to force a by-election. The Labour candidate was characterized by the press, without too great inaccuracy, as a left-wing, homosexual, Australian draft-dodger. Furthermore, when the local party first had wished to adopt him as its candidate, Michael Foot, the Labour leader, had said that he never would endorse him. Foot subsequently recanted and Labour offered a candidate who hardly could be improved upon if the aim was to lose the seat. The result was stunning; the Liberals, who had lost their deposit in 1979, won the seat with a majority of well over nine thousand votes over Labour.

Support for the Alliance jumped seven percentage points in the next Gallup poll to 29 percent, exactly where it had been immediately after the first shots were fired in the Falklands. The bandwagon was rolling once again and another by-election provided an opportunity for a further increase in support that could take the Alliance back to where it had been before the Argentine invasion. Darlington, which Labour had won by only a thousand votes in 1979, looked like a promising prospect for the Alliance, The class composition of the constituency was favorable, the Liberals had had some success in local elections, and the SDP candidate was a well-known local television reporter. Furthermore, Darlington was only a short distance from two constituencies held by Social Democratic MPs, one of them Rodgers. The SDP candidate proved, however, to be politically naive and uninformed. Not only did the Alliance fail to win, it finished a distant third. Everything that Bermondsey had achieved was lost and then some. The Gallup poll completed on the day that the date of the general election was announced showed support for the Alliance at 18 percent, exactly the same figure as the Liberals alone had had in January 1981. Slightly more than two years of fresh alternatives and new dawns—of mold breaking —had totally dissipated. The old two-party system apparently had reasserted itself and nothing had changed in British politics.

Could the Alliance Hold?

An electoral pact hardly was a new phenomenon in British politics. The Liberals had had an arrangement with the Conservatives in Bolton and Huddersfield in the 1950s and a secret agreement with Labour in the 1906 general election. The Liberal Unionists and the Conservatives had cooperated for several general elections at the close of the nineteenth century. Nonetheless, the Alliance was unique. Previous pacts had involved a dominant and a subordinate party; the Alliance was cooperation between equals.

Constituencies were divided almost equally between the two parties in 1983, 322 being fought by the Liberals and 311 by the SDP. Instead of each party having its own policies, the Alliance issued a joint manifesto. The campaign committee was composed of members from each party. The morning press conferences, held at Liberal headquarters because SDP headquarters lacked a room sufficiently large, always had a representative from each party. The press office, as distinct from the conference, was at SDP headquarters, so some Liberal staff shifted their offices over to SDP headquarters for the campaign.

The test at the grassroots level   Liberal experience with electoral pacts has not been pleasant. Usually they have been the prelude to being swallowed up by the Conservatives. This history, plus an innate local Liberal suspicion of national party headquarters, has helped to produce a fierce constituency party independence.[5]

Ensuring that such smoldering touchiness did not burst into internal strife demanded attention to what otherwise might be regarded as trivial details. While the Alliance manifesto appeared in only one version—the cover printed in the SDP's colors—the Alliance logos on the press conference dais alternated with first one in the SDP's red-white-and-blue and then the next in the Liberals' orange-and-black. The election rosettes used by campaign workers were manufactured separately by each party in its own color. The Liberals even went so far as to have two versions: one, like the SDP's, had the Alliance logo, but was in Liberal colors; the other, however, read "Vote Liberal Alliance," thus eliminating all reference to the SDP to avoid irritating those Liberal activists opposed to any cooperation.

Given the potential problems, the actual working of the Alliance at the constituency level exceeded expectations. In only three constituencies did Liberal candidates (none of them approved by national headquarters) oppose SDP candidates and in no case did this alter the results significantly, although it did cost one SDP candidate a lost deposit.[6] Constituency reports to Liberal headquarters after the election tended to be positive; SDP candidates welcomed the help of Liberal activists and, not infrequently, used a Liberal as their election agent. The main complaint was that in constituencies being fought by Liberal candidates not much was seen of SDP party workers. Liberal headquarters recognized this to be the result primarily of the SDP's inability to build up a substantial grassroots cadre in its brief life.

Since Steel had committed himself so wholeheartedly to an alliance between the two parties, one might assume that the successful functioning at the constituency level was evidence of his ability through strength of leadership to impose a desired relation upon a reluctant rank-and-file. This was not the view taken at Liberal headquarters, however, where Steel was regarded as willing to give away too much in the negotiations over constituencies. Unlike the SDP, whose negotiating team in each area was directed by a national leader, the Liberals turned the process over to their local activists. Liberal national headquarters briefed and trained these negotiators and sent representatives to the area meetings. These representatives were present merely to provide assistance if needed, however; the local activists were in charge. Where the Liberal locals were overawed by the prominence of their SDP opposite numbers, Liberal headquarters simply encouraged them to be confident and to use the approach that the Liberals were the givers and the SDP the takers. The terms of the negotiations should be to ask the SDP what it had to offer.

Having been allowed to negotiate their own deal, most Liberal activists were willing to live with the result. In fact, in some cases conflict was greater within the Liberal negotiating team than it was between the Liberals and the SDP. The Liberals knew that some seats in each area would have to be relinquished to the SDP, so the aim of some negotiators was to have a Liberal constituency party other than their own be the one to pay the price.

The test at the leadership level　The irony of the campaign was that the Alliance functioned more smoothly at the constituency level than at the national level. About two weeks before Prime Minister Thatcher revealed the date of the election, Steel announced that while he would lead the Alliance campaign whenever an election was called, Jenkins would be the prime minister-designate. This announcement was intended both to quiet those Liberal MPs who had been agitating for Steel to take command of the Alliance and to respond to the media's concern that two leaders could not hold the one office of prime minister. The arrangement provoked far more problems than it solved.

At least half of the first Alliance campaign telecast was devoted to emphasizing how unified the two parties were. Steel alleged that Thatcher's government wasn't a united team, while the Alliance was, even though composed of two separate parties. He and Jenkins were shown campaigning together and, subsequently, walking in the woods alone together, almost hand-in-hand. The mood recalled the intimate scenes employed by expensive cosmetics in their TV ads. Each leader praised the other at great length. Jenkins claimed not only to enjoy working with Steel, but noted that in his wide political experience actually getting pleasure from such a relationship was remarkably rare. Steel hailed Jenkins as a man of vision and leadership.

At Liberal headquarters this emphasis on personal chumminess was regarded as having been a bit much. The Alliance had hired a number of trucks carrying billboards to drive around populated areas. After this had been arranged, Liberal headquarters decided that the posters to be displayed showed Steel and Jenkins too close together. It proved too late, however, for the manufacturer to alter them.

The Alliance leadership problem derived from the fact that Steel had the most positive image of any British politician.[7] Jenkins, despite his standing as a senior politician of wide experience, was not perceived by the public to be an effective leader. When in March 1983 Gallup specifically asked whether Steel or Jenkins would be the better prime minister, 63 percent chose the former and only 23 percent the latter.[8]

Furthermore, Steel performs quite well on television, a considerable asset during an election campaign. Almost as many people heard Steel on television, radio, or in person during the campaign as heard Thatcher, and of those who heard them almost as many mentioned Steel (28 percent) as among the two or three politicians that had impressed them most as mentioned the prime minister (31 percent). What gave Steel the edge, however, was that 22 percent mentioned Thatcher as among those who had impressed them *least*, while only 2 percent said that of him. (Jenkins did not seem to have much impact one way or the other: only 2 percent mentioned him as among the most impressive and only 7 percent among the least.)[9]

To shunt Jenkins aside, however, would only fuel latent suspicions within the Alliance. The stress such a move would place on cooperation between the two parties can be seen in the results of a poll conducted in 116 marginal constituencies. Respondents were asked whether their vote would be affected were Steel, rather than Jenkins, the Alliance's choice for prime minister. While in Conservative and in Labour marginals over a third were more likely to vote Alliance if Steel were the potential prime minister (only a few said they would be less likely to do so), in the 27 SDP marginals only 29 percent were more likely to vote Alliance and 39 percent said they would be *less likely* to vote Alliance.[10] Thus in precisely those seats where the future existence of the SDP as a parliamentary group was at stake, replacing Jenkins with Steel would lose crucial votes.

When toward the close of the second week of the campaign the Alliance remained becalmed at under 20 percent in the polls, incipient panic produced action: the Ettrick Bridge summit. A regular meeting of the Alliance campaign committee had been scheduled for Edinburgh on 29 May. Steel not only shifted the site to his relatively nearby home at Ettrick Bridge, but was quoted in the press as saying, "*I have decided* we should have a major reassessment of the election strategy in the second half of the campaign."[11] Liberal headquarters regarded this as a demonstration that he was in command of the Alliance.

Nonetheless, Jenkins was not replaced as prime minister-designate; all that Steel told the press at the end of the campaign committee meeting was that he would be taking a greater role in the rest of the campaign. This was a rather curious result since, as noted already, the Alliance had intended from the beginning that Steel should have the lead in the campaign. The problem was that the Alliance could not order the media what to cover. If television news wanted to show Jenkins campaigning as much or more than Steel, the Alliance could not stop it. There is no evidence that media coverage of the Alliance leaders was any different after Ettrick Bridge than it had been before it.

The principal change, therefore, was that for each of the eight remaining morning press conferences Steel always attended, while the SDP representative varied from one day to the next. Furthermore, when during the next to last press conference most of the questions appeared to be directed to Jenkins, Steel interjected comments on his own even though the reporters had not asked for them.

Even after the election, SDP headquarters did not complain about the Ettrick Bridge summit. The view was that the meeting had gained the Alliance media attention that it otherwise would not have received and that the image projected was a positive one. Since the meeting did coincide with a surge forward in support for the Alliance, it appeared to have played a role in rejuvenating its campaign. SDP headquarters did not accuse the Liberals of a Machiavellian maneuver of emphasizing Steel's role in the campaign precisely at the point when they expected support for the Alliance to increase and thus of reaping acclaim derived from a spurious relation.[12]

Strain among Alliance leaders does not appear to have had a negative effect upon the voters. The election-day survey that Gallup carried out for the BBC found that in contrast to the 1979 general election, when 41 percent said Labour had the best team of leaders, 35 percent said the Conservatives, and only 17 percent the Liberals, in 1983 the Conservatives were the choice of 55 percent, then the Alliance with 23 percent, followed by Labour with only 16 percent.[13] Important though these figures are, they should not be interpreted as evidence that the complementary cooperation of the Alliance—Liberal grassroots organization married to SDP leadership credibility—had worked. A poll at the start of the campaign had found that 25 percent expressed very great or considerable confidence in Liberal politicians to deal wisely with Britain's problems and 37 percent had very little or no confidence at all in their ability to do so, while for the Social Democrats the figures were 14 and 48 percent.[14]

Despite serious problems, however, cooperation at the leadership level endured for the campaign and enabled the Alliance to appear to be a reasonably credible challenger for power.

The test of policy cooperation   While the date of the general election was a surprise to most everyone, the Alliance was not caught off guard. The SDP chief whip, John Roper, had prepared a number of timetables showing when certain things would have to be done for a variety of possible election dates. Several small groups of Liberals and Social Democrats had been working on formulating a common position from each party's stand on various policies. Eventually a comprehensive draft of their labors was prepared for the Leaders' Joint Advisory Committee (LJAC), composed—in addition to each party's leader —primarily of prominent party members not planning to contest constituencies in the election or standing for seats in the London area.

The LJAC had not been able to resolve by the first week in May all policy disagreements between the two parties. The remaining differences, however, hardly were fundamental. In Roper's view the Liberals were further away from the SDP on nuclear power than they were on nuclear weapons, a comment of some significance given an incident to be discussed shortly. As Thatcher's trip to Chequers on 8 May with her advisers to assess the results of the local elections and consider the timing of an election neared, Roper insisted that all policy disagreements had to be resolved just in case she were to announce the election date on 9 May. To expedite this, the LJAC empowered Roper and Alan Beith, the Liberal chief whip, to approve the final form of the Alliance manifesto. Thus on 12 May, only the third day after the date of the election was announced, the Alliance published its manifesto.

Finding anything in the manifesto that would not have been there were it a policy statement for the Liberal party alone is virtually impossible. This is not to say that the SDP was subservient to the Liberals, but merely to indicate how similar their policy views were. The SDP was willing to embrace PR with as much fervor as the Liberals had in the past. Devolution and decentralization, a written bill of rights, co-ownership with workers holding stock and sharing in the profits of their employing firms—all such traditional Liberal policies had their place in the Alliance manifesto.

Although the Liberals' 1979 manifesto had pledged to "introduce a sustained *prices and incomes policy* based on wide consultation and enforceable at law," both they and the Social Democrats had been divided within, not between, themselves on this policy. In 1981 the Liberal conference amended a motion favoring an entirely voluntary incomes policy to provide for statutory sanctions *as a last resort*. The debate indicated that while the party accepted that compulsion might be necessary in some circumstances, a judicious mix of carrots and sticks might be able to forestall such confrontations. Some SDP leaders, like Rodgers,[15] favored a statutory incomes policy, although not for prices as well. In October 1982 the SDP's council voted against such a policy, but the following January, considering the issue again with a differently worded motion, adopted a position quite similar to the Liberals'. Thus the Alliance manifesto's policy—a norm for pay settlements agreed among representatives of the government, the unions, consumers, and business; a commission to restrict price increases caused by paying wages in excess of the norm; and a tax to be levied on companies paying higher wages than the norm, unless justified by productivity increases—probably had as many Liberal, as SDP, supporters.

The overall theme of the manifesto, also emphasized in the Alliance's four campaign telecasts, was the Liberal eternal verity of cooperation and partnership as an alternative to the confrontation politics of Labour and Conservative. The key image was sensible, nonideological people working together for the national, not vested sectional, interest. To help ensure that this image was not blurred during the course of the campaign, the staffs of the two parties met together daily and decided upon common advice for the leaders. The leaders themselves were in frequent contact and sorted out any policy differences so that the Alliance projected a single position.

One area of potential disagreement remained and at the close of the campaign the *Times* and its political correspondent, Anthony Bevins, sought to manufacture a controversy over it. The Liberal 1979 manifesto had said, "*Europe's defence* must be a common defence, based on integrated forces and integrated command within the Atlantic Alliance," and in 1980 the Liberal annual conference had reaffirmed this opposition to an independent British deterrent. The following year the conference voted for a nuclear-free zone in central Europe and rejected the siting of cruise missiles in Britain; it specifically rejected a motion—the view of both the SDP and the German SDP—that a decision on cruise should be contingent on what happened at the disarmament talks in Geneva during 1983. Regardless of what was official Liberal party policy, however, Steel personally rejected the 1982 conference action.

On the day before polling day, the chief front page story in the *Times* was a report by Bevins of the previous day's Alliance press conference, headlined, "Jenkins and Steel split over future of nuclear deterrent." Bevins reported Jenkins as saying at the press conference that if the Geneva talks failed, an Alliance government would keep an independent British deterrent. Noting that such a statement was not in the Alliance manifesto, Bevins contrasted it with a speech that Steel had made six months earlier in which he had said that British Polaris missiles should be under NATO as a Western deterrent. Bevins quoted Jenkins, "We are not wedded to an independent British deterrent, but equally we do not believe in just throwing our weapons away. . . . We are going to continue with our independent deterrent for a substantial period ahead," and Steel, "There is no question of unilaterally phasing out Polaris." Bevins did not mention that Jenkins also commented that British Polaris could be included in the Geneva talks since the country could give it up because it did not need to have its own deterrent. All things considered the evidence for alleging a major policy split was rather flimsy. So trumped up was the story in fact that neither the *Daily Telegraph* nor the *Guardian* even mentioned it, to say nothing of giving it prominent coverage.

Only after the story had been published did Bevins, at the next press conference, directly challenge Jenkins and Steel on the question of a split. Jenkins responded that Bevins had manufactured a difference between the two leaders that didn't exist and that wasn't apparent to anyone else. Steel equally denied any disagreement. Nonetheless, Bevins's story on the front page of the *Times* on election day was headlined, "Owen statement confirms Alliance rift on defence." While reporting the denials of Jenkins and Steel, Bevins cited as evidence that the Alliance indeed was divided Owen's comment, during a radio discussion, that although Polaris was under NATO commanders, it could come under British control for use against a threat to the country's national interest. Again, this seems going rather beyond what the evidence justified.

Clearly the Alliance combined two parties that had more in common than a concern for self-preservation. Where they did differ on policy, the disagreement was not fundamental. Even when given an encouraging shove toward disunity, they maintained a common policy.

The Course of the Campaign

Support and strategy   The first half of the campaign was not encouraging to the Alliance, as can be seen from figure 4.2. In the closing days of the parliamentary session their support dropped. Then, with only a slight recovery once the campaign proper began with the dissolution of Parliament (day 4 in figure 4.2), their support stagnated. Of the fourteen surveys taken from 14 through 26 May,[16] thirteen were within two percentage points, plus or minus, of 17 percent. Since such a range is within the margin of error, the results suggest no change in total support. It will be recalled that the Ettrick Bridge summit occurred only a few days after this period and doubtless took the form it did because of this lack of movement in the polls.

The next week (27 May through 2 June) was the Alliance's best one in the entire campaign. Of the nine polls during this period, eight showed them to be within 1.5 percentage points, plus or minus, of 22.5 percent support. The striking way in which Ettrick Bridge was a pivot point in the Alliance campaign can be seen by noting that only the first and the last of all the polls from 10 May up to Ettrick Bridge showed the Alliance with as much as one-fifth of the vote; after Ettrick Bridge no poll ever showed them with less than one-fifth support.

Ettrick Bridge was not just a matter of leadership effectiveness and personality; it also produced a shift in strategy. The Alliance leaders decided, in effect, that Thatcher was unbeatable. The Labour campaign, on the other hand, ob-

Figure 4.2   Alliance strength in polls, May–June 1983

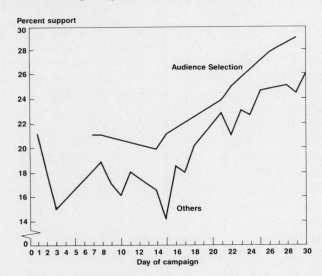

Source: Derived from MORI, *British Public Opinion*, nos. 5 and 6 (May and June 1983), p. 24.
Notes: Results are plotted by the day on which fieldwork was completed. Where more than one poll ended on a given day, the results are averaged. Day 1 is 10 May.

viously was crumbling. Therefore, the Alliance might credibly attempt to replace Labour as the official opposition. The emphasis of the Alliance campaign was to shift away from attacks on Foot and toward those on Thatcher. This, it was hoped, not only would gain the Alliance former Labour voters who had lost all belief in their party, but also those potential Conservative voters who feared, as even some members of Thatcher's cabinet seemed to, that a landslide victory for the prime minister would encourage her to implement rather extreme right-wing policies.

While this shift was occurring in the Alliance, the Conservatives also were changing gears. Just before Ettrick Bridge, Cecil Parkinson, the Conservative party chairman, warned that voting for the Alliance could cost the Conservatives so many seats that Labour would gain control of the government. Immediately after Ettrick Bridge, in her first major speech since returning from the international economic summit at Williamsburg, Thatcher, who until then never had so much as mentioned the Alliance, warned that voting for them could give power to Labour extremists. So great did she seem to regard the Alliance threat that as the week progressed she seemed to be urging people to vote Labour—paradoxically as a means of keeping Labour out of power by denying seats to the Alliance.

Figure 4.3   Alliance distance behind Labour, May–June 1983

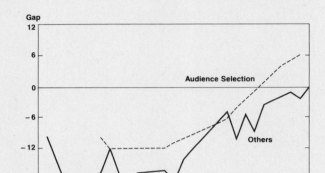

Notes and sources: See figure 4.2

The final week of the campaign (3–8 June) brought a further gain in Alliance support, although not as great as the increase of the previous week. Of eleven polls during this period, ten gave the Alliance 24.5 percent support, plus or minus 1.5 percentage points.

Success for the Alliance in the campaign was not only a matter of its share of the vote, but also of how its strength compared to that of Labour. Figure 4.3 charts the changes in the gap between them, indicating how far the Alliance was from a second-place finish. Using the same times as for the discussion of the Alliance share of the vote, from 14 through 26 May twelve of fourteen surveys indicated a sizable gap of eleven to nineteen percentage points. During 27 May through 2 June this narrowed considerably; seven of nine polls indicated that the Alliance was only four to nine-and-a-half percentage points behind Labour. Then in the final week, nine of eleven surveys showed the Alliance to be from four percentage points behind to *one percentage point ahead* of Labour. (Two of the final polls put the Alliance ahead of Labour. This is not clear in figure 4.3 because these results are averaged with three other polls that did not show the Alliance to be ahead.)

The role of the polls   In figures 4.2 and 4.3 the survey results obtained by Audience Selection are graphed separately from those for the other polling firms. Audience Selection's surveys for the 1981 GLC election and for the by-elections in Warrington, Crosby, and Hillhead all compared favorably with the actual results. But for the Bermondsey by-election Audience Selection underestimated Alliance support by sixteen percentage points. This may have caused the firm to attempt some correcting adjustment that went too far in the other direction. For in the Darlington by-election Audience Selection *over*estimated Alliance support by six percentage points.

While this is not the place to discuss polling methodology, a few comments are appropriate. Audience Selection, unlike other polling firms, does its field work by telephone. The raw results obtained from telephone polls must be weighted in some fashion to correct for the class bias in phone ownership in Britain. While such weighting is an objective procedure, no particular method clearly is most appropriate. To that extent weighting can be said to be subjective or, at least, judgmental. Some people wondered whether the quality of these judgments were affected by the fact that, in addition to the polling it had been commissioned to do by the *Sun* and *TV-AM*, Audience Selection also was conducting the Alliance's private polls.[17]

As can be seen in figures 4.2 and 4.3, in almost every instance Audience Selection polls showed the Alliance stronger than did the surveys of the other firms. The final surveys of the five other polling firms all agreed upon 26 percent for the Alliance—exactly what it did receive in the election—and showed Labour at 25 to 28 percent. Audience Selection's final poll gave the Alliance 29 percent and Labour only 23 percent. This inaccuracy suggests that Audience Selection had been wrong all along and that its surveys had a small bias in favor of the Alliance, primarily at Labour's expense.

Poll results were crucial to the Alliance; it needed some evidence that it was growing and overtaking Labour to seem a viable option. The Alliance leaders certainly were willing to milk the polls for all the benefit they could derive.[18] When they claimed that their support was starting to grow, the increase in the polls was within the margin of error and thus might not have been an actual gain at all. Only subsequently did it become clear that voters were shifting to the Alliance in significant numbers, although not to the extent that Audience Selection indicated.

Concern about the use of polling results in the campaign eventually led to a question at an Alliance press conference of why anyone should pay any more attention to the claims for increased poll support than they would to the typically inflated reports of canvassing results obtained by party activists. Steel's disarming reply was that they did not deserve any greater trust. He added that he disapproved of anonymous party officials leaking the results of private polls (as well he might, since doing so would violate the polling firms' code of ethics). However, he was not about to forego any advantage that the Alliance could obtain from reports of public opinion, for he went on to argue that what was important was not the exact figures of support for the various parties, but the trend: Labour was declining and the Alliance was gaining and eventually would overtake it. Finally, as British politicians always do when discussing this subject, he verified the trend by citing the huge attendance that Alliance public meetings were generating.

The Results

Half full or half empty?   The success of the Alliance in the 1983 election was truly remarkable, yet it was disappointing: 26 percent of the popular vote, but two percentage points behind Labour, and only 3.5 percent (23) of the seats in the House of Commons.

The Social Democratic MPs appear to have had a fairly sizable personal vote; their share averaged twenty percentage points higher than the 11.9 percent that the SDP gained of the total vote,[19] and they took nearly a third of the potential Labour vote.[20] It was not enough, however. Twenty-three of the twenty-eight SDP MPs standing for re-election (including two of the "Gang of Four") were defeated.[21] Here again the electoral system exhibited quirks. Shirley Williams received the third highest share of the vote of all SDP MPs— 42 percent—and took three-fifths of the potential Labour vote, but lost. Only one of the 283 SDP candidates who were not MPs managed to win election— thus giving the SDP its total parliamentary strength of six—and only two others came close.[22]

The Liberals did relatively better. All of their MPs but one were re-elected.[23] This was rather more of an accomplishment than it might appear. Due to the constituency boundary changes, four of the Liberal MPs were standing for seats that according to the notional figures would have been won by another party in 1979 with the Liberals coming third. In addition, all of the re-elected MPs won by a margin larger than that indicated by the notional figures.[24]

With little more than half as many candidates as they had offered by themselves in 1979, the Liberals won almost as many votes. Then they had averaged seventy-five hundred votes per candidate; in 1983 this rose to thirteen thousand. The average Labour vote was only four hundred greater than this.[25] Furthermore, that old nemesis of the Liberals, the lost deposit, was conquered. The Liberals lost only five and the SDP only six; Labour forfeited an incredible 119.

Yet, here again it was all not really enough. Only five of the 309 Liberal candidates who were not MPs were elected (excluding Grimond's replacement) to bring the total Liberal strength in Parliament to seventeen. The Liberals had hoped for more new gains than this through tactical voting, especially in the nineteen constituencies where the notional figures showed them second to the Conservative victor by twenty or fewer percentage points.[26] Tactical voting requires second-place Liberals to convince the supporters of the third-place party that since their party has no hope of winning, they should vote Liberal to defeat the party normally first, which, it is assumed, the supporters of the third-place party dislike more than they do the Liberals.

Given the recent interest in such attempts, the Gallup poll asked people in April 1983 whether they had heard anything about tactical voting. Less than a fifth—18 percent—said that they had. Furthermore, when asked what the phrase meant to them nearly three-quarters said it meant nothing. When presented with a detailed description of a tactical voting situation and asked what they would do, only 14 percent said they would think of voting for a party other than their own. Finally, when asked, "Have you ever voted tactically?" only 3 percent said yes.[27]

The Liberals, then, may have been basing their hopes too heavily on success in these nineteen seats, especially since nearly half of these seats were *not* tactical voting situations. Even if every Labour voter switched to the Liberals to keep the Conservatives out, the Conservatives still would have won the seat.[28] Therefore, these constituencies should be divided into two groups: ten tactical voting situation seconds and nine nontactical seconds. In the former the Liberal share of the vote increased by 9.3 percentage points, while in the latter it rose by only 1.6.[29] The Labour share of the vote declined by twice as much in the tactical seconds as in the nontactical ones: 8.1 percentage points to 4.2 percentage points. On average the decline in the Labour vote was less than a third of the gap between the Liberals and the Conservatives in the nontactical seconds, while it was more than three-fourths of the gap in the tactical seconds.[30] In six of the nontactical seconds the gap between the Liberals and the Conservatives actually increased, although for the entire group of nine constituencies the increase on average was only 1.2 percentage points. The gap narrowed, however, in all ten of the tactical seconds and declined on average by 9.1 percentage points. Finally, while the Liberals won none of the nontactical seconds, they did gain four of the ten tactical seconds, although not the first four on that list.[31] Thus some tactical voting does appear to have occurred,[32] but it was sporadic and rather limited. Like much else in the Alliance campaign, it was not nearly enough.

Who voted for the Alliance and why   One of the hallmarks of Liberal support has been its even distribution across the various demographic groups and regions of Britain. This rather diffuse support has combined with the form of the British electoral system to underrepresent the Liberals in the House of Commons drastically compared to their level of popular support. Despite the addition of the SDP—for the most part a former faction of the Labour party— the Alliance, exactly like the Liberals, failed to concentrate its support.[33]

The Alliance vote varied from 33 percent among white collar (ABC1) trade union members to 22 percent among young (18–24) manual workers (C2DE), a much narrower range than for either of the other main parties. Class had some limited effect upon union members and upon voters who were neither very young nor very old (25–54), with upper and middle class (ABC I) voters in these categories being somewhat more likely to support the Alliance than were non-skilled manual (DE) voters in these groups.[34] While the Alliance vote differed little by region, its support was somewhat lower in Greater London and the west midlands.

Alliance gains in support over that obtained by the Liberals alone in the recent past also were distributed evenly. The Alliance share of the vote in 1983 was seven percentage points higher than the Liberals had received in October 1974. The increase for eight of ten subgroups (men, women, union members, 18–24, 25–34, 35–54, 55 and over, ABC I, C2, and DE) was virtually the same, ranging from five to ten. The exceptions were union members, among whom the Alliance did thirteen percentage points better than the Liberals had in October 1974, and the youngest voters, among whom Alliance support was five percentage points *lower* than the Liberals had. Comparing 1983 with 1979, the Alliance improved on the Liberal share nationally by twelve percentage points. The increase was quite similar for each of the ten subgroups, ranging from ten to sixteen.

Introducing partisan considerations does indicate that the Alliance attracted some groups more than others. While the percentage of Conservative defectors going to the Alliance was the same as the percentage of Labour defectors doing so, the fact that Labour had so many more defectors meant that the Alliance got half again as many recruits from Labour as from the Conservatives.[35] Thus of those voting Alliance in 1983, only 29 percent had voted Liberal in 1979 and slightly more had voted Labour then, with about a fifth having voted Conservative.

Furthermore, the main parties lost different segments of their previous support. About half of those voting Conservative in 1983 were women, but nearly two-thirds of those who defected from the Conservatives to the Alliance were women. Those women especially likely to switch were upper- and middle-class (ABC I) ones who were neither very young nor pensioners (25–64). Such women were about twice as prevalent among those defecting from the Conservatives to the Alliance as they were among those voting Conservative. Ironically, the Conservatives were least able to hold women rather like Prime Minister Thatcher herself. Those defecting from Labour tended to be somewhat older (45–64) and their class background differed by sex. Among middle-aged men, professionals and managers (AB) were most overrepresented among Labour defectors, while for middle-aged women the nonskilled (DE) were. That the former should have deserted Labour hardly is surprising, but for the latter to have done so as well is further evidence of the party's inability to retain the support of those who would seem to be part of its natural clientele.

Much of this switching occurred in the closing days. Nearly half of those who decided how to vote in the two or three weeks prior to polling day, and even more of those making up their minds only a few days before the election, supported the Alliance. Thus while 6 percent of those voting Labour and 4 percent of those voting Conservative decided only in the last few days how they would vote, 17 percent of the Alliance voters decided then. Two-fifths of these Alliance late deciders said that their vote had been influenced by a TV broadcast and almost as many said it was affected by their desire to prevent the Conservatives from winning too big a majority or by the extremists in the Labour party (multiple answers were permitted).

Home ownership also had an impact upon Labour defectors. The proportion of upper- and middle-class home owners was twice as great among those who had voted Labour in 1979 but switched to the Alliance in 1983 as it was among those who voted Labour in 1983. Even for manual working-class home owners the proportion among defectors to the Alliance was almost half again as great as among those who voted Labour. On the other hand, manual working-class council tenants were less than two-thirds as prevalent among Labour defectors to the Alliance as they were among Labour voters. Late Alliance deciders tended disproportionately to be upper- and middle-class home owners.

What about those (about a quarter of those voting Labour or Conservative) who did not shift to the Alliance despite having considered doing so at some time during the two years prior to the election? Their chief reason for not switching, cited by about two-fifths, was simply that they saw no reason to change from their usual party. Among those new supporters recruited by either Labour or the Conservatives in 1983 the belief that the Alliance could not win was an important factor. As for those who decided only at the end of the campaign to vote for Labour, rather than the Alliance, dislike of Roy Jenkins was as important as perceived Alliance weakness, while for late Conservative deciders fear of letting Labour in was the most crucial consideration.

A few of those who originally had intended to vote Alliance shifted to other parties, about as many going to the Conservatives as to Labour. These switches, especially those to Labour, tended to occur either early in the campaign or somewhat before it formally got under way. As the campaign developed the Alliance eventually was picking up about twice as many Conservative intenders as it was losing Alliance intenders to them and about four times as much support from Labour as it was losing to it. Even a substantial number of those who planned to vote Labour as little as two weeks before polling day eventually swung to the Alliance.

A variety of reasons can be offered to explain why an electorate votes as it does in an election. The democratic ideal would cite the policies that the parties offer on the issues of the day. Equally legitimate would be the electorate's assessment of the quality of leaders offered by each party. Rather less acceptable would be the motivation of those voters deciding on the basis of party image. Still more questionable would be the behavior of those who allow themselves to be influenced by the public opinion polls. Finally, least respectable would be the voting of those who support a party not because they like it but because they dislike all the other parties even more. To what extent can support for the Alliance be explained by each of these five reasons?

The Liberals are widely said to have no, or vague, policies. What this demonstrably silly statement really means is that the person saying it has not bothered to find out what the policies are. Nonetheless, in this, as in many other aspects, the Alliance resembled the Liberals. A variety of polls consistently found that the Alliance on every specific issue inquired about always came third in the proportion of people saying they had the best policy. A poll toward the latter part of the campaign found that little more than a quarter of all voters and less than a half of those who planned to vote Alliance knew that proportional representation was Alliance policy and only 11 percent of all voters and little more than a fifth of Alliance intenders knew that the Alliance was pledged to introducing an incomes policy.

Voters did not expect election of the Alliance to make much difference. Early in the campaign people were asked whether they expected more or less inflation or no change if the Conservatives won the election and what effect such a victory would have on eleven other subjects as well. These questions were repeated for Labour and for the Alliance. In each case for the Alliance about a third said they didn't know what the effect would be (about three times as many as gave this response for Labour or the Conservatives) and the proportion expecting no change was sufficiently large for eleven of these twelve subjects that more than half were saying that election of the Alliance would make no difference—they either expected no change or didn't know whether they expected any. For the Conservatives, who, after all, were in power and whose reelection would not be expected to produce many changes, only on five of the twelve subjects did a majority indicate that winning the election would not matter and for Labour only on three. Generating enthusiasm for a party when most people feel that its policies will have no impact is rather difficult.

On the other hand, some evidence suggests that policies may have played a crucial role in gaining the Alliance the additional support that put it above a quarter of the vote, challenging Labour for second place. Shortly before the campaign started only 30 percent were willing to characterize the Alliance as having sensible policies. Less than a week before polling day 42 percent of these same respondents had come to see the Alliance that way. Not only was this twice as many who thought this of Labour, it was one percentage point more than for the Conservatives. When at the start of June people were asked whether they had seen or heard anything in the last seven days that had affected their attitude toward each of the parties, more mentioned policies (35 percent) than anything else as making them more favorable to the Social Democrats.[36] Among those who defected from the Conservatives or from Labour to the Alliance, almost three-fourths regarded the Alliance as having the best policies. Among those who had not voted in 1979 but supported the Alliance in 1983 the proportion thinking this was even greater.

As was the case with policy, so also the campaign helped to increase public appreciation of the quality of Alliance leaders. Before the campaign started only about a quarter of the public saw the Alliance as having a good team of leaders, while by the closing days of the campaign this had risen to 35 percent, nearly three times as many as regarded Labour this way. In the case of the Liberals the question about whether anything in the last seven days had affected attitudes revealed that 41 percent of those becoming more favorable attributed this to Steel.[37] While the 25 percent of the public who thought he would make the best prime minister was considerably smaller than the 46 percent who thought that Thatcher would, it was considerably better than the 15 percent who preferred Foot for the job. Furthermore, more than two-thirds of those defecting from the Conservatives or Labour to the Alliance saw Steel as the best person for prime minister. Going beyond Steel, more than half of those switching from the Conservatives to the Alliance and nearly three-quarters of those coming over from Labour saw the Alliance as having the best leaders, while among former abstainers who changed to the Alliance the proportion was even higher.

Turning to party image, after those who said that their opinion of the Liberals had improved in the last week had mentioned Steel, the next most frequently cited explanations were the Liberals' honesty (22 percent) and that they were "coming across better" (25 percent). The latter rather vague attribute probably relates to the previously noted increase in the proportion thinking that the Alliance had sensible policies and to a similar increase in those believing that it understood the problems facing Britain. By the closing days of the campaign nearly half of the public felt that the Alliance had such an understanding, more than believed this of Labour and almost as many as thought this of the Conservatives.

Half of those asked regarded the Alliance as moderate and as representing all classes (the classic Liberal image), far more than thought this of either Labour or the Conservatives. On the only image characteristic where Labour had some strength—concern about people in real need in Britain—almost as many attributed this to the Alliance as to Labour with the Conservatives well behind.

A poll midway through the campaign provided striking evidence of the Alliance's positive image. Respondents were asked whether since the start of the campaign their opinion of each of the parties had improved, stayed the same, or gotten worse. For the Conservatives 13 percent said it had improved and 28 percent gotten worse; for Labour only 8 percent improved and 47 percent worse; for the Alliance 22 percent improved and only 14 percent worse. Thus only the Alliance, on balance, had gained in the public's estimation in the campaign. Even more remarkable are the views of those who had voted for one of the two main parties in 1979. Of the 1979 Conservative voters 18 percent said their opinion of their party had improved and 14 percent that it had gotten worse. When those same people were asked about the Alliance, 23 percent said their opinion had improved and only 12 percent that it had worsened. And while only 14 percent of 1979 Labour voters said that their opinion of their own party had improved in the 1983 campaign and 31 percent said that it had gotten worse, 25 percent of them said that their opinion of the Alliance had improved and only 18 percent said that their opinion was worse. Thus the Alliance enhanced its standing considerably more among voters for the other parties than did those parties themselves.

Finally, to look at a negative image characteristic, half the public thought that Labour would promise anything to win votes, more than a third believed the Conservatives would, but only a sixth saw the Alliance in that light. Clearly, the Alliance's image was perceived more favorably than was Labour's and overall was the equal of the Conservatives'. While this image strength doubtless was an asset in gaining the Alliance the measure of support it received, the fact that it came third in share of the vote indicates the limited impact of image on voting behavior.

Constituency opinion polls can make tactical voting a significant campaign objective. While such polls have become common for by-elections, they remain rare in general elections where polls involve a national or, at times, regional sample, but seldom a constituency one. Nonetheless, even national polls could help to convince voters that the Alliance was a serious contender in their particular constituency.

Ascertaining how many people actually were influenced by the Alliance's position in the polls is difficult because few people care to admit that this, rather than more elevated concerns such as policy and the quality of leaders, affects their voting behavior. Responses to survey questions about the impact of polls probably understate their effect; nonetheless, the pattern is revealing. While only 4.7 percent of all voters said that the polls influenced their vote, 8.9 percent of those who voted Alliance admitted being affected and in the crucial Liberal/Conservative marginal constituencies the proportion increased to 10 percent. While only 7 percent of those defecting from Labour to the Alliance admitted the influence of the polls, 15 percent of those switching to the Alliance from the Conservatives acknowledged this. Nearly a fifth—17.6 percent—of those who decided in the last few days of the campaign to vote for the Alliance were influenced by the polls.

Furthermore, the public's knowledge of the polls' findings was fairly accurate. More than half knew that the Alliance was third but close to Labour and nearly a third believed that Labour was third but close to the Alliance (which indeed was the case in some polls). Interestingly, among those who voted for the Alliance in the Liberal/Conservative marginals the figures were reversed and somewhat more than a third believed the polls showed the Alliance third and close while nearly a half thought that they put Labour third and close. Thus precisely where tactical voting could be most effective, the national polls were perceived to depict a tactical voting situation favorable to the Alliance.

Mention of tactical voting leads to the last of five possible reasons for supporting the Alliance—dislike of the other parties—since such voting involves voters departing from their first preference to defeat their least desired alternative. The contrasting patterns of partisan strength in marginal constituencies provides evidence that dislike of some parties affected the vote. In the Liberal/Conservative marginals the Alliance gained 39 percent and Labour only 12.6 (just at the deposit-saving level), while in Labour/Conservative marginals Labour received 36.9 percent and the Alliance 18.9.

When Alliance voters were specifically asked which was stronger, their preference for the Alliance or their dislike of Labour and the Conservatives, 57 percent said their dislike was and only a third chose their like of the Alliance. While half of those who had decided to vote Alliance before the campaign started said their dislike was stronger, three-fourths of those who decided to support the Alliance in the last couple of days of the campaign said it was stronger. Dislike of the other parties was more prevalent among those 18 to 22 years old and among workers—either white collar or manual (C1C2DE). It was most common among those who were unemployed. Thus the Alliance gained a good bit of support not because of what it was, but because of what its opponents were.

People also were asked whether they supported the Alliance because of something in particular they liked about the party or because they just thought it was time for a change. Combining the two questions produces a fourfold categorization of Alliance voter motivation. Those who said their dislike of the other parties was greater than their preference for the Alliance *and* who said they supported the Alliance simply because they wanted a change can be labeled negative and general; two-fifths of all Alliance voters—the largest group of the four—fell in this category. Furthermore, among those who decided only in the last couple of days of the campaign to vote Alliance the proportion rose to 57 percent. While this may be a means of winning some additional votes in a given election, it does not seem to be a sound basis for a durable political movement.

Each of the five influences—policies, leaders, image, polls, and dislike of other parties—played a significant role in motivating support for the Alliance. Without suggesting that everyone went through each step of the process, the following can serve as a schema of the interplay of the five motivations. Dislike of Labour and the Conservatives was a key initiating factor, as can be seen from the fact that those who thought about voting Alliance, but did not, most commonly explained that it was because they were not dissatisfied with their current party. Furthermore, the Alliance recruited the bulk of its new support from Labour, where dissatisfaction with the party was rampant. The positive image of the Alliance helped to fan any spark of dissatisfaction into full flame since one's usual party would show up badly in any comparison. Alliance strength in the polls was important in offsetting to at least some extent the belief that was important among those who were recruited to Labour or the Conservatives, rather than to the Alliance, that the Alliance could not win. Finally, the growing attractiveness of the Alliance policies and leaders helped to provide some positive and specific justifications for voting Alliance to go along with the negative and general ones. Thus defectors could feel that they had indeed weighed the merits of parties and found the Alliance to be preferable just as the ideal democratic citizen should.

Coats Off for the Future!

The heading for this final section, which was the title of the Report of the Committee on Party Reconstruction prepared for the 1946 Liberal annual assembly, suggests that no matter how much things have changed in the early 1980s in British politics they have not yet ceased to be fundamentally the same.

The SDP has only six MPs and only one of them (and he in the farthest reaches of mainland Scotland at that) won by more than eleven percentage points. A modest swing of six percentage points at the next election and all but one are gone. The Liberals are somewhat better off: only nine of their seventeen MPs won by margins of less than eleven percentage points. Yet here again a modest swing of six percentage points and the Liberals are back to the level of representation that they had for most of the quarter of a century from 1950 to the mid-1970s.

But, it will be said, the Alliance came second in 313 constituencies (compared to only 132 seconds for Labour) and is posed for a major breakthrough in the next election. Unfortunately for the Alliance, this is less impressive than it sounds. In only sixty-three of its seconds did the winning party poll less than a majority of the vote. Even if tactical voting were to operate to the full and the Alliance were to gain every single vote cast for the third party in 1983 in each of these constituencies and lose none of the votes it obtained, it still could not win 250 of these seats.

Even in the sixty-three tactical seconds the Alliance faces a major task. In twenty-eight constituencies the SDP finished second to the Conservatives. To win these seats the SDP needs on average to gain two-thirds of the votes that went to Labour in 1983. The Liberals were second to the Conservatives in twenty constituencies and they need almost as much—nearly three-fifths of the Labour vote on average—to win them. In eight constituencies the SDP is second to Labour and needs, on average, nearly half of the 1983 Conservative vote to win these seats. The Liberals were second to Labour in seven constituencies and require more than two-thirds of the Conservative vote to win these. It is hard to believe that either major party is going to collapse to such an extent that it will lose half or more of its vote in a large number of constituencies. But only if that occurs can the Alliance make a significant breakthrough.

In the meantime, what about the loyalty of those who did vote Alliance in 1983? Whereas 43 percent of those who voted Labour consider themselves very strong Labour and 37 percent of those who voted Conservative very strong Conservative, only 13 percent of those who voted Alliance feel a strong identification with the Alliance. Considering only the 1983 recruits to the Alliance, the figure drops to 9 percent and for those who decided only in the last couple of days of the campaign to vote Alliance only 1 percent. In fact among these late Alliance deciders 32 percent regard themselves as either fairly strong Conservative or fairly strong Labour. The Alliance may have to run faster just to stand still.

Then there is the question of whether cooperation can be maintained between the SDP and the Liberals. Only days after the election Jenkins resigned as SDP leader in some apparent bitterness at the treatment he had received at the Ettrick Bridge summit. Apparently the great pleasure that he professed to derive from working with Steel had declined somewhat since he invited only his chief SDP colleagues to his home to learn of his decision.

Jenkins's replacement was Owen, the only other member of the "Gang of Four" still in the Commons. Owen and Steel were widely believed not to get on well together because they are of virtually the same age and are both politically ambitious, thus making it difficult for either one to defer to the other. Apparently, however, their relations were more a matter of not having had much personal contact than of rivalry. Their contacts during the campaign are supposed to have gone smoothly and a personality clash has come to seem less likely.

Personalities aside, a serious question of strategy remains. Owen firmly opposes any merger of the two Alliance parties. He apparently anticipates another installment of defections from the Labour party and believes that such people can be recruited more easily to a Social Democratic party than to an organization calling itself something like Liberal Alliance. Given the smooth functioning of the Alliance at the grassroots level, as discussed earlier, many local activists in both parties favor closer relations that would come quite close to merger. The sharing of constituencies between the two parties was to be for the 1983 election only. Virtually no one wants to go through such a set of negotiations again, but something must be decided about who is to fight which seat in the next election now that actual election results are available for the new constituency boundaries to provide a more reliable indication of relative party strengths.

Meanwhile Steel was under increasing pressure from those Liberal MPs who had taken a rather dim view of the Alliance from the start and who saw the election results as confirmation of their view that the Liberals could advance on their own. Some of them were coming close to saying that the SDP with its handful of MPs should join the Liberal party. Steel's response was to suggest— only two days after Jenkins had resigned—that he might resign as Liberal leader. When this threat—which, if carried out, would be certain to have a disastrous impact upon Liberal strength—failed to keep the troops in line, Steel decided to take a sabbatical for the rest of the summer and went home leaving the Liberal chief whip as acting leader.

While regarding the controversy within the Liberal party as another personality conflict is easy, the argument really is not about which individual shall be dominant nor even about which party shall have place of pride in the Alliance. The issue rather is one of strategy and tactics, and the opposing sides in the Liberal party are arguing from perceptions shaped by their personal experiences. Steel is lowlands Scotland and his political experience in winning support from the voters (which he has done very successfully) varies considerably from that of David Alton, Michael Meadowcroft, and Cyril Smith in the urban settings of Liverpool, Rochdale, and Leeds. Community politics clearly has worked for these three, all of whom have been cool to close cooperation with the SDP to say nothing of a merger, and they naturally regard such tactics as most likely to bring success to the Liberals.

Can anyone seriously believe, however, that community politics is the way to win Eastbourne, Bournemouth East, and Hereford? Community politics is largely irrelevant in Conservative-held constituencies in southern England and, to that extent, this prescription cannot be a panacea for the party. On the other hand, the future of the Alliance does not lie in southern England; despite having replaced Labour as the second party in this area the prospects of ever winning many seats from the Conservatives are slim. To succeed the Alliance must rout Labour from its northern fortresses. Only when the seismograph registers a major tremor in the north will there be an earthquake sufficient to break the mold.

In the north community politics may well be the key to success. So the Altons, Meadowcrofts, and Smiths do not speak for the area where the Liberals have been showing their most striking advances; they do, however, speak for the areas where the Alliance must flourish if it is to replace Labour as the official opposition. Such a change in emphasis does not require repudiating Steel or abandoning cooperation with SDP; it does mean increasing Liberal involvement in community political life, hardly likely to be an onerous burden for the party.

For not only has grassroots organization been the Liberal contribution to the Alliance, but participatory community politics has been identified as the fundamental motivating value of those who began to revive the party in the latter part of the 1960s.[38]

Unfortunately for the Alliance, its future may lie not so much with its own efforts as with the behavior of others, especially the Labour party. Labour is rather like the drunkard who has been advised to join Alcoholics Anonymous. If it does so, then it may return to full vigor. After all, the Conservative party suffered a landslide defeat in 1945 and Labour an even more crushing one in 1931, although even then the share of the vote it received was greater than that it obtained in 1983. But if the party cannot swear off old rotgut, then it is only a step away from the gutter. Should Labour continue on the course that brought it disaster in 1983, then an Alliance prime minister before the end of the century is a good possibility. Should it take the pledge and truly reform, however, then the Alliance, despite its achievements in 1983, would face a nearly insurmountable obstacle—in which case 1983 would not have been a fundamental divide in British politics.

Opinion Polls as Feedback Mechanisms:
From Cavalry Charge to Electronic Warfare

RICHARD ROSE

I have been attending a different election from the one described in the polls. — Michael Foot, Labour party leader, press conference, 5 June 1983

It would be fascinating to study the role of opinion polls in this general election campaign. — Cecil Parkinson, Conservative party chairman, press conference, 8 June 1983

——— The idea of elections as feedback mechanisms is far older than the use of public opinion polls.[1] The basic concept is simple: the actions of government and opposition parties stimulate a response by the electorate, which sends back judgments on each party. During the life of a Parliament the parties adapt their behavior in response to this feedback. The general election result is a judgment of their relative success in adapting. The development of public opinion polls offers politicians and voters a chance to improve the steering capacity of the electoral process by providing more accurate information about voters' views than politicians otherwise could obtain at the ballot box. The feedback model of elections does not assume naively that voters are the directive force in government nor does it assume that politicians can compel voters to respond as politicians would wish.

Polls have been used in political campaigning in Britain for a quarter-century, but the process of learning how to use sample survey technology is slow. The 1983 election was a landmark in British politics because of the extent to which politicians, the media, and voters made use of polls to inform themselves and inform others about what was happening in the election campaign.

British politicians now have shifted from cavalry campaigning, a phrase that aptly describes an earlier but long-lasting tradition of British electioneering, to electronic warfare, using contemporary computerized technology. In old-style cavalry campaigning, politicians charged about the country looking for an enemy to engage. Sometimes the enemy confronted was surprisingly strong and sometimes it was surprisingly weak. By contrast, in an electronic era computers can process information rapidly and produce results relevant to campaign needs. Opinion polls can be used like radar signals, giving information to campaign planners about obstacles in their path. Just as television makes widely available to viewers the chance to assess politicians, so the polls make widely available to politicians a common basis for assessing the views of voters.

An Odd Parliament

If the 1979 general election was a move toward political normality, the 1979–83 Parliament was a move away from normality. In 1979 the vote for the two major parties rose from that of the previous general election; voters gave a clear-cut endorsement to one of the two major parties; the party winning the largest share of the vote also won an absolute majority in the House of Commons; and public opinion polls therefore had little difficulty in correctly forecasting the election outcome.[2]

The Parliament elected on 3 May 1979 started off in a seemingly normal pattern but it soon developed in novel ways. The first phase of the Parliament displayed a normal swing in public opinion from the government to the opposition. The Labour opposition moved ahead of the Conservative government in the first opinion polls taken after the general election. The second phase of the Parliament opened when the Labour party unintentionally destabilized the established party system by fundamentally altering its internal decision-making procedures. In consequence, a number of former Labour cabinet ministers resigned from the Labour party, the Social Democratic party was created in January 1981, and a Liberal–Social Democratic party alliance was founded soon thereafter.

The surge in support for the Alliance faced pollsters with difficult problems. Readers of the polls could regard a forecast of a 5 or 10 percent Alliance nationwide lead in votes as promising an Alliance government, but psephological calculations showed that this would not necessarily follow.[3]

The unexpected outbreak of the Falklands war in April 1982, when the Conservatives already were beginning to regain support, gave the governing party a great boost in support in public opinion polls, by-elections, and the May 1982 local government elections.[4] Events, not opinion polls, caused the great strategic shifts in popular support during the 1979 Parliament. The slump in the national economy and the rise in unemployment explains Labour's surge in support. The polls were simply the means by which politicians could monitor what was happening.

By-election results, public opinion poll evidence, and the inexorable progress of the calendar combined before Easter 1983 to make Prime Minister Margaret Thatcher focus on the choice of an election date. Every prime minister knows that the object in timing a general election is to pick a date when the government is likely to win. However, in half the general elections since the war, the prime minister has picked the wrong date and lost. Sir Alec Douglas Home,

Edward Heath, and James Callaghan each lost the only election they called, and soon lost their posts as party leader as well. By Easter 1983, the pressures on Thatcher were such that after the 5 May local elections she had to announce whether or not there would be a June election.

When the prime minister sat down to consider a June election date, she had three types of statistical evidence available. First, there were by-election results, which tended to show a swing from the Conservatives, though not necessarily a big enough swing to give Labour a general election victory. Second, there was the evidence of Conservative Central Office's massive analysis of 5 May 1983 local election results, conducted on its own ICL ME29 computer. The Central Office interpretation was that the results were favorable for a June election. Other commentators interpreted the results less favorably for the Conservatives. In the *Times* on 7 May David Butler described the local election results as showing "even the omens don't know," and the *Economist* of 13 May concluded that local elections indicated a Conservative lead less than that of the 1979 general election.

Opinion polls gave much more positive encouragement to the Conservatives for an early general election.[5] The average Conservative lead for the first four months of 1983 in the Gallup poll was 10 percent, 13 percent in Market and Opinion Research International (MORI) polls, and in monthly Marplan surveys 16 percent. To test the lead further, Conservative Central Office commissioned two large nationwide surveys of more than two thousand interviews each from the Harris Research Centre and the Gallup Poll immediately after the local elections, on Friday and Saturday, 6–7 May, including those parts of England and Scotland where local elections had not been held. The report was delivered directly to a special weekend meeting at Chequers of the prime minister and her advisers. Polls commissioned by the party confirmed the evidence of the published polls: the Conservatives were well ahead with the electorate, leading Labour by 44 percent to 34 percent in the Harris poll, and 46 percent to 31 percent in the Gallup poll.

Although Conservative Central Office advisers were agreed that a June election would be best, the cavalry section of the party preferred postponement. The arguments against calling an election in June were varied, e.g., some advisers said it would harm Thatcher's resolute image to call an election before it was legally necessary; some based their postponement arguments upon speculative hope that the economy might improve; some were derived from parliamentarians' obsession with not interrupting a legislative session; while others argued mechanically from precedents from the past, notably Harold Wilson's defeat in 1970 after calling an election when the polls momentarily showed Labour ahead. Labour politicians, familiar with much the same poll data as that available to the prime minister, tried to turn Thatcher against a June election by alleging that it would be a panic choice. Most Conservative MPs sided with the view of the Labour party. According to a survey by a TV program, *A Week in Politics*, 50 percent of Conservative MPs favored an autumn 1983 election, as against 36 percent favoring June, and another 14 percent don't knows.

In the event, an odd Parliament ended with the prime minister doing a perfectly normal thing, timing the election for a moment when she thought her party would win. On 9 May Thatcher announced that a general election would be held on the first possible date, 9 June. This was entirely consistent with opinion poll evidence that if a general election were held immediately, the Conservatives would win with a comfortable majority.

A New Level of Polling

When the 1983 general election campaign opened, for the first time since 1966 it looked like the polls couldn't miss getting the result right. The Conservatives had enjoyed a double-digit lead in most polls for many months previously. From May 1982 to April 1983, the Conservatives averaged a 13 percent lead in the Gallup Poll and a 12 percent lead in MORI polls. The Conservatives enjoyed a 95-seat lead over Labour in the old House of Commons and their opponents were divided into two separate parties. One pollster privately remarked, "If we don't get this one right we ought to be shot."

The unique features of the 1983 general election campaign gave both cavalry types and computer analysts some grounds for pause. The old-fashioned campaigners simply repeated their understanding (or misunderstanding) of the performance of the polls in the 1970s. Pollsters themselves were concerned about the prospect of a volatile election campaign, in which swings in public opinion might occur more rapidly than they could track or produce a late swing vitiating eve-of-poll forecasts. Equally important, the division of the country into contrasting battlegrounds between Conservatives and Labour, as against Conservatives and Alliance, created the prospect of tactical voting with electors voting for their second-choice candidate in order to avoid wasting a vote for a party likely to finish third locally, but not nationally. The prospect arose of a great disjunction between seats and votes with no overall majority in Parliament. The polls could not forecast a winner, if the queen herself were unsure after election day which party had won the right to form the government in a hung Parliament.[6]

The demonstrated readiness of voters to move between established parties, and to or from the Alliance, appeared to be encouraged by the new technology of campaigning, and the polls themselves were seen as a potentially destabilizing element in the election. In the Bermondsey by-election, where three different candidates sought to defeat a visibly unpopular Labour candidate, Peter Tatchell, the polls were credited by many political journalists with identifying the Alliance candidate as most likely to win, thus creating a bandwagon effect resulting in a massive Alliance victory. But the Bermondsey campaign was unique in many respects. The polls did not cost Labour the Bermondsey seat; Labour's own actions did. In the Darlington by-election, held a month later, Labour won and Alliance came a poor third, despite early polls showing Alliance and Labour fighting hard for first.[7]

Notwithstanding the residue of cavalry officer skepticism, in 1983 opinion polls conducted far more nationwide surveys of the mass electorate than ever before; 48 nationwide pre-election polls were published compared to 35 in 1979, 23 in October 1974, and 26 in February 1974. There was an average of twelve polls a week during the election campaign. Given a British electorate of more than 40 million persons, there was no risk of saturating the electorate with interviews, but there was a possibility of saturating the media and the electorate with publicity about poll results, and same-day publication of results showing conflicting trends.

Since published polls normally are commissioned by media sponsors at a cost of from £3,000 to £8,000 per survey, the volume of polling reflects the readiness of the media to spend money. One reason why more media spending occurred in 1983 is that there were more potential sponsors. *TV-AM* and the *Star* newspaper did not exist in 1979; between them they underwrote eight polls in 1983. A second reason is the increased realization within newspapers that sponsoring a poll is a good way to secure free television advertising of the paper the night before. Each poll was released in time for BBC and ITN to report the results in their evening news bulletin. The cost of a poll could be offset at least in part by the publicity it gained. In the extreme case of the *Observer*, its poll was charged against the budget of the marketing department, not the editorial department. The television programs that sponsored polls could gain newspaper publicity by follow-up publication of the results, and could try to boost their viewership by releasing results in advance. Finally, editorial staff increasingly are accepting polls as a normal part of an election campaign. In 1983 only one popular paper did not sponsor a poll, the *Mirror*, still dominated by the belief that it knew what its readers wanted, although falling circulation figures might spur questioning of that judgment. Only one quality paper, the *Times*, did not sponsor a poll, but it did retain Robert Worcester of MORI to advise its staff about reporting other papers' polls, to which it gave substantial prominence.

In the 1983 general election, six different organizations produced nationwide polls for publication (see table 5.1). Five of the six worked for at least two clients; the exception was National Opinion Polls (NOP), a subsidiary of the *Mail* publishing group. The most polls (and the most clients) were claimed by Robert Worcester's firm, MORI, which conducted thirteen nationwide published surveys, plus private surveys for the Labour party and constituency surveys. Only one firm active in 1979 was not active in 1983, Research Services, which

Table 5.1 Nationwide polls during the 1983 general election campaign

Polling organization	Place of publication	No. of surveys	Range of sample size
MORI	*Sunday Times*	3[a]	Panel 1216
	Express	4.5[b]	867 (reint)–1,100
	Star	4.5[b]	867 (reint)–1,090
	Evening Standard	1	1,100
	Labour party	(20)	Quickies + panel
		13	
Audience Selection	*Sun*	5	Phone 504–1,100
	TV-AM	4	Phone 1,056–1,154
	Alliance frequent	9	
Harris Research Centre	*Sunday Observer*	4[c]	567 (reint)–1,052
	TV Eye/Thames TV	4	1,034–1,053
	ITN exit poll	1	10,141
	Conservative Central Office	(7)	1,049–2,307
		9	
Marplan	*Guardian*	5	1,276–1,457
	Sunday Mirror	3	1,250–1,325
		8	
Gallup Poll	Daily, Sunday *Telegraph*	6	918–2,015
	BBC	1	4,141
		7	
National Opinion Polls (NOP)	*Daily Mail, Mail on Sundays*	5	1,040–1,584

[a] Plus one survey conducted 21–25 April to establish the panel for campaign monitoring.
[b] Election day story jointly published by the *Express* and *Star*.
[c] Includes a survey released for election day, 9 June, through Press Association services.

conducted unsuccessful surveys for the *Observer*. The one new polling organization was Audience Selection Ltd., a subsidiary of AGB Research, specializing in telephone polls. Although a relatively new organization, it was headed by John Clemens, an experienced market researcher who had been with Marplan when it conducted eight surveys in the 1979 general election.

The great majority of the polls had many common technical features. A poll was typically a quota sample of about one thousand interviews with respondents selected according to quotas stratified by age, sex, and social class, as well as region and constituency. A concern with speed in identifying respondents as well as a marked deterioration in the electoral register meant that no polling organization wanted to undertake pure random samples, with all the additional expense in time and in money. The Gallup Poll was distinctive in regularly undertaking campaign surveys with up to two thousand respondents.

Developments in computer technology made it possible for opinion polls to conduct elaborate analyses of their data. Polls commissioned by the popular press found, however, that their sponsors usually were not interested in the vast quantity of information that a computer could generate. On the other hand, Conservative Central Office used its in-house computer heavily.

One polling organization, Audience Selection, stood out from the rest because it conducted telephone interviews exclusively. Telephone interviewing for commercial market research surveys has grown rapidly in Britain; Audience Selection had a turnover of more than £1 million annually within two years of being founded in 1980. The use of telephones for interviewing is normal in the expanse of the United States, where interviewing face-to-face involves a variety of obstacles, and there is a wide diffusion of telephones. While telephones cover approximately 72 percent of households in Britain, the proportion without telephones are not a normal cross section of the population in socioeconomic terms, and have been disproportionately Labour. The results of telephone interviews therefore must be weighted to correct for this bias. A proponent of the use of telephones for interviewing, Dr. William Miller, sought to demonstrate the efficiency of telephone sampling in the 1982 Glasgow Hillhead by-election. Of the three weighting methods used in the final survey of his Television Survey Research Unit, two gave the Social Democrat a lead, and one projected a Labour victory; the average placed the Social Democrats ahead of Labour by 0.3 percent. In the event, the Social Democrats won with a 7.6 percent lead over Labour.[8] Audience Selection sought to compensate for the known bias of telephone ownership by asking individuals their past voting record in 1979, then weighting their sample to produce figures that matched the 1979 election result. In their eyes, this made the results representative in 1983.

Given that the 1983 election campaign was unusually concerned with whether or not voters would change opinions, it is particularly noteworthy that only one poll—MORI for the *Sunday Times*—was a panel survey. The MORI panel could compare the difference between *aggregate* change in each party's share of the vote (which was generally low or well within the margin of normal sampling error fluctuations) and *individual* change (which was much greater, but often with results that cancelled out in aggregate).

In addition to the polls conducted with cross sections of the British electorate, polls were undertaken in Scotland sponsored by the *Scotsman* (MORI), the *Glasgow Herald* (System Three), and the Scottish *Daily Express* (MORI). In Wales pre-election polls were sponsored by Harlech TV (Research and Marketing, Wales and the West). Northern Ireland had its first British general election poll, sponsored by the *Irish News* of Belfast (Market Research Bureau of Ireland).[9]

The most imaginative set of specialized polls was commissioned by London Weekend Television's *Weekend World*, which employed the Harris Research Centre to conduct surveys weekly in three different types of constituencies: seats marginal as between the Conservative and Labour parties, conventionally the decisive seats in a general election; constituencies where the Liberals were challenging Conservative incumbents; and constituencies where Social Democratic candidates were fighting to represent what was normally a Labour seat. The results, televised each Sunday, consistently confirmed the Conservative lead over Labour and the relative weakness of each wing of the Alliance. On the Tuesday before the election, Yorkshire Television featured a MORI survey of 2,966 respondents divided into three equal groups: Conservative-held marginals, Labour-held marginals, and seats being defended by Social Democratic MPS. It showed an average 4.5 percent swing to the Conservatives, close to the actual result.

Among samples of special groups within the electorate, the most interest was occasioned by an NOP survey of 1,096 youths between 18 and 21, reported on Jimmy Young's popular BBC Radio 2 program. In previous elections young voters usually have been pro-Labour and a high incidence of unemployment among youths caused politicians to assume that youths would be even more pro-Labour in 1983. The NOP survey caused a stir when it reported that young voters gave the Conservatives a 10 percent lead, less than the Conservative lead in an NOP survey published in the *Daily Mail* at the same time, but a clear rejection of Labour. Postelection surveys confirmed that young voters did favor the Conservatives, though not by as much as middle-aged voters.[10] Other special-purpose surveys were conducted: among blacks by the Harris Research Centre for Channel 4's *Black on Black* program (a Labour lead of 60 percent); among teachers by NOP for the *Times Educational Supplement* (Conservative lead 16 percent); and among women by *News of the World* (a 17 percent Conservative lead over Alliance in a telephone survey conducted by Audience Selection).[11]

Among a host of constituency polls, unique attention was focused briefly on the *Sun* commission of an Audience Selection telephone survey of 503 electors in Bristol East, where Anthony Wedgwood Benn was the Labour candidate. Benn's left-wing views and vulnerability to defeat in a seat made marginal by redistribution justified the attention of a national newspaper. However, Benn took exception to the *Sun* survey, alleging that questions asking voters whether or not they agreed with Benn's views on disarmament, nationalization, and union power were an attempt to influence them. Benn threatened legal action on the grounds that spending money on such a poll was a "corrupt practice" intended to benefit his opponents. No suit was filed and Benn lost his seat, even though the *Sun* poll reported that in early May he was ahead by 6 percent.[12]

The bulk of the constituency surveys followed a pattern made familiar in previous general elections, typically being sponsored by local newspapers or regional TV companies to provide a local angle on nationwide opinion polls. Often the constituency polls had inadequate samples, for sponsors usually were not prepared to meet the cost of a proper size sample, which can be almost as big for a constituency survey as a nationwide survey. In Finchley, the prime minister's constituency, Dr. Julienne Ford, a sociology senior lecturer at Middlesex Polytechnic, reported conducting a telephone survey of 244 people on 5 June and finding a Labour lead of 15 percent. Later in the week, Thatcher won the seat by 24 percent.

The political parties commissioned their own polls during the campaign as well as reading with great interest but varying degrees of satisfaction the results of the published polls. For the sixth successive election, the Conservative party used the same polling organization, albeit Opinion Research Centre now was merged under the name of its parent company, the Harris Research Centre, directed by John Hanvey. Internal reorganization at Conservative Central Office transferred polling from the Research Department to the Marketing Department, with Christopher Lawson as director and D. Keith Britto as the staff specialist in data analysis. The organizational shift reflected a desire to integrate polls and advertising better, to develop political communication within the party, and to use survey data in formulating and monitoring the impact of the party's actions on the electorate.

Conservative Central Office was well prepared for analyzing public opinion during the campaign, having had a continuing program of monitoring feedback from the electorate since the mid-1960s. Immediately after the 1979 general election, it commissioned a postelection survey to find out more about the causes of its victory. In the interelection period the party commissioned annual surveys of popular reactions to the budget and studies of attitudes toward issues of particular importance (such as unemployment) and also subscribed to detailed monthly analyses of Gallup Poll omnibus surveys, which provided an unusual amount of reliable information about subgroups of the electorate. It read with interest surveys independently commissioned by a variety of institutions on matters affecting public policy, such as public transport, private medicine, and home ownership. The Conservative surveys took policies as given. Information was sought to assist in presenting government policies in ways most likely to appeal to the electorate. Surveys avoided asking about political personalities; Thatcher's character was taken as a given too.

During the election campaign Central Office each weekend commissioned a nationwide survey of two thousand interviews, especially useful for regional analysis, plus surveys of one thousand during the week. There were recurring questions about issues and party preferences, as well as ad hoc questions about topics of the moment, such as remarks by Denis Healey that the Conservatives believed were gaffes but wished to verify whether the electorate thought the same. The Marketing Department could provide the campaign committee with fresh input based on unpublished research three times a week, as well as daily input about published polls. It also could relate already collected data to topics arising unexpectedly in the campaign. John Hanvey of the Harris Research Centre came to Central Office each day to discuss polls and their implications.

The first private poll report from Harris, 13–14 May, gave the Conservatives a 14 percent lead. By 31 May its poll was giving the party a 19 percent lead. The total campaign expenditure on polls was in excess of £100,000, but substantially less than initially budgeted. In 1983 there was no anxiety about possible defeat to stimulate a frantic and expensive search for information.

The Labour party once again retained Robert Worcester's firm, MORI, first used in 1970, to carry out its opinion polls. The constitutional changes of the previous Parliament, the election of a new party leader, the appointment of a new party secretary, and even the shift of party offices to a new headquarters building in South London meant that the 1983 Labour campaign was not simply a repeat of the 1979 campaign. There was no broadcasting officer to consider the implications of opinion polls for strategy, and the new press officer, Nick Grant, was hardly in place before the election started. Ironically, MORI polls were atypical because they were an element of continuity in a much changed campaign staff. But even MORI's involvement was only confirmed by Labour committing itself to a contract in February 1983.

MORI's series of surveys started with a base line nationwide poll, developed after group discussions designed to identify the way in which ordinary voters discussed the parties and issues. MORI then conducted about twenty "quickie" ad hoc polls of about five hundred face-to-face interviews each with nationwide samples and target groups in the electorate in order to monitor the progress of the campaign and to deal with issues as they arose. MORI's specialization in quickie polls—surveys launched with an early morning strategy meeting agreeing on a final questionnaire, fieldwork conducted during the day, and the result available late the same night—was particularly relevant to an election campaign. Campaign staff could get information as quickly as it could review it, agreeing on final details one morning, and receiving results the next morning. In view of its large volume of published polling, MORI sought insofar as practicable to separate conduct of its private Labour polls from the conduct of published polls, using separate field interviewers and drawing a separate constituency sample. The total Labour party expenditure on campaign polls was about £60,000.

In the case of Labour, the client rather than the polls was the chief handicap.

MORI polls identified the distance that the party was behind the Conservatives, points in the party's manifesto that were unpopular (e.g., nuclear disarmament) and potentially popular (e.g., unemployment policy). But an opinion poll organization could not take the actions needed to make the party popular with the electorate. As Geoffrey Smith of the *Times* commented:

> The weakness of the Labour strategy lies not so much in its approach to salesmanship as in the goods it has to sell. . . . Labour's task, in other words, is not to show that there is a problem but to prove that they have a solution. But this would require a different manifesto and a different leader.[13]

The creation of the Alliance expanded the demand for opinion polls by political parties. Previously, the Liberal party headquarters had not commissioned public opinion polls. Liberal candidates usually have stressed local issues, seeking to insulate their constituency from a nationwide battle between the big Labour and Conservative battalions. In the words of one veteran Liberal constituency agent, "Our philosophy is to create a by-election atmosphere in the midst of a general election campaign." By contrast, the Social Democratic party was launched with technical support by advertising and public relations experts, and computerized membership lists and dues collection.

In planning for the general election, the Social Democratic party conducted in-depth qualitative interviews with the assistance of the Specialist Research Unit, commissioned two large national surveys by the Gallup Poll, and carried out reinterviews with a thousand people previously interviewed in person. Unlike the established parties, the SDP could not use such social characteristics as trade union membership or home ownership as a means of identifying its potential support. The SDP sought to make a cross-class appeal, even if appealing to only a minority of both the working class and middle class. Surveys for the SDP sought to identify a distinctive cluster of attitudes or issue positions among would-be SDP supporters. However, SDP voters turned out not to be distinctive but to differ only in the mix of attitudes, agreeing with Labour voters on some issues, with Conservative voters on others, and with supporters of both major parties on a third set.[14]

During the election campaign the Social Democrats commissioned a series of Audience Selection telephone surveys to monitor party support, the likelihood of tactical voting, and issues. The reports were presented to the Alliance campaign committee, which brought together both SDP and Liberal party leaders, by Sarah Horack, an SDP official who formerly worked in the United States with the American firm of Yankelovich, Skelly, and White. The total SDP expenditure on surveys during the campaign was upward of £30,000.

It had a particular interest in evidence indicating that the Alliance was gaining support, since it had been running a poor third in the polls in the weeks before the campaign was announced. Alliance politicians were predisposed to use the polls as ammunition in their campaign to boost the belief that Alliance votes would not be "wasted," rather than as feedback indicating whether their shots were hitting targets. As the Conservative and Labour parties each had an interest in the Alliance bandwagon not starting to roll, the Alliance interpretation of poll figures was a subject of political controversy during the campaign.

The Accuracy of the Final Forecasts

As the election campaign progressed, the anxieties of pollsters fostered by three abnormal elections in the 1970s gave way to relief. Of the forty-nine surveys taken during the campaign, forty-six showed the Conservatives with a double-digit lead. Moreover, of the ten polls showing the Conservatives with a lead of 20 percent or better, eight were taken within four days of the election. When election day came, the polls published their findings without qualification. The stories reporting these figures concentrated upon the size of the anticipated Conservative landslide.

The Conservative landslide victory made the 1983 election the easiest for the polls to forecast since 1966, when Labour won a very large majority. All polls correctly forecast a Conservative victory, differing only in the size of the margin. The fairest test of the accuracy of the polls is their estimate of the voting strength of each of the three major parties (see table 5.2). In 1983 the polls on average came to within 2.7 percent in predicting the Conservative share of the vote. All seven polls erred on the same side, predicting a higher Conservative vote than actually was achieved. The average error in the predicted Labour share of the vote was less, 2.1 percent, and every poll underestimated Labour's share of the vote. The Alliance share of the vote was predicted exactly by five polls, if only because of its fluke achievement of a round number result, 26 percent; the average error in forecasting the Alliance vote was an underestimate of 0.4 percent. The average error in the twenty-one forecasts of major party votes was 1.7 percent, better than the margin of error allowed by sampling theory. Another way to describe the record is to say that on average the polls correctly estimated 98.3 percent of each party's vote.

Forecasting the gap between the parties is more difficult than forecasting a single party's share of the vote, because an overestimate of one party and an underestimate of another compound sampling errors in measuring one party. In 1983 the polls had particular trouble in estimating the gap between the parties. In consequence of consistently overestimating the Conservative vote and underestimating the Labour vote, the average error in the gap was 4.8 percent. Conceivably, the forecast 20 percent Conservative lead dropped in the final hours before polling day, but it is implausible to accept what this implies: a 2.4 percent swing to Labour directly from the Conservatives or over-

Table 5.2   Accuracy of the final poll forecasts, 1983
(error in forecast in parentheses)

Fieldwork date	Poll	Con.	Lab.	All.	Con. lead over Lab.	Average error, 3 parties
9 June	Election result, Great Britain[a]	43.5	28.3	26	15.2	
8 June	MORI, *Evening Standard*	44 (+0.5)	28 (−0.3)	26 (0)	16 (+0.8)	0.3
7–8 June	Gallup, *Daily Telegraph*	45.5 (+2.0)	26.5 (−1.8)	26 (0)	19 (+3.8)	1.3
6–7 June	NOP, *Daily Mail*	46 (+2.5)	28 (−0.3)	24 (−2.0)	18 (+2.8)	1.6
8 June	Marplan, *Guardian*	46 (+2.5)	26 (−2.3)	26 (0)	20 (+4.8)	1.6
6–7 June[b]	MORI, *Express/ Star*	47 (+3.5)	26 (−2.3)	25 (−1.0)	21 (−5.8)	2.3
7–8 June[b]	Harris, *Observer*	47 (+3.5)	25 (−3.3)	26 (0)	22[c] (+6.8)	2.3
8 June[b]	NOP, Northcliffe chain	48 (+4.5)	24 (−4.3)	26 (0)	24[c] (+8.8)	2.9
Average, 7 polls		46.2 (+2.7)	26.2 (−2.1)	25.6 (−0.4)	20.0 (+4.8)	1.7
7 June	Aud. Sel., *Sun* (phone)	45 (+1.5)	23 (−5.3)	29 (+3.0)	22[b] (+6.8)	3.3

Note: The polls included in this table are the nationwide polls that commenced interviewing in the final three days of the campaign and concluded interviewing before voting commenced on Thursday, 9 June.

[a] Northern Ireland votes omitted, since polls do not survey there.

[b] Reinterviews of earlier sample.

[c] Labour placed third.

confidence in the election outcome causing 6 percent of committed Conservative voters to stay home. Some polls also had trouble in placing the second and third parties correctly; two of the seven put Alliance second, and a third forecast a tie for second place. The average error for the gap between these two parties, 2 percent, was smaller than that for the front-runners.

The most accurate poll based on interviews undertaken the day before the election was produced by MORI for the London *Evening Standard*. With allowance for rounding, it was spot on in forecasting the final result for all three parties. The importance of sampling fluctuations, even in the work of one organization, is illustrated by the fact that the MORI poll published in the *Express* and *Star* on the morning of election day was one of the less accurate polls. NOP similarly published final forecasts in two different places and these varied substantially. By contrast with the 1970s, none of the face-to-face polls felt any need to apologize for their performance once the actual election result was known. Robert Worcester, currently president of the World Association of Public Opinion Research (WAPOR), as well as head of MORI, told the *Times*, "I am very pleased. It vindicates the accuracy of the polls." He added, "Ninety-five per cent of polling is science; the other five per cent is luck. If you are not lucky, it is not a good business to be in."[15]

Insofar as elections are reckoned to be influenced by last-minute events—the so-called late swing that pollsters like to use to explain any difference between their results and the actual election outcome—then surveys conducted on election day ought to be the most accurate surveys. However, superior accuracy of late polls cannot be assumed. Whereas in 1979 the Gallup Poll for the BBC was very high in accuracy, the Opinion Research Centre exit poll for Independent Television News (ITN) was not as accurate as most final pre-election forecasts.

The BBC and ITN each sponsored election-day "exit poll" surveys for use in programs commencing as soon as the polls closed. ITN commissioned an exit poll from Harris Research Centre, interviewing a sample of voters as they left the place of voting. Each voter was asked upon leaving a polling station to complete a mock ballot and place it in a box provided by the interviewer. Its survey forecast a 14 percent Conservative lead and had an average error of 0.6 percent in votes attributed to the three major parties, more accurate than polls finishing a day or two before the election (cf. table 5.2).

The BBC commissioned a detailed Gallup Poll with 4,141 respondents selected by conventional quota sample methods the day before the election and on election day. The Gallup survey oversampled for Scotland. It gave the Conservatives a lead of 15.2 percent among those showing a voting intention, exactly the same figure as the actual result. The Conservatives were credited with 43.9 percent of the vote, Labour with 28.7 percent, and the Alliance with 25.7 percent, for an average error in estimating the parties' share of the vote of 0.4 percent. However, when Gallup adjusted the figure to take into account only those reporting that they definitely would vote, the basis of their final *Telegraph* forecast, the Conservative vote share rose to 45.8 percent, increasing the gap between the parties to 17.1 percent, and the average error in estimating the parties' share of the vote rose to 1.6

The telephone polls of Audience Selection were a controversial innovation. The director of Audience Selection, John Clemens, argues that telephone polls have five advantages over conventional face-to-face interviewing.[16] The sample can be scattered to every parliamentary constituency rather than restricted to fifty or a hundred constituencies by the need to limit the travel time of conventional interviewers. Respondent selection occurs randomly by drawing telephone numbers, without the interviewer discretion that occurs in a quota sample. Evening interviewing is done easily at all times of year. Interviewers are more easily supervised and briefed, because telephoning is done from a central location. Results can be produced within an hour of the completion of the final interview.

The use of telephone polls by Audience Selection Ltd. was criticized sharply by politicians and pollsters during the campaign, because of the possible bias in political preferences of telephone owners. In 1979 Gallup Poll surveys had found that within the upper middle class, Labour voters were 8 percent fewer among telephone owners than among people without telephones, in the lower middle class 7 percent, and among manual workers 10 percent fewer.[17]

Telephones now cover approximately three-quarters of the British electorate. Because Audience Selection interviewed a quota sample of telephone owners, it did not underrepresent manual workers per se, but only workers without telephones. In theory, the effect of omitting electors without telephones can be removed by correctly weighting the results to compensate for Labour's underrepresentation among telephone owners. A polling organization conducting face-to-face surveys as well as telephone interviews could derive a precise estimate of the within-class difference between telephone owners and nonowners, and adjust its results to remove the estimated degree of bias, but Audience Selection could not readily do this because it concentrates exclusively upon telephone surveys. To correct for the expected bias, it asked people how they voted in 1979. This introduced a new set of difficulties, for measures of voting intention from four years ago are subject to error in recall, and it is difficult to be sure of the base line for assessing recalled vote.[18] In the event, the weights derived by Audience Selection from 1979 voting had the effect of increasing the share of both the Alliance and Labour support almost equally (1.068 and 1.075, respectively), and decreasing the Conservative share (0.875).

Notwithstanding the use of weighting procedures intended to reduce the bias in a telephone sample, all nine of the Audience Selection polls showed a consistent pro-Alliance bias by comparison with face-to-face interviews conducted about the same time. Skeptical readers of Audience Selection polls could compare its findings with the average showing of the parties on the previous seven days; the average overestimate of Alliance support at any given time was 4 percent. The Conservatives suffered the greater degree of underestimation of support by the weights employed by Audience Selection, averaging a 3 percent loss. Labour support was underestimated by 2.5 percent by comparison with other polls; the discrepancy was most marked in the last ten days of the campaign. The final forecast of Audience Selection put the Alliance in second place and Labour a poor third.

Theoretically, the logic of the Audience Selection surveys sought to balance two competing sets of considerations: the disadvantages of interviewing a less than fully representative sample of the electorate, as against the advantages argued by John Clemens and William Miller. If the advantages and disadvantages had cancelled out, the Audience Selection record would have been about average. If the advantages were greater than the disadvantages, then the record would have been above average, but if the disadvantages were greater than the advantages, then the record would have been worse. In fact, the net result was worse: the final *Sun* poll underestimated the Labour vote and overestimated the Alliance vote more than any other poll. Equally critical, the Audience Selection method polls were *consistently* out of line with other polls, overestimating the Alliance support in every poll during the campaign by an average of 4 percent, and underestimating both Labour and Conservative support in every poll. Immediately after the election, John Clemens of Audience Selection ruefully admitted, "It doesn't look too good, does it." [19]

The inability of Audience Selection to produce results similar in accuracy to other polls reflects one correctable bias in their telephone sample. The Audience Selection sample greatly underrepresented council house tenants. Even after applying its standard weighting, council housing tenants constituted 21.4 percent of their sample, compared to 29.5 percent of respondents in the Gallup Poll campaign surveys, a figure consistent with census data. The underrepresentation of council tenants is particularly crucial in voting studies, given that since 1970 an elector's type of housing is more likely to be associated with party preference than occupational class. [20]

In effect, the Audience Selection survey compounded problems of *non*representation of telephone owners with *under*representation of council tenants. The actions required to correct for the reinforcing biases are different. Refining the selection of respondents to include a quota for council tenants (or any other politically significant group that happens to be underrepresented among those with a telephone) is a relatively straightforward task. If Audience Selection had done this, its sample would have been improved. The second problem is inherent in telephone interviewing, namely, determining what allowance to make for the quarter of the electorate presently without a phone. To conduct parallel face-to-face interviews with people without telephones is technically feasible but costly, and defeats much of the purpose of using telephone surveys.

Setting aside the unique problems of the Audience Selection poll, sample surveys necessarily must differ slightly from each other and from the actual election result. After an election it is tempting to assume that the differences between the polls and the result are systematic and persisting. In fact, they are usually random. Many seemingly plausible generalizations that might be drawn from the 1983 record are refuted by previous experience.[21] For example, in 1983 the polls reported a widening of the gap between the first- and the second-place party, whereas in the 1970s the gap usually narrowed.

Statements about the performance of the polls only can be true generalizations if they fit a number of election campaigns. To generalize solely from the result of the 1983 election campaign is to assume that all general elections are alike. Unlike generalizations about voting behavior, few propositions drawn from polls in the 1983 election will stand up to systematic testing against the polls' record at the four general elections of the 1970s. The one exception is: *the government's vote is usually overestimated by the polls.* 4.8 percent in 1983 compared to a 1979 overestimate of 1.4 percent in favor of the Labour government.

The Uses (and Abuses) of the Polls

The contents of opinion polls vary far less than do the interests of their users. Most polls ask the same types of questions about the parties, the personalities of leaders, issues, and social characteristics of voters. However, newspaper editors and television producers, party politicians, and ordinary voters can make very different uses of the information common to polls.[22]

The opinion polls, in the words of Robert Worcester, "are the handmaidens of the press."[23] All the nationwide published campaign polls were commissioned by the media but in no sense were the polls the chief story. MORI calculated that during the election on average 59 percent of front page news was *not* about elections, and of the 41 percent that was, only 4 percent concerned polls. Nearly half the polls were commissioned by popular papers, better described as feature-papers than news-papers, given the entertainment emphasis of Britain's tabloid dailies.

Since the polls were news, the popular papers gave the polls big headlines on page one, but ran stories of only 250 to 400 words. The papers thus were prepared to pay upward of £10 to £15 *per word* for their poll story. The popular press was interested in only two items of information: which party was leading and the size of the lead. Unfortunately, the size of a party's lead in the polls is doubly vulnerable to sampling error. The popular papers were ready to headline the least reliable element in poll findings, the change in the size of the lead.

The quality press sponsoring polls—the *Telegraph*, the *Guardian*, the *Sunday Times*, and the *Observer*—made better use of the results, giving more details of responses and even printing some complex tables. A reader of the serious papers could gain a significant amount of information from their published reports.[24]

The broadcasting media had the largest potential audience but is also the most evanescent medium for transmitting poll results. A three-minute segment devoted to poll results is equivalent to a news story of about four hundred words. Thames Television's *TV-Eye* and *Weekend World* on London Weekend Television each commissioned polls to provide a basis for questions to politicians being interviewed later in their program. However, there was no way for the interested viewer to examine the findings, except by hastily copying them down as they flashed quickly on the screen.

The failure to secure widespread attention for Harris Research Centre's imaginative marginal seats polls for *Weekend World* illustrates the ephemeral way in which polls are indiscriminantly treated. The Harris polls were unusual, concentrating attention upon marginal seats that would make or break each party's fortunes. No other poll regularly sampled this crucial set of seats. However, the press did not normally display these results the next day, even though they were issued midday Sunday and thus a godsend for a normally quiet Monday morning paper. When mention was made, it often was buried in an omnibus election story, and sometimes the reporting was so garbled that it was not possible to establish the overall electoral significance of the figures.

All the parties sought to make use of the polls in much the same way: to obtain information useful in developing and implementing their campaign strategy, and as feedback for evaluating their campaigns. In using polls to provide insight into popular opinions and to frame actions to influence opinion, rather than to forecast outcomes, the parties showed a sound awareness of the value of polls to them. The parties differed in their organizational capacity to make use of the information and in their readiness to welcome feedback, when it necessarily would be bad news for some politicians as well as good news for others.

From the beginning of the campaign, sophisticated journalistic questioning at press conferences and on TV made it evident that all parties would have to accept published polls as campaign facts. Party leaders were not asked how they thought their campaign was going, but how they reacted to reports of the public opinion polls showing their party doing well or badly. If unfavorable news was dismissed with the ritual statement "the only poll that counts is the poll on election day," the remarks carried no conviction. Sophisticated politicians shifted the ground of the question. For example, when Michael Foot was asked about Labour's standing in a BBC radio *World This Weekend* program on 15 May, he admitted that the position was "not very favorable at the moment" but added, "These are the very polls that are going to show a change in the next few weeks."

In the 1983 election campaign, both journalists and politicians were sensitive to the existence of unpublished polls conducted for the parties. Enterprising journalists sometimes pushed politicians to say whether their private polls showed results different from the published polls. An evasive or noncommittal answer was taken as a tacit admission that this was not the case. Upon occasion politicians sought to abuse the distinction between published media polls and unpublished party polls by selectively leaking information from unpublished party polls that they thought to be to their advantage.

The Alliance started the one significant controversy about poll interpretations and leaked polls. From the beginning of the campaign, the Alliance leadership promoted the idea that the polls would show a steady and large rise in Alliance support. This was not evident in the first two weeks of the campaign; Alliance support actually fell slightly. By the end of the second week of the campaign, the Alliance was down to an average of 17 percent—except in Audience Selection polls. When opinion polls in the third week of the campaign, especially Audience Selection, began to show a rise in Alliance support, an enthusiastic member of the SDP staff leaked an Audience Selection poll purporting to show that the Alliance soon would catch up with the Labour party in the race for second place. The fact that Audience Selection was using disputed telephone polls meant that politicians from other parties had both motive and materials with which to attack the Alliance. Both Conservative and Labour party politicians retaliated by referring to their own unpublished polls, which did not show a similarly high standing for the Alliance. Journalists then challenged the parties' pollsters to release the full results of surveys referred to selectively. The Harris Research Centre and MORI did so. The Harris poll for the Conservative Party on 3–4 June, for example, showed the Conservatives with a 17 percent lead—Conservatives 45.4 percent, Labour 28.4 percent, and Alliance, 23.9 percent—virtually the same as the results published by Harris in the *Observer* on 5 June.[25]

At the constituency level, Alliance candidates sought to boost their election prospects by referring to vaguely defined poll results purporting to show the Alliance candidate running a close second. This was intended to encourage voters favoring the party said to be in third place to switch to the Alliance. In Liverpool Broadgreen, for example, the Liberal candidate issued a leaflet featuring what was said to be the latest poll in the constituency. It showed the Liberal only 4 percent behind the Labour candidate. In the event, the Liberal finished third, 25 percent behind the winner. An SDP press officer, Roger Carroll, described this tactic, used in a number of constituencies, as candidates making "overoptimistic" references to canvass returns. He added, "Candidates should use them with circumspection, but few from any party ever do."[26]

As the consistently front-running party, the Conservatives had no difficulty in reading the polls with approval. The feedback from the polls offered independent confirmation of what the party leaders most wanted to hear, namely, that they would win the election. But this was not the only reason for attending closely to poll evidence. The party had integrated polling into its campaign strategy for more than a decade, and experienced staff was at hand to commission polls, to interpret them, and to offer ideas about how the data could best be used to maintain the party's lead. Insofar as the polls warned Conservatives that a few issues were not popular, for example, cutting expenditure on the welfare state, they were useful in preventing politicians from confusing the relatively extreme ideas of political coteries at Westminster with mass opinion. During the election campaign there was a visible "moistening" of Margaret Thatcher, as she embraced publicly her government's record of increasing public expenditure on the welfare state, a wet action consistent with public opinion data but not popular with the drys in her own party, who wished to cut rather than expand public spending.[27]

The polls were not the cause of Labour's difficulties in the 1983 election campaign; they simply brought home to party leaders their magnitude. Labour was shown to be trailing badly behind the government in the polls and its leader extraordinarily lacking in popularity. There was one encouraging element in the poll findings: unemployment was consistently the most important issue in the minds of the voters, and when the campaign opened the Gallup Poll showed that more voters had confidence in Labour handling unemployment. The Labour party could not change its leader at the outset of the campaign—but it could seek to use the feedback from the polls to adapt its course to win more votes.

The Labour party was doubly handicapped in using opinion poll data. In 1983, by contrast with the Wilson era, the groups dominating the party's policy-making apparatus were less sensitive to electoral opinion. The whole point of the left's battle within the Labour party from 1979 was to secure a party manifesto that expressed the values of the left, not to adopt a manifesto in keeping with majority opinion.

When the Labour leader proclaimed a few days before election day that he had been attending a different election from the one described in the polls, he spoke truer than he knew. Michael Foot made his declaration in response to journalists asking how he reacted to polls giving the Conservatives a lead of 12 to 18 percent. He claimed that the campaign was proceeding well because of the enthusiasm shown by the party faithful. The old cavalry campaigner's model of an election was that of a battle in which the general enthused the troops and the troops then won victory. In his eve of poll message, Foot proclaimed, "I believe we can win."[28]

Symptomatic of the introverted outlook of the Labour campaign was a press release issued two days before the election by David Hughes, national agent of the party, headed, "Good News for Labour." The press release chronicled the lead that Labour was enjoying among various minorities, such as ethnic voters, Scots, and voters in Labour seats held by SDP defectors. No attention was given to opinion poll evidence showing that the Conservatives were ahead among the white electorate, in England, in constituencies not held by SDP defectors, and among home-owning manual workers. So great was Labour's aversion to thinking in terms of broadening its appeal that its marginal seats campaign was directed as much toward holding the seats it already had as to gaining Conservative-held seats needed to constitute a Labour majority.

Labour's campaign committee did make some positive use of information gleaned from the polls. The campaign committee used poll evidence about issues (and about the parties favored on the issues) in selecting themes for highlighting at daily press conferences. It emphasized unemployment and the social services, where the party was shown to be relatively popular, rather than nuclear weapons and trade unions, where it was not. When poll evidence showed Denis Healey far more popular and trusted than Michael Foot, he was given a more prominent role in the campaign, until Healey's controversial statements on nuclear weapons and his gaffe on the Falklands caused him to be shunted to the sidelines.

When all was failing, the Labour leadership turned to the prerogative of losers: it abused the polls. The Labour vitriol was stimulated by poll evidence vigorously promoted by the Alliance, indicating that the Alliance might succeed in finishing ahead of Labour. Michael Foot referred to such a possibility as "absolutely ridiculous" and said it could only come from "cooked polls." Denis Healey alleged, "The polls have already discredited themselves. They disagree violently with one another." Healey even went so far as to identify himself with the cavalry wing of the Labour party, asserting of the polls, "What they say bears no relation to what we are hearing on the doorstep."[29]

As a so-called media party, the Alliance was not lacking in sophisticated personnel with a general understanding of public opinion polls, sensitive to the need to make a big impact on the mass electorate in order to "break the mold" of British politics. David Steel's strategy was based on the assumption that once a general election campaign started the Liberals inevitably would gain support, due to the greater broadcasting exposure given a third party then, because the broadcasting media adheres to proportionality among parties in election campaigns. Steel also hoped that the sight of both major parties attacking each other night after night on television would drive voters to the Alliance. In fact, the pattern of campaign trends was much less clear-cut than Steel's confident assertions made it appear. In 1979 polls had registered an increase in Liberal support during the election campaign. In February 1974 the same had happened. The result was that final polls *over*estimated the actual level of Liberal strength. In October 1974 the polls showed virtually no movement in Liberal support during the campaign. In 1970 the polls showed a slight rise and then a fall in Liberal support. The claims being made by Alliance representatives about an assured rise in support were based more on faith than historical precedent.

In one respect the polls did force the hand of the Alliance, by spotlighting the different levels of popularity of the SDP leader (and Alliance prime minister-designate), Roy Jenkins, and the Liberal leader, David Steel. In April 1983, just before the campaign started, the Gallup Poll reported that 64 percent thought Steel was proving a good leader of the Liberal party, as against 31 percent approving Jenkins as SDP leader. During the campaign, several published polls sought to test-market the relative attractiveness of the two Alliance leaders. An Audience Selection poll for *TV-AM* found that when people were asked how they would vote if David Steel became Alliance leader, Alliance support increased from 20 to 29 percent.[30] The pressures culminated in a summit meeting of Alliance leaders on the penultimate Sunday of the campaign, a high Steel profile in the remainder of the Alliance campaign, and bruised feelings among the followers of Roy Jenkins.

Voters could make use of the polls in two ways: to communicate their views to politicians, since an opinion poll reflects popular views with greater precision than statements by MPs; and to monitor the progress of the parties during the campaign, a point of particular importance to individuals wishing to use their vote to greatest tactical advantage in a three-cornered contest in their constituency.

Polls asking voters to rank the issues of greatest importance consistently showed that unemployment came first by a wide margin, usually followed by worries about inflation, defense, and law and order. All the parties received similar information about electoral priorities from their private polls and this influenced their selection of campaign themes. For example, the Conservatives devoted more campaign attention to unemployment, where the party was on the defensive, than to inflation, where its record was an improvement on its Labour predecessor. For internal political reasons, the Labour party was incapable of altering its policies, however unpopular they might be with the electorate; its manifesto was a reprint of a previous policy document embodying difficult-to-negotiate bargains. It could use poll findings to decide which issues not to highlight but it could not abandon unpopular positions. The Alliance was most flexible, if only because of a lack of an established record. Fewer voters were clear about the position of the Alliance, a fact that was both an advantage and a handicap.

Granada Television provided a unique opportunity for two-way electronic communication between voters and politicians in a twelve-part series of Channel 4 TV programs, the *Granada 500*. The audience for the program consisted of five hundred people from the northwest of England, selected by AGB Cable and Viewdata as an approximate cross section of the electorate. In each program the audience questioned a different group of experts or politicians about major issues. In addition, Granada TV arranged through AGB for a cable connection with 550 households. Viewers could be quizzed about their opinions and respond electronically, making the results instantly available on screen.

Remote interactive participation, an extension of participation via phone-in quizzes of politicians, is at an experimental stage. It was nonetheless an experiment on a grand scale, costing Granada upward of £125,000 for the cable connection to viewers' homes, a connection that also is used for testing audience reaction to TV commercials and current affairs issues.[31]

Before the campaign commenced, there was widespread expectation that the electorate would use the polls to assist in tactical voting. Polling evidence of a close race between Labour and the Conservatives was expected to squeeze the Alliance vote, just as evidence that Alliance would win many seats was assumed to create a bandwagon effect benefiting the Alliance. However, a Gallup Poll survey on tactical voting, undertaken a month before the campaign began, found the great majority of voters were not inclined to vote tactically. Voters were asked, "If the opinion polls in a general election said that a party you disliked most was going to win, with your party in third place but that the party in second place stood a chance of winning, would you stick to voting for your own party, seriously think of voting for the party in second place, or decide not to vote?" A total of 77 percent said they would stick to their own party, as against 14 percent prepared to think of voting for another party.

The high level of public opinion polling in the 1983 general election made it easy for voters to see public opinion poll forecasts on the television or in the press. The consistency in the Conservative lead made it easy to gain an accurate picture of which party was ahead. In an election day poll, Gallup found that 67 percent recalled hearing a public opinion poll result, the same as in 1979. What was different was that 61 percent now correctly perceived poll findings as showing a big Conservative lead; the rest thought the polls showed a small Conservative lead. By contrast, in 1979 only 36 percent correctly perceived the polls as showing a Conservative lead, as against 25 percent perceiving a Labour lead, and 6 percent a neck-and-neck race.[33] Moreover, in 1983 a total of 89 percent said they thought they knew which party was third in the polls; 54 percent correctly perceived the third place party as Alliance, as against 31 percent perceiving Labour.

While the conditions for tactical voting were widely met—either to favor a Conservative bandwagon or, equally possible in the abstract, to encourage a "counterbandwagon" effect—the polls appear to have had little or no actual influence on the outcome. First of all, the Gallup Poll found that only 8 percent of voters had not made up their mind until a few days before polling day, and 78 percent said they had decided a long time ago. Second, only 14 percent of respondents thought that the polls had a lot of influence on voters generally; the median respondent thought the polls had only a little influence. Third, when voters aware of poll results were asked whether they were influenced by the polls, 95 percent said no. A breakdown of the responses by party preference shows that among the small group who said they were influenced by the polls,

Table 5.3 Influence of the polls

Reports self influenced by opinion polls	Percentage of voters			
	Con.	Lab.	All.	Total
Yes	2	3	9	5
No	98	97	91	95

Source: Unpublished cross-tabulation provided by the Gallup Poll from 8–9 June 1983 survey for the BBC.
Note: The question was worded, "When you finally decided which way to vote, were you influenced at all by what the opinion polls were saying?" (Asked of the 67 percent recalling seeing an opinion poll during the campaign.)

Alliance supporters were most numerous (see table 5.3). The numbers are so small, however, that this differential impact can have had little net effect upon the election result. The 5 percent of the electorate saying they were influenced by the polls undoubtedly would have divided three ways had they voted differently in the absence of poll information. At most, one of the parties might have added 1 percent to its share of the vote thanks to the polls, and another party lost 1 percent.

The Unresolved Issues

The performance of the polls cannot be evaluated independently of what we expect the polls to do. The media that sponsor them are clear about this: the polls should "get it right," that is, correctly forecast the election winner. The social science techniques on which the polls are based do not recognize the concept of "rightness"; they recognize only expected margins of sampling error.

By the crude criterion of predicting the winner, all the polls "got it right" in 1983. Political factors were responsible for this as well as technical features of the polls. With the Conservatives victorious by a margin of 15 percent, a poll could make a sizable error in estimating the share of the vote for individual parties, yet still name the winner correctly. Where the margin between the parties was small, the 2.3 percent Labour lead over Alliance, two of the seven polls mistakenly placed Alliance ahead of Labour, and another placed them even.

By comparison with previous general election polls, the 1983 performance was only average. In the seven elections since 1964, when numerous professional polls first occurred, the average error in forecasting the gap between the parties has been 3.6 percent. Five of these elections showed polls more accurate in forecasting than 1983; only the 1970 record was wider of the mark (see table 5.4). In forecasting the share of the vote for each of the three parties, the polls'

Table 5.4   Accuracy of 1983 polls compared to polls in previous elections

Year	Mean error gap	Average error per party	Number of polls
1964	1.8	1.3	4
1966	3.9	1.7	4
1970	6.7	2.6	5
1974 Feb.	2.5	2.2	6
1974 Oct.	4.2	1.6	4
1979	1.7	1.0	5
1983	4.8	1.7	7
Average	3.6	1.7	5

Source: Richard Rose, "Opinion Polls and Election Results," in R. Rose, ed., *Studies in British Politics*, 3d ed. (London: Macmillian, 1976), table 2, updated by the author. Calculated for major parties (Conservative, Labour, and Alliance) only.

mean error of 1.7 percent in 1983 was the same as the average for the period as a whole.

By conventional standards of sampling, 98 percent-plus accuracy in estimating a party's vote and a margin or error of 3.6 percent in estimating the difference between two groups is a very good record. While the calculation of sampling error differs with the specific design of a poll (and purists would argue that sampling error cannot be calculated at all for quota samples), pollsters say that their results should be within 3 percent of the underlying distribution of opinion in 95 percent of all cases, and within 6 percent in measuring gaps between parties. The postelection assertion by Ivor Crewe of Essex University that polls should be accurate to within 1 percent was an assertion regarded as unrealistic by polling organizations, and not endorsed by sampling theory.[34]

While the professional respectability of the polls depends upon forecasting the vote within an acceptable margin of sampling error, the political credibility of the polls depends upon correctly forecasting the winner. The average 3.6 percent error in estimating the gap between the parties is greater than the lead of the winning party in seven of the previous ten general elections. To be sure that a poll accurately forecasts the winner, the final forecast must be within the margin of sampling error *and the winning party's lead should be greater than the margin of sampling error*. The ability of the polls to meet journalistic as well as sampling criteria is dependent upon political factors outside the control of the pollsters and polling techniques.

Most campaign polls are not final forecasts of the state of the parties, nor are they taken as such. The overwhelming majority of polls are published before election day; they measure trends during the campaign. The use of a panel survey greatly improves the accuracy of an opinion poll as a trend measure, for the changes reported are true changes, that is, they represent different views held by the same person. By contrast in successive one-off surveys, the answers are given by different people. In nonpanel surveys the changes reported each week combine random fluctuations inevitable in the sampling process plus actual changes in public opinion. The two types of change may or may not be the same in magnitude or direction. In 1970 a simulation of election polls conducted by the author illustrated how sampling fluctuations could make a campaign appear full of movement without any change whatsoever in the opinions of the hypothetical electorate.[35] The 1983 election offers empirical evidence to support the hypothetical example.

The MORI panel survey for the *Sunday Times* shows that there was very little net change during the election campaign from its base-line panel survey of late April, a survey closely in line with the final 9 June election outcome. The MORI panel showed an average fluctuation of less than 1 percent in support for the Conservative and Labour parties, and 1.7 percent for the Alliance. By contrast, MORI's two nonpanel surveys averaged much greater weekly fluctuations in Conservative support (5.3 percent each) and Labour support (3.7 and 4.7 percent). The average fluctuation in Alliance support in the nonpanel surveys was double that in the panel survey. In 1979 too, panel surveys showed much less movement in voter preferences than did nonpanel surveys.[36]

The distortion in feedback introduced by sampling error can be illustrated simply by comparing actual net changes in the Conservative lead over Labour, as reported in the MORI panel survey, with changes reported in its nonpanel surveys. In each of the panel surveys the net lead of the Conservatives fluctuated only 1 percent each week. By contrast, in the nonpanel *Express* poll the Conservative lead fell from 15 to 9 percent, then zoomed to 22 percent and fell to 11 percent. In the *Star* nonpanel poll, the Conservative lead fell by 8 percent, then jumped to 18 percent, and fell again to 12 percent. Headlines emphasized the size of the fluctuations in the polls. There was no mention of sampling error as a principal cause.

The existence of large weekly differences in reported changes among three sets of MORI polls does not mean that the two nonpanel polls were inaccurate. Taking the election as a whole, all three MORI samples averaged virtually the same division of opinion among the voters, a division that was in line with the actual results. The difference is that only the panel consistently reported a lead close to this average; the nonpanel surveys arrived at an accurate figure only by a process in which overestimates in one week were offset by underestimates in another week, each appearing at the time as if it were a major swing in the actual views of voters.

The arguments for using panel surveys to measure campaign trends is strong in principle, given their ability to reduce greatly the random week-to-week fluctuations inherent in conventional sampling. But running a panel survey also presents problems. However representative of the electorate a panel may be when drawn, the fact of being a member of a panel may make respondents less representative as the panel continues. The repeated interviewing of a group of individuals (particularly a group that may learn the result of their responses from the national media) may bias the panel, or make it more attentive to the election campaign than voters only interviewed once or not at all. Panel members may maintain more consistency in what they tell an interviewer than other electors. Insofar as those who drop out of a panel are not a cross section of the panel, then the panel may become biased by a process of attrition. If the panel happened to be a rogue (that is, atypical) sample, nonrepresentativeness could increase during its life. Notwithstanding these difficulties, panel surveys have been less prone to fluctuations, and major academic surveys of voting in Britain since 1963 consistently have made use of panels to measure changes in voters' outlooks.

Speed is as important to journalists as accuracy. Moreover, in an election campaign in which there is a significant last-minute change in electoral opinion, the ability to poll up to election day can be crucial in accurate forecasting. Because conducting an opinion poll is a complex process, the speed with which a poll moves from questionnaire design to publication depends upon a number of separate considerations. All the polls have taken major steps since 1970 to accelerate the conduct of polls, especially the final poll forecasting the result, but organizations differ in what they do, and there is no agreement about how best to conduct a poll quickly as well as accurately.

One innovation of the 1983 general election was the widespread use of one-day "quickie" polls. Whereas in 1979 only six of twenty-seven polls were undertaken in one day, in 1983 there were twenty-seven one-day quickie polls. These included all the MORI surveys for the popular press except for one reinterview, all the Audience Selection telephone polls, five Marplan polls, three NOP, and one Harris poll. In addition, fourteen polls were completed within two days. The Gallup Poll was alone in spreading its interviewing over a number of days. Two Gallup reports based upon weekly omnibus surveys were spread intentionally over six days, two polls were done in three days, and the final pre-election poll in two days. The Gallup Poll relied upon the return of questionnaires by post for all but its final pre-election survey. Given the deterioration in the postal service, it experienced irritating delays in the processing of results.

While polling organizations are agreed in principle about the desirability of speed, they disagree about the safest speed at which to conduct interviews. All polling organizations want to minimize the amount of time taken to send out and return questionnaires. In 1983 polling organizations usually employed a standard questionnaire that could be sent by post well ahead of interviewing dates, or else a questionnaire that had only a few variable elements that could be transmitted to interviewers by telephone immediately before fieldwork was due to commence. Most poll organizations also had their interviewers phone results directly to headquarters or used regional field staff as centralized collectors of questionnaires. The advantage of phoning in answers is speed; replies even can be punched directly into a computer as they are received. However, the process is labor-intensive and there are few checks on accuracy.

Even before the 1983 election, polling organizations had been experimenting with electronic and cable technology in search of economical methods of communicating questionnaires and receiving results. The ideal would be for a survey organization to transmit its questionnaires directly to the homes of interviewers by cable. Interviewers could use handheld electronic devices to record answers from respondents, machines that could be programmed to flash questions in the correct sequence and to correct the interviewer if an illogical answer is recorded. The results of electronically recorded interviews could then be transmitted by cable to the polling organization and fed directly into its computer for checking and processing. The main inhibition to greater use of electronic and cable technology has been cost.

Given the tendency for the cost of new technology to fall rapidly as equipment is developed, it is possible that by the time of the next British general election most polling organizations will have equipment capable of eliminating some delays now inherent in transmitting questionnaires and interview results. Since it is already possible for the final details of a poll to be agreed at breakfast and the results available by midevening, new technology can add little to the speed already obtained by quickie polls.

One unresolved question remains: how quick *should* polls be? Constraints of media publication schedules, as well as interviewer and respondent work schedules, now force a compression of one-day polls into far less than one day. Quickie polls conducted in the 1983 election were not one day, that is, covering twenty-four hours, or from breakfast until late evening. They were eight-hour polls. MORI started its polling in the morning and fieldwork had to be completed by 6 P.M. in order to meet deadlines of newspapers going to press later that evening for publication the following morning, and to publicize the results in late evening TV news programs. Compressing interviews into ordinary working hours raises problems in securing a fully representative sample. In an effort to guard against the biases thus arising, MORI included in its quota sample design a requirement that at least half of the interviews be done between noon and 2 P.M., and 4 P.M. and 6 P.M. when employed people could be taking a lunch break or could have finished work. Audience Selection's telephone interviews spread calls from midafternoon to 9 P.M. in order to catch people at home who would be out at work all day.

The chief argument in favor of quickie polls is also the chief argument against them. A quickie poll is most sensitive to abrupt shifts in popular opinion in response to a particular speech by a politician or a major national or international event, producing a prompt reaction when an event occurs. Insofar as each day of an election campaign produces fresh happenings, quickie polls will exaggerate electoral trends by emphasizing day-to-day political fluctuations, many of which may cancel out. The results of a poll taken on a single day will be less stable than the results of polls taken over two days. Party organizations may want polls quickly in order to influence such changes, but serious media sponsors of polls are likely to want greater stability rather than gain greater speed at the price of increasing fluctuations beyond that inherent in sampling.

The greater stability of two-day (or longer) polls as against quickie polls is shown by comparing the range of support attributed to each of the parties by the two types of polls. Excluding Audience Selection, quickie polls reported the Conservative lead ranging by 9 percent during the campaign; polls interviewing for at least two days reported a range of only 4 percent. Quickie polls reported Labour's vote varying by 12 percent; polls taking more time for interviewing reported a range of 11 percent in Labour support. Alliance support, according to quickie polls, was said to range by 13.5 percent. By comparison, polls interviewing for at least two days found a 9 percent range in Alliance support. However, Audience Selection telephone polls show a substantial degree of stability, with a range of 5 percent for the Conservatives, 10 percent for Labour, and 9 percent for Alliance overall in its polls.

By definition, political questions about the use of the polls are subjects for dispute. However, political parties in Britain today no longer debate whether to pay heed to the polls; the question at issue is how the polls are to be used. The Labour party leadership illustrated how polls can be used and abused, leaking polls in efforts to deflate talk of Alliance overtaking it, and simultaneously attacking polls that showed the Conservatives with a landslide lead over Labour. The practice of abusing the messenger who brings a distasteful message dates back at least to the Greeks. The Labour party was not so much stuck in a cavalry age as it was stuck in a timeless conflict between what its leaders knew was true and what they wished to admit was true.

The ambivalent Labour attitude toward the polls was revealed in the post-election issue of the party's paper, *Labour Weekly*.[37] It carried the full text of Michael Foot's postelection resignation statement to the parliamentary Labour party, in which he attacked the polls for playing "a larger—and in a sense a more malign—role than in any previous election." Concurrently, the paper drew upon MORI and Harris polls to give its readers an insight into how different social classes voted. It also featured prominently a photograph of a Campaign for Nuclear Disarmament lobby at the House of Commons, in which demonstrators displayed posters citing opinion poll findings showing opposition to Trident and cruise missiles.

In British politics in the 1980s each of the political parties can expect the polls to give it good news and bad news in turn. Polls in the 1979–83 Parlia-

Table 5.5 Popular views about the banning of opinion polls (in percentages)

	Con.	Lab.	All.	Total
Should ban polls	28	34	31	40
Should not ban polls	59	47	55	53
Don't know	14	19	16	17

Source: Unpublished cross-tabulation provided by the Gallup Poll from its weekly omnibus survey of 13–19 April 1983.
Note: Wording of the question, "It has been suggested that opinion polls should be banned during an election campaign. Do you think the publication of opinion polls should or should not be banned during an election?"

ment showed each of the parties with up to 50 percent of popular support in the polls—only to chart the downfall of two of them in reaction to the surge in Conservative support. In a competitive party system there are always losers as well as winners, and also-rans as well as front-runners. The most and the least that the polls can do for politicians is to feed back information about public opinion independent of partisan sources. It is then up to the politicians to decide whether or how they wish to react to this news.

Ironically, public opinion polls offer the only source of information about popular views of polls. A Gallup Poll question about banning polls, asked prior to the start of a general election campaign, found that among those with a view, more than three-fifths were in favor of polls continuing; less than one-third positively supported banning polls (see table 5.5). Moreover, differences in views were very little affected by party. Ordinary people, like the popular media, appear to regard polls more as a diversion. The chief reason given for allowing polls during an election campaign was that they are harmless; 44 percent said that polls don't affect how people vote or are harmless, as against 28 percent who favored publication of polls because they give people an idea of how things stand.[38] A postelection MORI survey for the *Daily Star* found that 37 percent said they had not seen any pre-election polls and only 33 percent could name the poll they thought they had seen.

Free elections presuppose that all contending groups, and the electorate as a whole, are able to enjoy the full advantages of free speech. During an election campaign, it is not possible to prevent politicians from making claims about the state of public opinion or asserting that the electorate favors their particular cause. The question is whether or not the electorate is to be trusted with other sources of information beside the *parti pris* views of politicians. British polling organizations have a body of professional expertise and are open about their methods. Moreover, the record of the pollsters, measured against the actual election results, is far better than that of self-interested politicians, relying upon "horse-drawn" methods of public opinion analysis in an electronic age. The voters can be trusted to take what they wish from the polls and, on 1983 evidence, not to be stampeded into voting for a party because of poll findings. As former Prime Minister James Callaghan once remarked, "If the people cannot be trusted with opinion polls, then they cannot be trusted with the vote."[39]

The Ethnic Minorities' Vote

MONICA CHARLOT

——— Just over thirty years ago citizens of the New Commonwealth began arriving in Britain in substantial numbers, using their right to enter Britain on the same terms as the British.[1] Many received active encouragement to come from British public corporations and industries. Legislators since then have progressively limited their right to entry,[2] which under the 1981 Nationality Act[3] virtually has disappeared.

Today they and their children, born in Britain, constitute a "recognizable" minority—for the simple reason that they are nonwhites. There is debate as to their number and their importance in the electoral contest. Yet, at the same time, they are wooed actively by all the political parties. The 1983 situation with new constituency boundaries[4] and three major parties fighting for power increased party efforts, for in three-cornered fights small numbers of votes weigh more than in two-party elections in which most seats are safe.

The Numbers Game

Between 1971 and 1981 the number of immigrants living in Britain increased by 13 percent to 3,374,000. Six percent of the total population thus was born abroad.[5] The increase was due essentially to New Commonwealth and Pakistan-born immigrants (see table 6.1) who now number just over 1.5 million. These figures do not include the children born in Britain to those from overseas, since the 1981 census unfortunately offers no information concerning second generation nonwhites.

The 1981 census was to include a question on race or ethnic origin. Different versions of the question were tried out between 1975 and 1977.[6] Meanwhile opposition to the whole idea of counting the heads of immigrants and their descendants had been building up. It came essentially from the left and held that the whole operation was dangerous because it was incipiently racist, based on the notion that there was some basic difference between people of different descent. There was no justification whatever, claimed the critics, for picking out nonwhites in this fashion.

Table 6.1   Places of birth outside the United Kingdom

	1971		1981	
	Number	Percent of total	Number	Percent of total
Irish Republic	709,000	24	612,000	18
Old Commonwealth	143,000	5	155,000	5
New Commonwealth and				
Pakistan	1,151,000	39	1,517,000	45
Other countries	980,000	32	1,090,000	32
Total	2,983,000	100	3,374,000	100

Source: Adapted from *Census 1981* (London: HMSO, 1983).

The result of these criticisms and the debates that followed was that the population in question, as represented in their associations and organizations declared they would not answer such a question because of its racist bias. There was no option but to drop the question and thus no British census up until now has included questions on ethnicity. There may be a danger in asking questions in such a way that they create artificial social groupings and antagonize respondents. The absence of solid data, however, enables those who wish to do so to advance exaggerated estimations of numbers to fuel racist arguments.

Aware of this, the Government Statistical Service has tried to fill the gap in information. Estimates of the various minority groups are based on answers to questions about ethnicity asked in sample surveys conducted on a voluntary basis and on information about birthplaces in the census itself. In fact some 90 percent of the total population of New Commonwealth and Pakistan (NCWP) ethnic origin live in households headed by a person born in the NCWP. The 10 percent who are not covered by this household classification are essentially the U.K.-born of NCWP ethnic origin who head their own households.[7] Currently, because the West Indians settled earlier in Britain than the other subgroups of the NCWP, such households are mainly of Caribbean origin. The census estimates the population of NCWP ethnic origin resident in Great Britain at 4.1 percent while the *Labour Force Survey* puts it at 4.3 and the *General Household Survey* at 4.5 percent. There is a broad consistency among the various sources when sampling variability and differences in definition are taken into account.[8]

The House of Commons Home Affairs Committee recommended in May 1983 the inclusion of a question of ethnic origin in the next census, expected in 1991.[9] At the same time the committee recommended that in order to allay immigrants' fears that a government might use the information to identify individuals for repatriation, all the forms should afterward be destroyed. It stressed that "census data on ethnic origin are crucial to identify effectively, in conjunction with other data, the nature of racial disadvantage and indirect discrimination." This is also true for analyses of voting behavior. A lack of precise data makes it difficult to assess the number of potential voters in Britain's Asian and Afro-Caribbean families. The ethnic minority proportion of the electorate is certainly less than the ethnic minority proportion of the population; the NCWP population has a higher proportion of children under voting age. The number of potential NCWP electors varies according to whether or not those of mixed origin and those of Arab and Chinese origin are included in the NCWP statistics. It is at most 3.4 percent, at least 2.7 percent.[10] It is not unreasonable to estimate those able to register at roughly two-thirds of a given NCWP population.

Although the percentage is low, the concentration of Britain's Asian and Afro-Caribbean families in certain areas means that they have a greater influence in some localities than the national figures might suggest. Immigrants essentially were used as replacement populations in those regions that, despite demand for labor, had failed in the fifties and sixties to attract a white population. They thus filled a vacuum in the run-down inner city areas of London, the West and East Midlands, and the West Riding. Clustering was the result of labor demand linked to family migration with relatives joining one another. This is known to be particularly strong when the contrast between the homeland and the new area is great and when the immigration occurs within a limited time span. Housing shortages, prejudice, and discrimination intensified the concentration. At the 1983 election 19.5 percent of all constituencies had no blacks in them and 59.8 percent had less than 5 percent, representing some 3.3 percent of those of voting age.[11] At the other end of the spectrum forty-five constituencies (6.9 percent) had an NCWP population of over 15 percent: 10 percent of the over-eighteens. The nonwhites constituted over 20 percent of the population, 13.3 percent of the over-eighteens, in twenty-seven constituencies. Of these, six had between 30 and 40 percent (20 to 26.6 percent of the over-eighteens), three over 40 percent (26.6 percent). Clearly the impact of black electors on the results must not be exaggerated.

Registration

The right to vote is, with certain qualifications, assured to all male and female British subjects, including citizens of commonwealth countries over eighteen years of age and normally resident in the United Kingdom on 10 October preceding the election. With the exception of citizens of Eire,[12] aliens living in the United Kingdom are not able to vote.[13]

Table 6.2   Registration by sex and age, 1983 (in percentages)

	Asians		Afro-Caribbeans	
	Male	Female	Male	Female
Registered	94	93	77	87
Not registered	3	4	15	8
Don't know/Not sure	3	3	8	5
$N =$	331	196	222	241

Since 1918 the compilation of the electoral register has been the responsibility of the registration officer. Each autumn forms are sent out to all heads of households who are required to enter the names of all residents aged eighteen or over on the qualifying date, plus those who will have their eighteenth birthday during the life of the register. A provisional register is compiled that is open to public inspection from 1–16 December. Those who think they have the right to vote and have not been included may ask to be put on the register. The final register is in force from 15 February each year. The system is complicated. The procedure is not always understood by Asians and Afro-Caribbeans; some of them do not even realize they have the right to vote. In other cases a householder deliberately may omit to register immigrants because he does not declare the revenue he receives from the rent they pay him. Some immigrants may suspect the motives of those who seek information or simply fear the consequences of giving it.[14]

Since 1974 Opinion Research Centre has been monitoring registration of ethnic minorities. Their first registration survey carried out in seven constituencies[15] showed that 30 percent of eligible Asians and West Indians were not registered as against 6 percent of whites. In May 1979 another survey, this time in twenty-four constituencies,[16] showed that 22 percent of nonwhite respondents were not on the electoral register compared with 7 percent of white respondents. A breakdown of nonwhite respondents showed that 19 percent of West Indians and 23 percent of Asians were not registered.

In May 1983 a more complete survey dealing specifically with the black vote was carried out throughout the urban areas of England by Harris Research for London Weekend Television.[17] It showed that 94 percent of Asians and 82 percent of Afro-Caribbeans were registered. The trend toward a higher level of registration is clear within both groups. Among the Asians registration increased marginally between 1974 and 1979 (rising from 73 to 77 percent, +4 percentage points) and then massively between 1979 and 1983 (from 77 to 94

	Asians				Afro-Caribbeans		
18–24	25–34	35–44	45+	18–24	25–34	35–44	45+
88	94	96	96	76	81	87	84
6	3	1	4	15	14	8	9
6	3	3	0	9	5	5	7
113	170	141	102	98	148	125	183

Source: *Black on Black/Eastern Eye*, London Weekend Television (Harris Research Centre, May 1983).

percent, +17 percentage points), attaining at the 1983 election a level roughly equal to that of whites. Among Afro-Caribbeans the great surge forward occurred between 1974 and 1979 (+18 percentage points) and then remained stable in 1983 (+1 percent).

Asian registration is significantly higher than Afro-Caribbean registration. Its structure is also very different (see table 6.2). The level of registration of Asian men and women is roughly equal, whereas within the Afro-Caribbean community the women are much more likely to register than are the men. This may stem from the position of women in the Caribbeans. The slave legacy of instability in sexual relationships has led to a loose family structure. Serial concubinage—faithful while it lasts—is widespread. This leads to the reinforcement of the mother's role and in many cases to the total absence of the father. West Indian women may take their civic duties more seriously than their male counterparts.

The youngest group of both Asians and Afro-Caribbeans, the 18–24-year-olds, register less than their elders but in no case do less than three-quarters register. The work status of those registered shows that the fact of being unemployed and even more of not working plays a much greater role in nonparticipation within the Afro-Caribbean community than within the Asian community. The Asian family is close-knit. In the Asian culture the wishes of the individual are considered of less importance than the preservation of family prestige and respect for parents. This may well mean that the family acts as a buffer in times of stress and maintains the integration of the individual in the social structure. Whatever the causes of nonregistration it is obvious that from election to election the situation changes.

The ethnic minority groups were more likely to register in 1983 than they had been in 1979. It is therefore less legitimate to take differential registration into consideration today since the rates of minority and white registration are drawing nearer together and this gives greater strength to the NCWP electorate.

Wooing the Ethnic Vote

The Commission for Racial Equality (CRE) claimed in 1974 that the ethnic minorities had determined the outcome in February and in October: "It is likely that without the minorities' support Labour would not have won more seats than the Conservatives in February 1974 and would not have won an overall majority in October 1974."[18] They clearly overstated the case. Although this had been shown in several academic articles, the CRE nonetheless succeeded in convincing politicians that ethnic voters had become a decisive factor in a number of marginal constituencies and that the ethnic vote should be courted more actively.

In January 1976 the Conservative party set up a new Department of Community Affairs at Central Office, within which was the Ethnic Minorities Unit. The task of the unit, headed by Mervyn Kohler, was to liaise with ethnic organizations; a budget of £2–3,000 was available to help set up new community groups. Two new associations were formed: the Anglo-Asian Conservative Society and the Anglo–West Indian Conservative Society under the direction of Narindar Raj Saroop and Basil Lewis, both local councillors. The West Indian Association never really took off. The Asian was more successful; by 1983 it had over a thousand members in fourteen branches, mostly in London and the South East. It appealed above all to businessmen, doctors, and accountants.

The Labour party, disquieted by the idea that the Conservatives might make inroads into the Asian vote, sent out a questionnaire to its constituency parties early in 1981 to assess to what extent they maintained contacts with the NCWP communities. The response was disappointing. Only 132 questionnaires were returned and only six constituency parties claimed that they met with ethnic minorities regularly. However, 38 percent of the 132 had included an ethnic minority member on their panel of local candidates.[19] The Labour party also relied to a great extent on antiracist organizations and campaigns to persuade the ethnic minorities that it was in their interests to vote Labour.

The 1982 local council elections in London encouraged the parties to woo black electors.[20] Before the elections there were fifty-one NCWP councillors in London; after the elections there were seventy-seven. The percentage of NCWP councillors in London thus rose from 2.7 percent to 4.1 percent. Only one out of every four boroughs had no minority councillor. The voting system with multimember constituencies favors the integration of nonwhite candidates in multiracial wards.

The real lesson for the parties was that there had been major changes in ethnic clustering since the sixties. Immigrant groups had been leaving the decayed inner city areas at a much faster rate than the indigenous population.[21] There thus had been a relocation of areas of concentrated settlement. Brent, for instance, which is outside the inner London area, is now Britain's "blackest borough." The number of areas where the black vote might be important thus was increasing.

At the same time the threat of the creation of independent black groups fielding their own candidates increased. Many of the new black councillors were members of the London-based left-wing Asian Labour Party Alliance (ALPA) that had successfully elected candidates in many wards. ALPA also was developing support in Coventry, Birmingham, and Leicester. Into the bargain Ealing Southall—with the second highest nonwhite electorate in any constituency—had elected six independent Asian councillors representing a distinct political grassroots movement.

The 1982 local elections thus confirmed that the parties would be wise not to neglect the ethnic voters. Accordingly in 1983 all three major parties organized what might be called an ethnic drive. All three parties prepared numerous leaflets in various languages other than English. The courting of the ethnic vote was not without its pitfalls. Shyam Bhatia revealed that a Conservative party slogan in Punjabi was withheld from distribution because of mistranslation,[22] while some of Labour's election posters in Gujarati intended for circulation within London's Islington ward also had to be withdrawn because the lettering had been printed upside down.

The manifestos of the three parties all made gestures toward the black communities. The Conservative manifesto claimed that its policy on immigration was "firm and fair" and that it was "utterly opposed to racial discrimination wherever it occurs" and determined to see "that there is real equality of opportunity."[23] The Alliance promised to repeal the British Nationality Act of 1981, which it judged "offensive and discriminatory" and made a blanket promise to "protect and promote individual and minority rights" through a Bill of Rights.[24] The Labour party would repeal both the Nationality Act of 1981 and the Immigration Act of 1971.[25] It also pledged itself to a positive action program in favor of greater ethnic participation and declared it would "expand funding to ethnic minority projects" and "ensure that ethnic minorities receive a fair deal—in employment, education, housing and social services."

Each party also produced a special statement on race relations. The Conservatives stressed their rejection of "calls for massive repatriation" and their policies on urban aid and on the encouragement of small businesses. The Labour party and the Liberal party expanded on the statements made in their general manifestos. In fact all three parties made pious statements, weak on new ideas. The only original element during the campaign was the controversial advertisement put out by the Conservatives. In the last week in May a £16,000 advertising campaign was launched to persuade members of the ethnic minorities to vote Conservative.[26] The campaign relied on advertisements that featured a smartly dressed West Indian or Asian.[27] The copy read, "Labour says he's black. Tories say he's British." The small print compared Labour promises with Conservative action and stressed that the Conservative economic strategy was working. The minister for Home Affairs, Timothy Raison, defended the advertisement as an attempt to unite the country:

> We want to get away from the idea that we are a divided country. I don't think we'll get away from it by constantly stressing that people are different. Citizenship represents a bond which unites the country rather than divides it. The implication is that British people who have our citizenship are equal.[28]

The Labour party had, as part of its overtures to the NCWP minorities decided that the shadow home secretary, Roy Hattersley, would hold a special press conference for the ethnic press. It fell on the day the advertisement was published. At the conference Hattersley claimed that the advertisement was an insult: "Those of use who know about ethnic communities know that they want to be—indeed insist on being both black and British. It is an insult to them to imply that they have a choice between the two."[29]

The advertisement was to figure in sixteen black papers. The *Caribbean Times*, Britain's largest ethnic minority newspaper,[30] refused to carry it and instead printed a front page lead story calling it "insulting, obnoxious and immoral." The editor of the paper, Arif Ali, announced the paper's decision during a Conservative Central Office press conference chaired by Cecil Parkinson, and distributed to the other journalists copies of statements from William Trant, chairman of the West Indian Standing Conference, and Clem Byfield, secretary of the Association of Jamaicans, expressing their indignation at such low-level advertising. Cecil Parkinson retorted that the paper's refusal was in fact "a censorship in advertising which I totally deplore." The *West Indian World* justified publication of the advertisement by saying that the Conservative party was a "political force that traditionally has not enjoyed much support in the black community. . . . But our pages are open to all shades of opinion no matter how unpopular."[31] It claimed that it reserved the right to criticize any party whether or not it advertised in the paper's pages. *Voice* did not comment at the time of publishing but in the next edition an editorial defended its decision, "As company policy we will only refuse advertisements on the ground that it is racist or sexist."[32] After the election the journal was still smattered with justifications for having printed the advertisement.

Criticism came in from all sides. Peter Newsam, chairman of the Commission for Racial Equality, said he failed to understand the distinction between black and British. Labour politicians had a field day. Faced with mounting controversy Conservative Central Office acknowledged that the advertisement was "a bit more punchy" than previous attempts to win black votes. It was in fact based on the idea that underprivileged racial groups only favor the left so long as their minority status is stressed and preserved. The aim of the conservatives

Table 6.3 Turnout by ethnic group, 1983 (in percentages)

	Likelihood of voting[a]		Voting intention or vote[b]	
	Absolutely certain	Certain	Probably will	Definitely will/ have voted
Asians	61	23	10	68.3
Afro-Caribbeans	33	18	21	61.5
Whites[c]				74.6

Sources: (a) *Black on Black/Eastern Eye*, London Weekend Television (Harris Research Centre, 30–31 May 1983). (b) BBC Election Survey, 8–9 June 1983, Gallup Poll. (c) The Harris poll has no white control group.

was to free what they considered a captive group and detach some blacks from the Labour party claiming Labour operated a system of electoral apartheid.

Turnout

Over the past two decades turnout at British general elections has fallen steadily. It averaged 80.5 percent in the 1950s, 76.4 percent in the sixties, 74.7 in the seventies. The turnout of ethnic groups is difficult to assess, first because the exact number entitled to vote in any constituency is not known and second because the British system of bringing all the ballot boxes to one central place in the constituency and mixing up the ballot papers prevents ecological analysis.

It is possible to identify Asian names and to check on the electoral register whether or not they have voted. This has been done by Dr. Le Lohé in his studies on Bradford[33] and by the Commission for Racial Equality. In all these studies it has been shown that the Asian level of turnout has been consistently higher than that of all non-Asian minority groups. The differences have not been negligible: in the nineteen constituencies studied by the CRE Asian turnout was on average 18 percentage points higher.

The opinion poll done for London Weekend Television at the end of May, nine days before the election, gives an approximate idea of turnout (see table 6.3). It shows that there was a certain reticence on the part of West Indians to vote, maybe reflecting their dissatisfaction with the Labour party. Michael Phillips, a black journalist and former editor of *West Indian World*, saw the figures as a protest against Labour "not having done anything to repay the attachment of the black community for a long time."[35] He stressed in particular the failure of the party to select black candidates for safe seats.

The Gallup poll taken on the eve of the election and on election day would seem to indicate that turnout had indeed been lower than that estimated by the CRE for 1979, with 68.3 percent turnout for Asians and 61.5 percent for Afro-

Table 6.4   Voting intention of Asians and Afro-Caribbeans (in percentages)

| | All respondents | | All naming a party | |
	Asians	Afro-Caribbeans	Asians	Afro-Caribbeans
Conservative	7	5	9	6
Labour	65	67	82	88
Liberal/SDP	7	4	9	5
Other	1	2	0	1
Don't know/ Refused/Won't vote	20	22	0	0

Source: See note to table 6.3.

Caribbeans; the white vote was estimated at 74.6 percent.[36] However, the 80.3 percent CRE estimate seems rather optimistic.

Voting Patterns

With regard to the voting patterns of Asians and Afro-Caribbeans the major question is: Is there an ethnic vote and if there is does it play a decisive role in some marginal constituencies?

The elements that enable us to reply are few. For 1983 the most usable data come from the Harris poll carried out for London Weekend Television. It alone enables us to study subcategories though even here the numbers are such that we must proceed with caution. The voting intentions recorded just over a week before the election (see table 6.4) showed that of all those naming a party 82 percent of Asians and 88 percent of Afro-Caribbeans intended to vote Labour. Even if we take into account those who were not sure of their vote, those who did not intend to vote, and those who refused to answer, the Labour party still obtains 65 percent of Asian votes and 67 percent of Afro-Caribbean. Despite their efforts the Conservatives and the Alliance had not succeeded in turning away the nonwhites from the party they had long considered their natural defender. When asked why they normally voted Labour, 64 percent of Asians and 76 percent of blacks said it was because Labour supported the working class, 7 percent of blacks and 31 percent of Asians that it was because Labour supported blacks and Asians.

The differences between the voting intentions of the two ethnic groups and the final election result are so marked that we are probably in the presence of a specific ethnic vote. We can verify this by showing that Asian and Afro-Caribbean voters behave differently from white voters with similar demographic characteristics. An analysis by social class (see table 6.5) shows that Asians and Afro-Caribbeans vote massively Labour with one notable exception: the routine nonmanual (CI) voters, whose score (59 percent) is low by nonwhite standards.

The increasing fluidity of allegiance among British electors has been charted by Ivor Crewe.[37] In 1979, for instance, the Labour party lost its lead over the Tories among skilled workers. Hilde Himmelweit and colleagues argue, too, that strong class-based party identification is a thing of the past.[38] For Asians and Afro-Caribbeans, however, loyalty to a given party is the rule with 81 percent declaring that they vote for the same party every time.

Two other variables that influence voting behavior—sex and age—also show that the nonwhite vote is specific. Afro-Caribbean men and women give their votes in exactly the same proportion to the Conservative and Labour parties, while Asian men vote slightly more to the right than Asian women. In neither group does conservatism increase with age. In both groups it peaks among the 25–34-year-olds and then declines. These patterns are markedly different from those of the electorate at large.

The ethnic vote is therefore specific and massively Labour. It is interesting, though, to note that the Conservatives are making inroads into the Asian vote. This can be seen by the relatively high proportion of CIs who vote Conservative (table 6.4) and also by a study of voting intention among first-time voters (see table 6.6). Here the difference is marked sharply with the Afro-Caribbean vote if anything more Labour-inclined than ever.

Table 6.5 Social class and voting intention, 1983 (in percentages)

	Voting intention					
	Asians			Afro-Caribbeans		
Class	Con.	Lab.	All.	Con.	Lab.	All.
AB	0	80	20	0	80	20
C1	30	59	11	4	89	7
C2	12	79	9	4	90	6
D	2	90	8	7	90	3
E	2	94	4	7	92	1

Source: See note to table 6.3.

Table 6.6 Voting intention, first-time voters, 1983 (in percentages)

Voting intention	Asians	Afro-Caribbeans	Total
Conservative	18.2	5.1	11.65
Labour	61.4	86.0	73.7
Alliance	20.4	8.9	14.65
N =	44	79	123

Source: See note to table 6.3.

The preoccupations of the different ethnic communities during the election were somewhat different. Not unnaturally unemployment was the dominant issue for all groups. The cost of living also ranked among the three major issues for all three groups. The remaining issue (among the three first) differed for each group. For whites it was defense and nuclear weapons, for Asians immigration and nationality, for blacks education. Blacks considered immigration and nationality much less important than did Asians and for whites the issue had ceased to be of importance at all. For blacks the police and law and order was twice as important as for Asians and three times as important as for whites.

The number of constituencies in which the ethnic minorities might influence the outcome of the election is open to discussion at each election. It obviously depends on the degree of marginality of the constituency and on the strength and cohesion of the immigrant voice. Assessment was even more complex in 1983 given the extensive redrawing of constituency boundaries and the intervention of the Alliance. A list of marginals however could be drawn up on the basis of the notional results.[39] The number of such marginals differed according to the method employed by the experts to draw them up. The Runnymede Trust found 37 ethnic marginals in 1983,[40] based on Ivor Crewe's definition of an ethnic marginal (a constituency, with a nonwhite electorate of at least 5 percent, that would be lost, in the case of Conservative-held seats, on a 5 percent swing to Labour or, in the case of Labour-held seats, on a 7.5 percent swing to the Conservatives).[41]

The statistics available for determination of the nonwhite vote have from the first been unsatisfactory. They have been made even more so by the use of the notional calculations—themselves approximations—as points of comparison. Our remarks with regard to the impact of the nonwhite vote in 1983 therefore will be tentative.

All nine Conservative marginals save one, Birmingham Erdington, remained Conservative. The notional result gave the constituency, which had a Labour MP, a Conservative majority vulnerable to a swing to Labour of 1.8 percent. This may well reflect the problems of notional calculations rather than an ethnic minority vote, first because the seat only had lost a few thousand electors in the redistribution and had been Labour for forty years and, second, because the nonwhite electorate was only around 4.8 percent (population 7.2 percent). The Liberal marginal remained Liberal and of the twenty-seven Labour "ethnic marginals," sixteen remained Labour and eleven were lost to the Conservatives. Irrespective of the level of their nonwhite population all but one vulnerable on a swing of under 4 percent went to the Conservatives.[42] All vulnerable on a swing of over 4 percent and under 8 percent remained Labour. The constituency that remained Labour against the swing was the Lancashire textile town of Blackburn with a nonwhite electorate of around 9.8 percent. More important, it still bears the mark of Barbara Castle who represented the constituency from 1945 to 1979.

The uncertain nature of the figures available makes it imprudent to attempt a more sophisticated analysis. It seems probable that the following conclusion can be made: the scale of Margaret Thatcher's success and of the Labour party's failure in 1983 was such that at best the nonwhite voters were able to consolidate seats already won by the Labour party and not in great danger at the 1983 election.

Ethnic Minority Candidates

Since 1945 there has been no Member of Parliament from NCWP groups.[43] If membership of the House of Commons reflected accurately the 3 percent of the electorate of NCWP origin there would be twenty MPs from these groups. However, the House of Commons is not a reflection of the electorate. If it were there would be 338 women instead of 23!

White, middle-class, male supremacy is obvious in the House of Commons but are the nonwhites unrepresented because they do not stand or because electors do not vote for them? It was not really until 1970 that nonwhites began to be drawn into politics at the national level. David Thomas Pitt, a West Indian doctor established in London since 1947, had been adopted as Labour party candidate in 1959 for Hampstead; A. M. Abbas, a Pakistani, stood as an independent in Holborn and St. Pancras South in 1964, aroused much hostility from Pakistani organizations and obtained 226 votes; but these were isolated cases.

In the 1970s the major parties put up very few nonwhite candidates. One reason may well have been a belief in the reluctance of white voters to vote for nonwhite candidates. In 1970 the Labour party presented Dr. Pitt again, this time in a safe Labour seat in London: Wandsworth Clapham. Although he was a respected doctor and a GLC councillor he lost the seat on a swing of 10.8 against him, a figure double the regional average. In 1974 Michael Steed noted, "The South London constituencies to which parts of Clapham had been attached all showed high swings to Labour as the Labour voters who had declined to vote for a black Labour candidate in 1970 returned to their party allegiance."[44]

In February 1974 the Labour party again presented a single nonwhite candidate, Bashir Maan in East Fife. Comparison with the result achieved by a white Labour candidate in the same seat in October 1974 showed clearly that the white candidate was able to mobilize more votes than the nonwhite. In

1979 the only nonwhite Labour candidate was Russell Profitt in London, West-minster South. The vote for the party dropped from 30.9 percent to 25.4 per-cent. This was, however, little different from the swing against Labour in other parts of inner London.

The Liberal party fared no better than Labour with its nonwhite candidates. The three Liberal candidates in 1970 were all of Asian origin and they all did badly: in East Bradford and Smethwick the Asian candidates obtained only half the vote achieved by Liberal candidates in any other constituency. In Sheffield Hallam, where a Sikh candidate stood, the Liberal decline between 1966 and 1970 was three times the national average.[45]

In February 1974 the Liberals lost only four deposits in England. One of them was that of their Asian candidate Dr. Prem in Coventry South East. Once again a white candidate in the same constituency, six months later, fared much better, actually increasing the Liberal vote, against the trend for Liberals both nationally and regionally. In 1979 the two nonwhite Liberal candidates again did badly. Liberal scores dropped from 15.4 percent of the votes cast in Coventry North East to 4.9 percent, from 18.6 percent to 9.8 percent in Nuneaton.

The Conservative party presented nonwhite candidates for the first time in 1979: one in Glasgow Central, the other in Greenwich. Neither had any chance of being elected since both stood in safe Labour seats. In Greenwich the Conservative candidate increased his vote with a swing of 5 percent (English average 5.8 percent) and in Glasgow the swing in favor of the Conservative candidate—1.6 percent—was higher than the Scottish average (0.7 percent). There were also in the 1970s a smattering of ethnic minority "fringe" candidates, two to four at each election. They tended to be extreme left-wing, belonging to the Marxist-Leninists, the International Marxists, or the Workers Revolutionary party.

Throughout the seventies the two major parties thus presented a mere hand-ful of nonwhite candidates. When the Labour party adopted such candidates it tended to be in areas where they had some chance of winning. Their poor scores undoubtedly increased the apprehension of the party and kept the num-ber of such candidates down to a token. In the only election prior to 1983 in which the Conservative party presented nonwhites its electorate did not seem as hostile as that of the Labour party.

In 1983 the list of black candidates was longer than in any preceding election. The major parties put up eighteen: Conservatives, SDP, and Liberals four each, the Labour party six.[46] Five candidates in 1979, eighteen in 1983—it might seem as if the main parties had made a gesture in favor of ethnic minority repre-sentation. This is, however, illusory. The only candidate to have a notional majority in his favor was Paul Boateng, a Labour West Indian, and even then the seat was marginal and his selection had been surrounded by bitter confrontations since he was a left-wing councillor on the controversial GLC. Russell Profitt, another GLC councillor and one of the authors of the *Black People's Manifesto*, had been a candidate in 1979 and for 1983 had been selected for a solidly safe seat (Battersea). When the seat disappeared in the boundary changes and two seats became one, it was the white candidate for the other seat who was adopted. There was much disillusion among nonwhites when the Labour party failed to select black candidates in any safe seats. This led three ethnic minority organizations—the Conference of Indian Organisations, the West Indian Standing Conference, and the Federation of Bangladeshi Organisations—to put up five candidates of their own. Their best results were in Brent South and Birmingham Ladywood, two of the least white constituencies in Britain, where they obtained a mere 0.9 percent of the vote.

A study of the biographies of the eighteen major party nonwhite candidates shows that their profile was broadly similar whatever party they stood for. All of them had gone on studying for a further diploma after leaving school. Thirteen were members of the professions, seven of the legal professions (two barristers, five solicitors, one counsellor), three teachers, two doctors, and one architect. The remainder was made up of an estate agent, a housing advice officer, a director of community development organization, and a housewife. Roughly a third had stood as candidates at local government elections and a sixth were local councillors. Four were women. Half were in their forties, seven under forty, and two over fifty. Asians represented two-thirds of all nonwhite candidates. this profile shows that thew were as sociologically unrepresentative of black electors as white candidates are of white electors.

Did nonwhite candidates prove an electoral liability? Their fortunes in fact varied widely. The two who did least well were those who had been expected to do best: Paul Boateng in West Hertfordshire and Pramila Le Hunte in Birmingham Ladywood. The first was the Labour candidate in a notionally marginal seat. He ended up third with 22.3 percent, dropping 23.7 percent of the Labour vote. The second was the Conservative candidate in Birmingham Ladywood (which includes the city center and Soho), the most heavily non-white area in the city with 71 percent blacks and Asians.[47] Although the seat was in notional terms a safe seat, the Conservatives hoped that their candidate, an Indian, might capture the nonwhite vote in the second least white constituency in Britain. She obtained 27.1 percent, a 10.6 percent drop in the Conservative vote. It is of course impossible to draw from these two examples general notions as to whether or not nonwhite candidates are a handicap. In each case specific reasons for doing badly may be found that have little to do with color. After all in the other constituencies Labour and Conservative nonwhite candidates fared neither better nor worse than their white counterparts in similar seats.

The story for the Alliance's eight Asian candidates was different. Michael Steed's analysis shows that

> comparing their performance with the average rise since 1975 and 1979 and with regression estimates produces a consistent figure of about 5 percent for the proportion of the voters in those constituencies who failed to vote Alliance because of the colour of the candidate.[48]

The Alliance attracted, as the Liberals before it, some protest voting. In the 1970s the interchangeability between National Front and Liberals had been noted with, for instance, the National Front losing votes in October in seats where no Liberal had stood in February.[49] It is probable that the racist element in Alliance voting stems from protest voters whose general commitment to the ideals of liberalism is weak.

Conclusion

Since the 1960s the nonwhite electorate has increased from one election to the next. Its influence depends on the closeness of the election in a given constituency and in the country. As interest in the question grows it is to be hoped that better data will be available in the form of regular opinion polls and, later, census material. This would enable us to chart the qualitative change that will occur as the young people born in the U.K. gradually become the majority of the nonwhite electorate.

As electors of NCWP origin leave the safe Labour areas in city centers will they improve the prospects of Labour elsewhere or will they become as volatile as the white electorate? Be that as it may there seems little doubt that the next decade will see a nonwhite representation in the House of Commons. Whether the newcomers stand for the major parties or endeavor to represent the nonwhites on their own depends mostly on the actions of the parties.

How to Win a Landslide without Really Trying: Why the Conservatives Won in 1983

IVOR CREWE

──────── When Margaret Thatcher first became prime minister in May 1979 she inherited from the defeated Labour government an unemployment rate of 5 percent and an inflation rate of 9 percent. Both were at a postwar high for an election. In the circumstances it was perhaps not surprising that the Conservative majority (in votes), and the "swing" that secured it, were also the largest since 1945.

In the early 1980s, however, the British economy entered the worst recession since the 1930s. Bankruptcies soared and manufacturing output slumped. By the 1983 election unemployment had almost tripled to 13 percent. The inflation rate, it is true, had fallen to 5 percent, but only after first soaring to 22 percent. According to the "misery index" (the addition of the inflation and unemployment rates) the British economy was in a sorrier state at the end of the Conservative government than at the beginning. In almost every other Western democracy a rising misery index has taken its electoral toll.[1] In Australia, Austria, Canada, France, Greece, the Irish Republic, Norway, Portugal, Spain, Sweden, the United States, and West Germany the most recent elections turned out the government. In Finland, Italy, and Japan the latest elections recorded the lowest support for the permanent party of government for generations. However, in Britain the 1983 election not only rewarded the Conservatives with a second term, but added the bonus of a massively increased majority in Parliament.

The Conservative government was reelected with a crushing majority of 188 seats over Labour and of 144 overall. Reendorsement of a government after a full term is rare for Britain. The last occasion was Harold Macmillan's victory in 1959, when the economy was buoyant. Such handsome reendorsement is rarer still. The Conservative majority, in votes and seats, was the largest secured by one major party over the other since 1935. The Conservatives' advance since 1979—an additional 58 seats on a 3.9 percent swing—had never been surpassed by a government at one election.[2] For once nothing but the word "landslide" will do. How did it happen?

The British electoral system provides part of the answer. The relation between votes and seats is never proportional under the single-member simple-plurality system. Its exaggerative properties magnify a small swing into a large turnover of seats and overreward the winning party. In 1983 the vote-to-seat distortion was the worst since universal franchise was introduced in 1918.[3] The Conservative party's seat landslide, the tripling of its parliamentary majority from 44 to 144, was not based on any ground swell of popular support. Its share of the vote actually fell, by 1.5 percentage points, to 42.4 percent,[4] by past standards low, not high. For example, its share fell well below that obtained by the Conservative governments of the 1950s, when it averaged 49 percent, or even that recorded in 1964 (43.4 percent), an election it lost. Its share of the registered electorate also fell, by 2.5 percentage points, to 30.8 percent, marking its third lowest point this century, a level barely above that in 1945 (30 percent) when it went down to a crashing defeat. Only twice before has a government secured an outright majority with less popular support.[5] Never in the field of electoral conflict was so much owed by so many Conservative MPs to so few Conservative voters. It was a landslide by default.

Britain's electoral system overrewards the winning party according to the margin of its vote majority, not the size of its vote. The 1983 margin was a postwar record not because the Conservative vote was unusually large but because the Labour vote was exceptionally small. Only the word "disaster" does justice to the enormity of Labour's defeat. It lost a quarter of its 1979 vote, itself the lowest for almost half a century. It lost 119 deposits (the £150 sum forfeited by candidates if they fail to obtain one-eighth of the total constituency vote), by far the severest losses in its history. It was virtually wiped out as a serious political force in the south of England outside of London, winning only three of the seats and being relegated by the Alliance to third place in 150 constituencies. Its 9.3 percentage point drop in the national vote was the sharpest collapse suffered by a major party in a single election since 1945. At 27.6 percent its support was at its lowest since 1918 when, unlike 1983, it failed to contest a third of the seats. Judged by the average share of the constituency vote obtained by Labour candidates the 1983 result was Labour's worst performance since the party was founded in 1900. An account of the 1983 election must explain not why the Conservatives did so well but why Labour did so badly.

The Conservative landslide also owed much to a split opposition. The Alliance's 25.4 percent share of the vote was only 2.2 percent behind Labour's. It was the best performance by a national party of the political center for sixty years.[6] Its 11.6 percentage point advance over the 1979 Liberal vote was the strongest improvement achieved by a party at a single election since the Conservatives in the crisis election of 1931. It lost only eleven deposits. It took second place in 312 seats, thus creating two parallel party systems at electoral ground level. In the industrial and urban areas of Scotland, Wales, the North, and Midlands the two main parties continued to take first and second place and the Alliance remained in a respectable third position. But in rural and suburban areas everywhere, and throughout the South outside London, the Alliance replaced Labour as the principal, if not always very threatening, opposition to the Conservatives.

This achievement, however, amounted to a cracking rather than a breaking of the two-party mold. The Alliance's 25.4 percent vote elected a mere twenty-three MPs (seventeen Liberals and six from the SDP). This was more than any previous Liberal total since 1931, but well short of a breakthrough. The electoral system is again a large part of the explanation. It always penalizes a small party, but does so mercilessly if its national vote is evenly spread (as the Alliance's was), rather than locally concentrated (as Labour's was). Thus the Labour party obtained 2.2 percentage points more of the vote than the Alliance but nine times as many MPs. Nonetheless, the Alliance's vote, as well as its seats, fell far short of its original expectations. In the first year after the SDP's formation in March 1981 the Alliance was gaining hitherto impregnable Conservative seats at by-elections and coasting ahead of the two main parties with more than 40 percent support in the opinion polls, enough to win an election outright. An account of the 1983 election must explain why the Alliance did well; but it also must explain why it did not do better.

The Conservative landslide came about by default in another sense. It owed little to the Conservative party's election campaign. On election day the Conservative majority over Labour (in Great Britain) was 15.2 percent; a month earlier, in the week following the election's announcement, the opinion polls already were putting them ahead by 15.8 percent. In fact Conservative support fell during the campaign (see table 7.1). In the first few days it stood at 47.5 percent and by the midpoint of the campaign (25–28 May), after minor fluctuations, had risen fractionally. By the final week, however, it had slipped to 46 percent and by polling day it was 43.5 percent. It was only the parallel fall in Labour's support—from 32.5 percent in the first week to 28.3 percent on election day—that enabled the Conservatives to maintain their commanding lead. Judged by the net movement of voting intentions during the four-week preelection period both Conservative and Labour party campaigns were relative failures. To be sure, campaigns can be assessed less narrowly. One might have expected underlying party loyalties to close the initial party gap. Against this assumption the Conservatives' retention of most of their early support might be judged a success and Labour's lack of recovery a failure. Moreover, the campaign was important for one aspect of the result. The rise in the Alliance's support in the final ten days saved it from near-oblivion. An election held in

Table 7.1   Party support in the opinion polls during the campaign

Fieldwork dates	Number of polls	Con.	Lab.	All.
9–13 May	6	47.5	32.5	18.8
24–28 May	6	48.4	30.8	19.5
3–8 June	11	45.8	26.2	26.0
Election result (Great Britain)		43.5	28.3	26.0

Source: British Public Opinion 5 (May–June 1983), p. 24.
Note: The figure for each party is the unweighted mean. Support for minor parties is omitted from the table, but not from the percentage base.

the first week probably would have left the Liberals with seven seats and the SDP with one. To explain why the Conservatives won, and won so decisively, one must turn to events before the campaign.

Before the Campaign: the Falklands Factor

To most observers the crucial precampaign factor is self-evident: the Falklands war. Daily for ten weeks television news bulletins and newspaper front pages were devoted to reports of the British task force setting sail toward, invading, battling for, and finally recapturing the Falklands Islands. Nothing comparable since World War II—not Suez, nor the Profumo and spy scandals under Macmillan, nor the miners' strike in 1974—had so dominated the headlines and captured the public imagination.

Its effect on the Conservative government's standing was electric. In 1981 it was in the doldrums. In the monthly opinion polls its average support over the year stood at 28 percent, behind both Labour, at 30 percent, and the newly formed Alliance, at an astonishing 42 percent.[7] In the Gallup polls the proportion "satisfied" with Thatcher averaged 31 percent; the proportion "dissatisfied" 64 percent. By this measure she was "the most unpopular Prime Minister since polls began."[8] In two autumn by-elections the Conservatives lost Croydon North West and the previously safe Crosby to the Alliance. In early 1982 the Conservatives' support recovered slightly, but not by enough to prevent the loss of Glasgow Hillhead to Roy Jenkins for the SDP, whereupon their support immediately slipped again.

The Hillhead by-election was held on 24 March. A week later Argentinian forces invaded the Falkland Islands. Conservative support in the March opinion polls stood at 32 percent; satisfaction with Thatcher at 34 percent. On 14 June British troops captured Port Stanley and took the surrender of the Argentine troops. Conservative support in the June opinion polls now stood at 47 percent; satisfaction with Thatcher at 51 percent. In the space of three months public opinion, and party politics, had been transformed.

Such a rapid transformation of public opinion was hardly surprising. All the ingredients of the war combined to boost the standing of the prime minister and her government. For one thing, it was from the beginning a popular war. Overwhelmingly the public thought Argentina in the wrong and supported the sending of the task force. A substantial majority, which grew after the bombing of British ships, approved of the invasion of the islands.[9] For another, it was a spectator war. On the one hand, the electorate was in no physical danger; on the other television enabled it to follow the progress of British forces and feel closely involved. Also, when the media's attention was not on the South Atlantic it turned to those prosecuting the war: government representatives, the "war cabinet," and, in particular, Thatcher. Finally, it was a successful war: casualties were limited, it was over quickly, and, above all, Britain won. For a country starved of international success, victory was exhilarating. It was Britain's first popular national triumph since winning the World Cup in football in 1966. For many voters made weary by economic and imperial decline it put the "Great" back in Britain.

Popular and successful wars inevitably make life difficult for the opposition. Public attention is diverted away from the opposition parties and domestic problems. For the Labour party a no-win political situation was turned into a sure loser by division and indecisiveness. A substantial minority of the Labour party, led by Tony Benn, opposed the sending of the task force from the start. Michael Foot spoke for most of the parliamentary Labour party (PLP), however, in demanding in early April a vigorous response to the aggression of the "fascist junta" in Argentina; this impression of a staunchly loyal opposition was vitiated in May when he drew back from unequivocal support for the invasion of the islands. In the polls support for Labour dropped from 35 percent in March to 27 percent in June.

The Alliance's backing of the government was constant and unconditional, yet in the polls its support fell by even more, from 34 percent in April to 24 percent, firmly back in third place, by June. For its previous success the Alliance, as a new party, had depended on momentum. Its pattern of support resembled a periodically pumped-up tire with a slow puncture. At times of intense and favorable publicity, such as a by-election gain, its support would be temporarily inflated only to subside until the next bout of good publicity.

The Alliance expected its win at Hillhead to be a launching pad for widespread gains in the annual local elections in early May. These in turn would have provided a stronger organizational base and sufficient momentum to retain Mitcham and Morden in the June by-election, from which it could proceed to further successes in the autumn. The Falklands war killed the momentum.

The Alliance was knocked out of the news. Roy Jenkins was deprived of the opportunity to exploit his reentry into Parliament. Foreign and military affairs were not his speciality, old-fashioned patriotism not his style. He left the speeches to the SDP's foreign affairs spokesman, David Owen. With only 26 percent of the vote and sparse gains the local election results were a sore disappointment. Mitcham and Morden was lost to a Conservative. The good ship Alliance appeared to be sinking under the waves of the South Atlantic, executed by General Galtieri.

The strength of the Falkland war's impact on public opinion was expected; the duration of that impact was not. The eruption of Conservative support it brought about did not subside even as the war gradually disappeared from the headlines. In June 1982 Thatcher's satisfaction rating in the Gallup Poll was 51 percent; almost a year later, in May 1983, it was 50 percent. Conservative support slipped from 47 percent in June to 44 percent in August but from then right up to the election it remained, steady as a Falklands rock, between 41 and 45 percent. The Falklands factor clearly amounted to something more than a mere rallying around the flag. To be sure, the Falklands war did not completely disappear from public view after the Argentine surrender. Massive media coverage of the returning ships, the Thanksgiving service, and Thatcher's visit to the Falklands in January 1983 kept it in the public consciousness.

The government's standing also was helped by a modest improvement in the economy. Unemployment remained unprecedentedly high but at least its growth was leveling off. The inflation rate was steadily descending, from 12 percent in March 1982 to 4.5 percent in May 1983. The public noticed; the proportion saying that over the previous twelve months prices were "very much" or "quite a bit" higher fell from 59 percent in March 1982 to 36 percent in May 1983.[10] Over the same period the proportion who considered that the "government is doing enough to control the rise in prices" rose from 29 percent to 49 percent. Optimism about the economy's future grew in tandem. In March 1982 pessimists about the "general economic situation in the next twelve months" outnumbered optimists by 40 percent to 31 percent; by May 1983 there were many more optimists (47 percent) than pessimists (20 percent).

These real and perceived improvements in the economy were gradual, however, whereas over the same period the government's popularity started—and remained—high. The Falklands war was indeed crucial, but for symbolic as much as substantive reasons. It served as a perfectly timed metaphor for all that the government hitherto had claimed about its domestic strategy. It would not duck tough decisions about the economy; it did not wriggle out of its commitment to the Falkland Islanders. It would stand firm against the militancy of some trade unions; it stood firm against the bullying of Argentina. It would not be deterred from its long-term objectives by temporary setbacks; it did not throw in the towel after the disaster of Bluff Cove. There would be no policy U-turns; the troops on the Falklands always pressed on, never retreated. Britain needed Thatcher's brand of decisive leadership; it got it in abundance during the war. The army term for the arduous forty-mile marches over moor and bog, the public learned, was "yomping." That, the government argued, was what it had been doing since being elected. It was called "The Resolute Approach."

The Conservatives entered the election campaign with the largest lead of one party over another recorded in the history of opinion polls. Yet the Falklands war played no explicit part in the campaign. It did not figure prominently in the Conservative manifesto or its leaders' speeches. It was two Labour politicians, Denis Healey and Neil Kinnock, who out of desperation late in the campaign clumsily raised the issue. By the conventional measure it was not salient to the public: in the campaign polls almost nobody mentioned it as an influence on his or her vote. But it did not need to be conspicuous. It existed in easily deciphered code. In the Conservative campaign there were constant references to the way Thatcher's strong leadership had restored Britain's self-respect and standing in the world. People knew what was meant. The Falklands war formed the permanent backdrop to an electoral drama whose finale was known to the audience from the start. In no previous postwar election had opinion shifted enough to overturn a 16 percent lead. The only uncertainties were whether the Alliance would be salvaged, and by how much, if at all, Labour would narrow the gap. Why the Alliance succeeded and Labour failed is the subject of the analysis that follows.

Organization and Publicity

As usual the parties entered the electoral arena as unequal contestants. The Conservative party's organization is superior in almost every respect to Labour's. It is better funded at both the national and local level; its local constituency associations have larger and more active memberships; it employs more headquarters and research staff; it has more agents and regional officials on its books; and it is more committed to the exploitation of modern advertising and public relations methods. In close elections these advantages can be, and have been, crucial.[11] They are insignificant, however, when compared with the enormous advantages that both major parties enjoy over the Liberals.

Without business or trade union funding, the Liberal party has had to conduct election campaigns on shoestring budgets. Its headquarters are tiny and at elections it largely relies on the unpaid assistance of supporters with professional expertise or political experience. It has no full-time agents. It rarely can afford private polls, press advertising, or nationwide poster campaigns. In a few areas, especially where it has gained significant local representation, it has built up large constituency associations but the typical local Liberal party has fewer funds or members than its Conservative or Labour counterparts. It therefore relies more on the limited state aid available to parties in Britain. Like the major parties its candidates receive free postage for their election address and it receives a standard, although unequal, allocation of time for party election broadcasts (PEBs) on television and radio.

These customary inequalities were mitigated slightly by the early and sudden calling of the 1983 election. Local parties, in the midst of reorganization occasioned by the constituency boundary changes, were caught unprepared. Scarcely any time was left for the parties to raise extra election funds or engage in a sustained bout of precampaign advertising, at both of which the Conservatives traditionally have an edge. Moreover, the existence of the SDP partly compensated for the Liberal party's poverty. It added sixty-five thousand members to those of the Liberal party, which this time had to contest only half the national total of seats. (However, some Liberal members in constituencies with SDP-Alliance candidates, and SDP members in those with Liberal-Alliance candidates, may have sat on their hands, although how many is impossible to tell.) The SDP brought more than members. Its headquarters staff was larger, and probably more professional, than that of the Liberals. It also attracted sufficient funds to pay for a limited poster campaign, private polls during the campaign, and professional filming (rather than nothing but "talking heads") for the PEBs, which it entirely financed. Most important of all, the formation of the SDP and the subsequent electoral strength of the Alliance persuaded the broadcasting authorities to allocate the Alliance an extra ten-minute PEB, thus raising the proportion from three in 1979 to four in 1983 for every five for the Conservative and Labour parties.

The Conservative party still outspent the other parties. Its central expenditure was about £3.8 million, the Labour party's £2.5 million, and the Alliance's between £1.3 and 1.5 million.[12] It made more use of its advertising agency, Saatchi and Saatchi, commissioned more private polls, and advertised more in the national press. The electoral benefits, however, appear to have been negligible. End-of-campaign surveys by Market and Opinion Research International (MORI) and Gallup both show that the Conservative and Labour campaigns reached almost identical proportions of the electorate (see table 7.2). Their PEBs on television were seen by about 70 percent apiece; their radio PEBs and phone-ins by 35 percent apiece.[13] Given the equal allocation of time to the Conservative and Labour parties on the broadcasting networks this is perhaps not surprising. However, party activities that depend on organization, party workers, and money, where on paper Conservatives had such superiority, also reached similar numbers. The identical proportion claimed to have been leafleted (54 percent) and canvassed (27 percent) by each of the two parties. Only 2 percent more remembered seeing a Conservative as opposed to a Labour poster. The Alliance, it is true, consistently failed to reach as many people as

Table 7.2 Impact of campaigning (percent of voters)

Question	Yes, Conservative	Yes, Labour	Yes, Alliance
Since the start of the election have you . . .			
seen TV PEBs?	71	72	65
been leafleted?	54	54	48
seen any posters? (G)	38	36	35
seen hoardings?	27	25	19
been called on by any of the parties? (G)	27	27	18
heard radio PEBs?	18	17	14
heard radio phone-ins?	17	18	13
been canvassed?	14	12	8
been called upon by anybody from any of the parties on election day itself? (G)	6	8	5
attended a meeting?	1	1	*

Sources: MORI survey for *Daily Express*, 2 June 1983 ($N = 1,067$). For the full set of findings see Market and Opinion Research International, *British Public Opinion, General Election 1983, Final Report*, p. 79. The Gallup questions are taken from the *Gallup Political Indexes* for June 1983 (p. 18), and for July 1983 (pp. 6, 25).
Notes: * = less than 0.5 percent. (G) denotes a Gallup question; all others are MORI questions.

the major parties did, but the differences were always slender, and certainly smaller than that represented by its financial and organizational handicap.

Effective campaigning is measured not only by the numbers reached but by the numbers persuaded, whether persuasion takes the form of defection to another party or swallowing doubts and remaining loyal. Once again, the easy assumption that the Conservative party campaign was by far the superior, or that the Alliance suffered severe disadvantages, are at odds with the survey evidence. To begin with, the form of campaigning that had overwhelmingly the most impact was television broadcasting, where the parties compete on almost equal footing, rather than advertising or house-to-house calls, where perhaps they do not. Asked to choose from a list of possible influences on how they "finally decided . . . to vote," 4 percent of all voters mentioned party advertising, 7 percent a personal contact (relative, colleague at work, party worker, etc.), but 20 percent a television PEB (see table 7.3). Television's preponderant impact was even more marked among waverers who only made up their minds in the closing days of the campaign: 13 percent mentioned personal contacts, 14 percent party advertising, but fully 52 percent referred to PEBs.[14] Elections are won and lost in sitting rooms, not on doorsteps or at poster sites.

A detailed examination of the net benefits accruing to each party from advertising and PEBs suggests that the Conservative edge over Labour was minimal and that overwhelmingly the Alliance did best. The net impact of

Table 7.3   Campaign's effect on vote choice (percent of votes)

Reason for vote choice	All voters	Late deciders	Loyalists	Switchers
Because of a				
Conservative broadcast on TV	6	14	5	8
Labour broadcast on TV	5	12	5	7
Alliance broadcast on TV	9	26	6	22
Because of a				
Conservative newspaper advert/ poster I saw	1	4	1	2
Labour newspaper advert/ poster I saw	2	5	2	1
Alliance newspaper advert/ poster I saw	1	5	1	4
Because I was persuaded by . . .				
my wife/husband	2	2	2	3
my parents/children	3	4	3	1
somebody at work	1	2	1	1
a party worker	1	5	1	2

Source: BBC TV/Gallup survey, 8–9 June 1983 ($N = 4,141$).
Note: Question was worded, "When you finally decided which way to vote was it for one or more reasons on this card?"

advertising was minuscule. In the BBC / Gallup survey only 28 respondents (0.7 percent of the sample) said they were influenced by Conservative advertising; of these 19 were loyalists, the rest an equal balance of 4 recruits and 5 defectors. The figures for Labour advertising are virtually identical: 20 loyalists, 5 recruits, 4 defectors. The Alliance fared better: of the 38 respondents claiming to have been influenced by its advertising, none were Liberal defectors and 22 were recruits—but they represent a mere 0.5 percent of all respondents. As regards television, one test of effective persuasion is the proportion of late deciders whose final decision, they claim, was influenced by a PEB and who voted for the party whose PEB it was. The results are: Conservative PEBs 48 percent, Labour PEBs 50 percent, Alliance PEBs 83 percent. Another measure, paralleling that used for advertising, is the net gain to each party among all voters, whenever they decided, who cited that party's PEB as an influence on their vote. Of the 102 respondents who said they were influenced by a Labour PEB, defectors outnumbered recruits by 21 to 14, a net loss of 0.2 percent of all respondents. Among the 128 respondents apparently influenced by a Conservative PEB, there was a tiny surplus of 24 recruits over 18 defectors—a net gain of 0.1 percent. Only the Alliance's PEBs had an impact of any consequence. Of the 184 respondents referring to them, 46 were loyalists, 5 defectors, and fully

133 recruits: a net gain of 3 percent. Taking these figures at face value, the absence of PEBs would have left the Alliance with 23 rather than 26 percent of the vote, at the probable cost of seven seats. What the Alliance lacked on the streets it more than made up for in the television studios.

Too much should not be made of these figures. Some of the respondents claiming to have been influenced by advertising or television would have voted the same way anyway. But the evidence does tally with the fact that, as we have noted already, during the campaign both major parties slipped in the opinion polls by the same amount to the benefit of the Alliance. It is accepted wisdom that Labour's advertising and PEBs were uninspired, its campaign organization amateurish and ineffective, whereas the Conservative campaign was a model of smooth-running professionalism. It is always tempting—and also politically convenient for the party—to pin the blame for defeat on its organization. The survey evidence suggests that the electoral importance of campaign organization is easily exaggerated. The Conservative party could have saved much of its advertising expenditure. It did more for Saatchi and Saatchi than Saatchi and Saatchi did for it. It was not the medium that hurt Labour but the message—and the chief messenger.

The Flow of the Vote

To explain the 3.9 percent swing from Labour to the Conservatives between 1979 and 1983 the natural point of departure is to ask, Who swung? From the net change in the three parties' share of the national vote—the Conservatives down 1.5 percent, Labour down 9.3 percent, and the Alliance up 11.6 percent—the conclusions seem obvious: the Conservatives owe their triumph, the Alliance its advance, and Labour its humiliation to a direct switch of votes from Labour to the Alliance. However, a preliminary analysis of the BBC / Gallup survey suggest that the true story is more complicated.[15]

Table 7.4 displays the flow of the vote from party to party between 1979 and 1983. There is one caveat about the table: it is based not on panel data, but on respondents' *recall* in 1983 of their vote four years earlier. Recall data are subject to well-known biases (including the underreporting of previous abstention and the projection of current party preference onto past party preference), leading to an underestimation of vote switching.

Nonetheless, table 7.4 leaves little doubt that Labour indeed suffered massive desertions. Well over a third (37 percent) of its 1979 support, itself reduced to what might have been regarded as a loyal core, defected. (Panel data probably would reveal the true proportion to be even higher.) However, by no means did all Labour deserters go over to the Alliance. For every three switching to the Alliance, one switched to the Conservatives, and another one stayed at home. Moreover, there was less than unswerving loyalty among 1979 Conserva-

Table 7.4   Flow of the vote from 1979 to 1983 (percent of voters)

Voted in 1983	Voted in 1979				
	Conservative	Labour	Alliance	Did not vote	Too young
Conservative	77	7	14	22	28
Labour	4	63	9	12	17
Alliance	13	22	72	14	20
Other	*	1	*	*	2
Did not vote	6	7	5	52	32
$N =$	1,521	1,252	382	357	396

Source: See note to table 7.3.
Notes: * = less than 0.5 percent. Percentages do not add to 100 because of rounding.

tives (of whom 23 percent switched) or even 1979 Liberals (of whom 28 percent switched). The contribution to the pro-Conservative swing made by Labour desertions to the Alliance (22 percent) was lessened by a reverse movement to Labour by 9 percent of ex-Liberals and by Conservative desertions to the Alliance amounting to 13 percent. The overall impact of the traffic between the Alliance and the two major parties was a mere 1.6 percent of the swing from Labour to Conservative, leaving the remaining three-fifths of the total swing of 3.9 percent still to be explained. For Labour to attribute its defeat entirely to an SDP "betrayal," however comforting, therefore would be far too simple.

The Alliance's differential impact on the relative fortunes of the major parties was only one of five components in the national swing, albeit the single most important. There were four other ways in which electors could have changed their vote between elections to return the Conservatives with an increased majority:

1. *Straight switching*: more defections from Labour to Conservative than vice versa.
2. *Differential abstention*: more former Labour than former Conservative voters deciding to abstain.
3. *Differential turnout*: more 1979 nonvoters turning out this time for the Conservatives than for Labour.
4. *Physical replacement of the electorate*: more deaths (or emigration) among previous Labour than Conservative voters, and/or a Conservative majority among those entering the electorate for the first time (through coming of age or immigration).

Straight switching was the second substantial contributor to the pro-Conservative swing. There were almost twice as many direct converts from Labour to Conservative (7 percent) as vice versa (4 percent), which added 1 percent to the swing. Straight switching was also significant as a measure of the Alliance's failure to make the most of disillusion with the two major parties. Had the Alliance succeeded in capturing all the straight switchers its national vote would have risen to 29 percent, relegating Labour to third place, and winning up to ten extra seats.

Labour also was hit by differential turnout. Former nonvoters gave the Conservatives a 10 percent majority over Labour, equivalent to an extra 0.5 percent on the swing. However, Labour's traditional problem of differential *abstention* ("we failed to get our vote out") did not occur, despite the rise in nonvoting since 1979. The abstention rates of those voting Conservative, Labour, and Liberal in 1979 were almost identical. Labour's supporters in 1979 did not stay at home in large numbers on 9 June 1983. They went to the polling stations where, in large numbers, they switched parties.

It is impossible to put a precise estimate on the partisan impact of the physical replacement of the electorate. As usual, there will have been more Conservative than Labour supporters among those who died between the two elections. In striking contrast to the past, however, there also were more Conservative than Labour voters among new electors. Until 1979, surveys consistently showed that, compared with the old, the young voted Labour in higher proportions and, in addition, swung more heavily against whichever party held office. Under Conservative governments, therefore, these two tendencies reinforced each other to produce substantial majorities for Labour; indeed, they were sufficient by themselves to give Labour its knife-edge parliamentary majorities in 1964 and February 1974.[16] In 1979, for the first time, new voters divided equally between Labour and the Conservatives. In 1983 the swing to the right among the young went further still. Labour came third among new electors, taking a mere 18 percent of their vote, 2 percent behind the Alliance and 10 percent behind the Conservatives. The result was another 1 percent on the swing and the final nail in Labour's coffin. That Labour should fail so dismally among the young at a time of severe youth unemployment must seem a mystery. Some light is thrown upon it in the following pages.

Tables 7.5, 7.6, and 7.7 put flesh on this skeletal analysis by showing how the 1979-to-1983 net change in the parties' share of the three-party vote varied among social groups. The main features of the tables are summarized below.

A glimpse of a gender gap?   For the third successive election the pro-Conservative swing was stronger among men (4.5 percent) than women (3 percent). This decade-long accumulation of undramatic differences produced an electoral landmark in 1983. A permanent feature of postwar elections until recently was the higher Conservative vote among women than men. The difference disappeared in 1979 and went into reverse in 1983 (see table 7.5). For the first time, and under Britain's's first woman prime minister, the Conservatives drew less support from women (43 percent of the three-party vote) than from men (46

Table 7.5   Vote by sex and age (percentage of three-party vote)

	Men		Women	
	1983	Change from 1979	1983	Change from 1979
Conservative	46	−1	43	−4
Labour	29	−10	29	−10
Alliance	24	+11	28	+13
Swing				
Lab. to Con.		4.5		3.0
Lab. to All.		10.5		11.5
Con. to All.		6.0		8.5
N =		1,649		1,853

Sources: BBC TV / Gallup survey, 8–9 June 1983; BBC TV / Gallup survey, 2–3 May 1979.

percent). Perhaps the "tough" style of Thatcherism, underlined by the Falklands war, had something to do with it; perhaps it reflected the apparent international trend for women to be moving leftwards. Whatever the cause, the Alliance, not Labour, benefited, taking 4 percent more of the women's vote (28 percent) than of the men's (24 percent).

Labour's failure among the young   The largest pro-Conservative swing was among new voters (6 percent), where the Labour vote fell by 13 percentage points. As usual, Conservative support steadily increased from young to old, but along a much gentler gradient than in the past. For the young to be the most volatile is normal but for that volatility to work against the Labour party when it is in opposition is unprecedented.

The other odd group out was the over-65s, among whom the Conservative vote fell by more than average and the Labour vote by much less, resulting in no swing at all since 1979. Labour policy and the government's record on pensions could be an explanation, although only a fifth of the over-65s cited pensions as an important issue. An alternative explanation is that the over-65s are the political generation of the interwar Great Depression and World War II. The majority first voted in, and preponderantly contributed to, the Labour landslide of 1945. Some of the Labour loyalty induced in their formative years may have lasted until today.

The Alliance did best among new voters (30 percent), worst among the over-65s (19 percent), probably because party loyalties are least fixed among the young and most ingrained among the old. The Alliance's campaign must have been particularly effective among first-time voters, since all precampaign surveys found lower than average support for the Alliance in this group.[17]

18–22 years		23–44 years		45–64 years		65 and over	
	Change from		Change from		Change from		Change from
1983	1979	1983	1979	1983	1979	1983	1979
42	−1	44	−3	46	−2	47	−3
29	−1	29	−10	27	−13	34	−3
30	+14	28	+13	28	+15	19	+7
	6.0		3.5		5.5		0.0
	13.0		11.0		14.0		5.0
	7.5		7.5		8.5		5.0
411		1,383		1,060		654	

Notes: Column percentages do not always add to 100 because of rounding. Swing figures are derived from vote shares estimated to one decimal point.

The class factor　It was not sex or age but social class that continued to be the primary shaper of party choice (see table 7.6). On climbing the class ladder the Conservative share of the vote rose and the Labour share of the vote fell. Among the professions and management the Conservatives led Labour by 61 to 12 percent; among semi- and unskilled workers the Conservatives trailed by 29 to 44 percent. However, the partisan slope of these class ladders was less steep than at any time since the war. The class polarization that was widely expected in the wake of mass unemployment did not materialize. Among the middle classes there was no swing to the Conservatives at all. The Conservative vote fell by 6 percentage points, well above the national average, in the professions and management. Among clerical and office workers there was actually a small swing to Labour. The shift to the right occurred in the working class, a 2 percent swing to the Conservatives among skilled workers and a 4 percent swing among semi- and unskilled workers. In the ranks of trade unionists it was a massive 8 percent (as against 1 percent among nonunionists) although this figure owes something to the growth in the white-collar proportion of trade unionists since 1979. These pro-Conservative swings occurred not because the working-class Conservative vote went up, but because the working-class Labour vote, which had already hemorrhaged badly in 1979, continued to bleed away, mainly to the Alliance. Only at the very bottom of the economic ladder, among the unemployed, was there a hint of a working-class backlash. Here the Conservative vote (which had risen sharply in 1979) dropped by 10 percentage points, Labour's by only 5, to produce what was technically a pro-Labour swing of 2.5 percent.

The Alliance vote was remarkably even across the class spectrum. There

Table 7.6   Vote by social class (percentage of three-party vote)

	Professional/ managerial		Office/clerical	
	1983	Change from 1979	1983	Change from 1979
Conservative	61	−6	55	−4
Labour	12	−6	21	−1
Alliance	26	+11	24	+4
Swing				
Lab. to Con.	0.0		−1.5	
Lab. to All.	8.5		2.5	
Con. to All.	8.5		4.0	
N =	708		844	

Sources: See note to table 7.3.
Notes: "Trade unionists" include respondents belonging to a household containing a trade union member.

Table 7.7   Vote by sector of employment and housing (percentage of three-party vote)

	Housing				Sector of employment			
	Owner-occupiers/ mortgagees		Council tenants		Private sector		Public sector	
	1983	Change from 1979	1983	Change from 1979	1983	Change from 1979	1983	Change from 1979
Conservative	55	−1	22	−5	49	+4	37	−1
Labour	17	−11	55	−7	26	−14	36	−9
Alliance	28	+12	24	+12	25	+9	27	+10
Swing								
Lab. to Con.	5.0		1.0		9.0		4.0	
Lab. to All.	11.0		9.5		11.5		10.0	
Con. To All.	6.0		8.5		2.5		6.0	
N =	1,847		863		1,764		1,031	

Source: See note to table 7.3.
Notes: The 1979 data used for comparison are taken from the 1979 British Election Study and standardized to the three-party vote share in the 1979 general election. Column percentages do not always add up to 100 because of rounding. Swing figures are derived from vote shares estimated to one decimal point.

Skilled manual		Semiskilled/ unskilled manual		Trade unionists		Unemployed	
	Change from		Change from		Change from		Change from
1983	1979	1983	1979	1983	1979	1983	1979
39	−6	29	−3	32	+1	30	−10
35	−10	44	−12	39	−16	45	−5
27	+17	28	+15	28	+14	26	+14
	2.0		4.0		8.0		−2.5
	13.0		13.5		15.0		9.5
	11.0		9.0		6.5		12.0
	959		964		1,252		319

Column percentages do not always add to 100 because of rounding. Swing figures are derived from vote shares estimated to one decimal point.

was not a trace of evidence that its supposedly middle-class image was anathema to the "real" working class or that as a middle-of-the-road party it had a particular appeal for the intermediate strata. It was as popular among the unemployed (26 percent) and the semi- and unskilled manual workers (28 percent) as among the professions and management (26 percent). The 32 percent Alliance vote among university graduates mildly corroborated its reputation as the "intellectuals' party," but was well short of the 43 percent Conservative vote in the same group.

Private versus public sector The 1979–83 Conservative government set out to curtail the role of the state in the economy. It reduced the number of civil servants, curbed local government spending, abolished industrial subsidies, denationalized industry, selectively cut welfare provisions, and generally sought to lower public expenditure. There were signs of a reaction against this by voters dependent for their livelihood on the state (see table 7.7). We already have noted the pro-Labour swing among the unemployed, who depend on unemployment pay (the real value of which declined) and other welfare benefits. Among public sector employees the pro-Conservative swing (4 percent) was half that among their private sector counterparts (9 percent). Indeed, private sector workers constituted one of the few segments of the electorate in which the Conservative vote actually increased. In the housing market the pattern was similar: among owner-occupiers a swing of 5 percent to the Conservatives; among council house tenants a tiny swing of only 1 percent.

Table 7.8   Defection rates among 1979 Labour voters

Group	% of group switching from Labour
All Labour voters, 1979	31
Nonmanual	38
Manual	29
Professional / managerial	45
Clerical / office workers	32
Skilled manual	31
Semi- and unskilled manual	29
Pensioners, welfare dependents	28
Member of white-collar union	36
Member of blue-collar union	27
Not a union member	33
Private sector	33
Public sector	29
Nonmanual, private sector	42
Manual, private sector	30
Nonmanual, public sector	31
Manual, public sector	28
Bought council house	59
Owner-occupier / mortgagee	44
Working-class home owner	42
Council tenant	21
White	32
Black	21
Ages 22–44	33
Ages 45–64	34
Ages 65+	25

Source: See note to table 7.3.
Note: Vote in 1979 is based on respondents' recall in 1983.

Labour's Constituency   The "swing" measure is based on changes in both parties' vote. Labour's spectacular collapse warrants a separate examination of the way defection rates from Labour varied among social groups. As table 7.8 shows, heavy Labour desertions occurred across the entire social spectrum. They were especially marked on the periphery of Labour's social constituency, among its middle-class, nonunion, and private sector supporters of 1979.[18] House ownership had most impact. Large-scale switching took place among owner-occupiers (44 percent), working-class owners as much as middle-class owners. Among council tenants who voted Labour in 1979 but subsequently

Table 7.9 Two working classes and the 1983 vote (percentage of three-party vote)

Vote in 1983	"New" working class			"Traditional" working class		
	Owner-occupiers/ mortgagees	Workers in private sector	Residents of South	Council tenants	Workers in public sector	Residents of Scotland/ North
Conservative	47	36	42	19	29	32
Labour	25	37	26	57	46	42
Alliance	28	27	32	24	25	26
Con. versus Lab. majority	Con. +22	Lab. +1	Con. +16	Lab. +38	Lab. +17	Lab. +10
Category as % of all manual workers	43	66	36	45	34	38

Source: See note to table 7.3.

bought their council house the defection rate was a massive 59 percent. The Labour vote held up best, although still not well, among the inner-city ghetto groups of council tenants, blacks, and the over-65s.

The 1983 election made the Labour party look like the party of a *segment* of the working class. In parliamentary terms it became a regional-class party; in electoral terms a party supported by the traditional working class of the council estates, of the public sector, of Scotland and the North—and then disproportionately among its older members. Among these slowly dwindling groups Labour remained the first, if not always the majority, choice (see table 7.9). However, it lost the "new" working class. Among private sector workers it ran neck and neck with the Conservatives. Among manual workers owning their house or living in the South the Conservatives had a commanding lead and Labour came third, behind the Alliance. Thus Labour's claim to be the natural party of the whole working class looked threadbare in 1983. The Labour vote remained largely working class, but the working class ceased to be largely Labour. Its vote split three ways, giving Labour a mere 5 percent lead over the Conservatives; among trade unionists the Labour majority was only 7 percent. Labour's share of the working-class electorate, as distinct from those who voted, was down to barely a quarter (27 percent). Why the working class should display such a lack of class consciousness and solidarity after Britain's worst recession in fifty years is one of the questions to which the next section will seek an answer.

Table 7.10   Motivation of party choice (percentage of voters)

| | Vote in 1983 | | | |
	Conservative	Labour	Alliance[a]	Total
Positive	45 (−3)	38 (−21)	37	41
Negative	55 (+3)	62 (+21)	63	59
	Decided how to vote during campaign			
	Conservative	Labour	Alliance[a]	Total
Positive	22 (−24)	30 (−17)	31	27
Negative	78 (+24)	70 (+17)	69	73
	Recruits from 1979 to			
	Conservative	Labour	Alliance[a]	Total
Positive	37 (−7)	25 (−20)	31	31
Negative	63 (+7)	75 (+20)	69	69

Source: See note to table 7.3.

Notes: Wording of question, "What would you say is stronger—your *like* of the Conservatives (Labour, Lib.-SDP Alliance) or your *dislike* of Labour (the Conservatives, the Conservative and Labour parties)?" The small number replying "both equally" are excluded. Figures in parentheses show change from 1979.

[a] The motivation question was not asked of Liberal voters in 1979. This makes comparisons with 1979 for all voters, as well as for Liberals, impossible.

Why the Switchers Switched

Having identified the movers let us proceed to ask what moved them. Before describing the specific factors that mattered most there is a general point to be made. In 1983 the British electorate, and especially the switchers, were moved by the forces of repulsion not attraction, by fear not hope. That the Conservative victory was a landslide by default is underlined by the preponderance—and growth—of negative voting (see table 7.10). The majority of voters (59 percent) disliked the other party or parties more than they liked their own. In the case of switchers and those who only decided during the campaign these negative majorities—69 percent and 73 percent, respectively—were substantial.

This begrudged vote was slightly lower among Conservatives (55 percent) than Labour (62 percent) or the Alliance (63 percent) but nonetheless it was the majority sentiment, it was up from 1979, and it was the overwhelming attitude of those persuaded to vote Conservative during the campaign. Moreover, asked whether they voted Conservative "because of something in particular" or because they "saw no need for a change of government," only 35 percent gave the first answer, 65 percent the second, an almost exact reverse of the 1979 position. None of this suggests a ringing endorsement of the government's record, the Conservative manifesto, or the "resolute approach."

Although the Labour posters said, "Think Positive Act Positive" the Labour vote owed far more to the Conservative government's record than to the Labour program. Sixty-two percent of all Labour voters, 70 percent of those persuaded during the campaign, and fully 75 percent of Labour recruits voted against rather than for. The increase in negative motives compared with 1979 was particularly marked among Labour voters—which puts to rest Tony Benn's comforting postmortem that the remaining bedrock of Labour support was a vote for the manifesto and a foundation for true socialism.[19] In fact the Labour vote was as much a protest vote as that for the Alliance. Without the rise in unemployment, the cuts in public services, and Thatcher's less attractive characteristics the Labour vote would have diminished further.

Granted that more voters were turned off than turned on, which of the many influences on their vote—leaders, party policy, self-interest, sheer partisan loyalty—had the most impact? All had some influence and disentangling precisely their separate effects is beyond the scope of this chapter. Yet for all the habitual complaints about the presidential style of the campaign, the evidence strongly suggests that, as in previous elections, policies counted for much more than personalities, and perceptions of the national interest for more than feelings of self-interest. One test is how people actually vote when they prefer the policies of one party but the leader of another. Among the 824 BBC / Gallup respondents in this position there was an 83 to 17 percent split in favor of the first. Also, faced with a dilemma between two parties, one with the "best policies," the other "best for people like me," voters divided by 72 to 28 percent in favor of the party with the "best policies."

This decisive although not exclusive dominance of national policy considerations is revealed when the actual vote is compared with people's choice of parties on different criteria (see table 7.11). If the election had in fact been presidential and votes cast solely for a prime minister, or for a cabinet, Labour's share would have dropped to about 15 percent, barely half of what it got, and the Alliance would have become the major party of opposition. If people had voted strictly according to their perceived self-interest, Labour's share would have been 5 percentage points higher, the Alliance's 4 points less. If policies were all that counted, however, the Conservatives would have won 50 percent of the vote and an even more staggering majority in Parliament. The fact that more people chose the Conservatives on each criterion than actually voted for it is testimony to the power of deep-seated Labour loyalties to induce in many what was clearly a vote of the heart rather than the mind.

Table 7.11   Party preferences on various criteria (percentage of voters)

Which party	Con.	Lab.	All.	Other
has the best policies?	50	25	24	1
is best for people like you?	43	33	22	2
has the best team of leaders?	58	17	24	1
do you generally identify with?	44	38	16	2
	Thatcher	Foot	Steel	Jenkins
Who would make the best prime minister?	46	13	35	6

Source: See note to table 7.3.

Notes: Wording of questions, "Taking everything into account, which party has the best policies?"; "And leaving on one side the question of which party you voted for, which party is best for people like you?"; "And which party has the best team of leaders?"; "Leaving aside this particular election, would you say you *generally* think of yourself as Conservative, Labour, Liberal, SDP, or what?" "Leaving aside your general party preference, who would make the best prime minister?" The small number of respondents answering "none," "all the same," and "don't know" have been omitted.

Issues

If it was not organization or personalities but issues that counted most, which issues in particular? The "right" issues for a party are those with the double advantage of being important to the electorate and being ones on which the party's record or proposals are preferred. Table 7.12 rank orders the two issues that electors said, on the eve and day of polling, most influenced their vote. Overwhelmingly the most important issue for voters was unemployment (mentioned by 72 percent), followed far behind by defense (38 percent), prices (20 percent), and the National Health Service (NHS) (11 percent). No other issue was cited by as many as 10 percent of respondents. Omissions from the list are conspicuous. References to strikes fell from 20 percent in 1979 (the election held shortly after the industrial Winter of Discontent) to 3 percent this time, reflecting perhaps the sharp fall in industrial disputes. The proportion mentioning taxes dropped from 21 percent in 1979, when it was a major plank in the Conservative platform, to 4 percent in 1983, when it was not. Immigration, the hidden mover of votes in the 1960s and 1970s, dropped to the bottom of the political agenda (1 percent). Copying the politicians, electors were staggeringly parochial. Foreign affairs and international peace came to the lips of only 24 out of 4,141 respondents (0.6 percent); Northern Ireland to a minuscule 3 people i.e., 0.072 percent. (The survey was confined to the British mainland.) And the Falklands? Precisely 1.4 percent claimed that it affected their vote.

The parochialism was national rather than local: different groups of voters largely agreed in their ranking of the issues, varying only in the degree of emphasis they placed on them. Concern about defense, prices, and the European Economic Community (EEC) pushed voters to the right, eroding the Labour vote and keeping Conservatives loyal. Concern about unemployment and the social services (especially the NHS but also education and pensions) pushed voters to the left, eroding the Conservative vote and keeping Labour supporters loyal.

Table 7.11 also shows the party lead on each issue among those mentioning it as personally decisive and comparison of the two sets of figures immediately poses a puzzle. For on the single most important issue of all—unemployment—Labour was the preferred party, by 16 percentage points. Moreover, references to unemployment as an influential issue were more frequent among new electors and semi- and unskilled manual workers, who swung strongly to the Conservatives, than among the over-65s and the professions and management, who did not. How, then, did Labour manage to lose so badly?

First, the Conservatives' advantage on their own best issues of defense (+54 percentage points) and prices (+40 percentage points) was much more decisive than Labour's advantage on "its" issue of unemployment. The Conservatives were overwhelmingly the preferred party among those concerned about defense (70 percent) or prices (61 percent) whereas among those concerned about jobs only a minority (43 percent) preferred Labour. Even in households that suffered unemployment during the Thatcher government under half (45 percent) regarded Labour as the best party for the problem.

Second, an election result arises from changes in the distribution of opinion and votes from one election to another. Such changes cannot be explained by issue data limited to one election. We require parallel data from the 1979 campaign to see how the relative importance of issues, and the electors' party preferences on each, shifted between that election and 1983. An issue could produce a swing to the Conservatives in either or both of two ways: first, if support for the Conservatives on the issue had grown, and second, if, in cases where the Conservatives were already the preferred party, the importance of the issue had grown.

Analysis of these changes shows why the electoral benefits to Labour from the issue of jobs was limited. The lengthening of the dole queues made more people put unemployment at the top of the agenda, but no more people than before were convinced that Labour would be better than the Conservatives at shortening the lines. In 1979 Labour's edge over the Conservatives as the party for jobs was 15 percent; after a tripling of unemployment in four years of Conservative government, its edge was 16 percent. The issue only half worked for Labour. It damaged the Conservative vote without doing much to repair Labour's; at best it prevented Labour's disaster from turning into a catastrophe.

Two other issues were ranked lower in importance yet made a bigger impact, compensating the Conservatives for what they lost on jobs. Defense is

Table 7.12   The issues that mattered, 1983

	Total	Change from 1979	Con. loyalists	Con. defectors	Lab. loyalists	Lab. defectors
		(Percentage mentioning an issue as one of the two most important in influencing their vote)				
Unemployment	72	+45	54	73	84	75
Defense	38	+36	46	41	33	42
Prices	20	−22	27	15	15	13
NHS/hospitals	11	+7	4	12	20	16
Pensions	8	+1	4	7	14	10
Education	6	−2	6	11	4	9
EEC	5	+1	7	4	2	9

the prime example. In 1979 only 2 percent said it influenced their vote; in 1983 38 percent did. Among the latter the Conservatives were preferred to Labour as the defense party by a huge 54 percentage points.[20] The campaign polls reported a mounting public rejection of (and puzzlement about) Labour's defense policies. A large majority opposed the unilateral renunciation of Britain's Polaris fleet in particular and of nuclear weapons in general, which appeared to be Labour party policy and were certainly Michael Foot's. And, in a reversal of earlier opinion, small majorities supported the government's intention to install NATO cruise missiles and purchase the Trident missile system, to which Labour was strenuously opposed.[21]

The other helpful issue for the Conservatives was prices. Its electoral impact has been underestimated by commentators because it dropped from first to third place in importance between 1979 and 1983, with only half as many (20 percent as against 42 percent) mentioning it as an influence on their vote. However, in 1979 Labour had a 13 percentage point edge as the party for low prices whereas by 1983 there had been a sharp turnaround and the Conservatives were preferred by 40 percentage points. The net impact was a potential swing to the Conservatives of 6 to 7 percent.[22] Contrary to the cynics, the government's reward for bringing down the rate of inflation was not apathy or public amnesia, but moderate gratitude.

On almost every other issue—education, the EEC, peace, crime, taxes, strikes, and prosperity—the Conservatives were the first choice, usually by a wide margin. The one exception was the NHS—on which Labour led the Conservatives by a commanding 46 percent—an issue that grew in prominence for voters as the campaign progressed.[23] However, even by election day it was something that consciously affected only one voter in ten; the scope for Labour gains was therefore limited. Had the Labour campaign devoted more time to attacking

Party preference on issue (among those citing it as important)	
1983	1979
Lab. +16	Lab. +15
Con. +54	n.a.
Con. +40	Lab. +13
Lab. +46	n.a.
Lab. +5[a]	Lab. +55
Con. +10[b]	n.a.
Con. +50	Lab. +8

Sources: (a) NOP poll, 16–17 May 1983, reported in National Opinion Polls, *Political Social Economic Review*, no. 42 (June 1983), p. 22; (b) MORI panel survey, 1–3 June 1983, reported in MORI, *British Public Opinion, General Election 1983, Final Report*, p. 120: For these two issues party preferences are those of all respondents, not just those citing the issue as important. All other figures are based on BBC TV/Gallup survey, 8–9 June 1983.

Notes: Wording of question, "Think of all the urgent problems facing the country at the present time. When you decided which way to vote, which two issues did you *personally* consider most important?" (This was an open-ended question. The issues above were those most frequently mentioned). "Don't know" responses have been excluded from the percentage base for party preferences; "no difference" responses are included.

the apparent provisions for cuts in the NHS contained in the allegedly "secret manifesto" of the Conservatives, some of Labour's leaking support might have been stopped.[24]

There is a third reason for Labour's puzzling failure to profit more from the rise in unemployment. In order to deliver votes to one party rather than another, it is not enough for an issue to be important and for that party to be preferred on it, as Labour still was on unemployment. The issue also must be regarded as soluble and the party's proposals as credible. Here lay Labour's problem. Its manifesto promised to cut unemployment from 3.5 million to 1 million within the lifetime of a Labour government. The electorate was profoundly skeptical. It doubted that any government could do much in the short-term. A MORI poll revealed that a majority of respondents expected the unemployed in two years to number 3.5 million if the Conservatives were reelected, but at least 3 million if Labour won.[25] According to three separate polls only 40 percent expected unemployment to fall under a Labour government, the rest expected no change or even a rise.[26] What was in doubt was not Labour's greater concern about unemployment, but its superior ability to do much about it.

Labour's credibility on other issues was even weaker. A majority (52 percent) thought that Labour's defense policies would make Britain a less safe place; only 14 percent took this view of the Conservatives' nuclear strategy (see table 7.13). On the question of prices the Conservatives had an easy task to be convincing, because the inflation rate had already tumbled to its lowest point in fourteen years. MORI reported that 71 percent agreed that the Conservative government had kept the inflation rate down; even higher proportions expected it to remain low, or ebb further, if it was reelected.[27] By contrast the majority view (53 percent) was that prices would again rise fast if Labour won.

Table 7.13   Expectation of the effect of each party winning (in percentages)

	Con. win	Lab. win	Con.-Lab. difference
Unemployment			
substantial reduction	16	40	−24
no real difference	46	43	+3
would get worse	33	14	+19
Inflation			
rate would be lowered	31	8	+23
no real difference	42	34	+8
would rise substantially	22	53	−31
Britain's defense			
would be safer	44	16	+28
would be no more or less safe	37	26	+11
would be less safe	14	52	−38

Source: Harris Research Centre poll of Con.-Lab. and Lab.-Con. marginal constituencies commissioned by London Weekend Television. The questions about a future Labour government were asked on 25–26 May; about a future Conservative government on 3 June (different samples). *Notes:* Wording of survey questions, "Do you think that a Labour/Conservative government would reduce unemployment substantially, make no real difference to unemployment, or make unemployment worse?"; "Do you think that under a Labor/Conservative government the rate of inflation would be lowered, there would be no difference in the rate of inflation, or the rate of inflation would rise substantially?"; "Do you think that the Labour's/the Conservatives' defense policies would make Britain safer, less safe, or no more or less safe?" The small percentage of "don't know" responses are omitted from the table.

The Labour campaign badly underestimated the inflationary fears its program provoked.

On a host of secondary issues people were more fearful of the consequences of Labour as opposed to the Conservatives winning. Substantially more assumed that the income tax would be higher, the trade unions more powerful, immigrants more numerous, "law and order" less in evidence, government controls more stringent, and personal freedom more curtailed under a Labour rather than Conservative government.[28] These changes were not wanted by the majority of voters. Labour's implausibility in the eyes of voters was summed up by a general question on the economy's future. Asked which party would do better "at making Britain more prosperous," 57 percent of the BBC/Gallup respondents replied the Conservatives, only 22 percent said Labour. The link to Labour's electoral collapse was striking. Among 1979 Labour supporters as many as 42 percent did not answer Labour; of these, three in four defected to another party in 1983. Many electors continued to recognize Labour as the best protector of the unemployed and the NHS, as the party that would seek hardest to relieve the pain of the recession, but few believed it actually could end the recession.

Impact of the Party Leaders

The effect of the party leaders cannot, of course, be ignored. Immediately before the campaign a MORI poll asked respondents how they would vote if the Labour leader were Denis Healey rather than Michael Foot. In this hypothetical situation an 11 percent Conservative lead over Labour melted away to nothing.[29] Not since the war (probably much earlier) had a major party leader been regarded as so implausible a prime minister as Michael Foot. The more he appeared on television during the campaign, the more implausible he seemed. Gallup asked viewers whether his appearances increased support for the Labour party. In the first week of May the preponderance of those saying that he did not was 19 percent; by the first week of June it was 33 percent. Over the same period the majority of positive rather than negative assessments of Margaret Thatcher and David Steel grew. By election day only 13 percent picked Michael Foot as the best potential prime minister; fully 63 percent picked him as the worst (see table 7.14). Labour loyalists certainly harbored doubts: less than half (44 percent) regarded him as the best potential prime minister, as many preferring David Steel or Roy Jenkins. The contrast with 1979 hardly could have been more striking. Then almost all Labour voters (88 percent) had been happy with Jim Callaghan. For many of these 1979 Labour supporters the misgivings about Michael Foot were too hard to swallow: among Labour defectors, only 4 percent thought Foot would make the best prime minister; fully

Table 7.14 The best (and worst) person for prime minister (percentage of voters)

| | Who would make | | | Overall score among | | | |
	the best prime minister?	the worst prime minister?	Overall score (% best minus % worst)	Con. loyalists	Con. defectors	Lab. loyalists	Lab. defectors
Thatcher	46	25	+21	+86	+12	−59	−8
Foot	13	63	−50	−89	−73	+34	−54
Steel	35	2	+33	+9	+58	+34	+56
Jenkins	6	10	−4	−7	+3	−9	+6

Source: See note to table 7.3.

Note: Wording of question, "Leaving aside your general party preference, who would make the best prime minister—Margaret Thatcher, Michael Foot, David Steel, or Roy Jenkins? And who would make the worst?"

58 percent thought he would be the worst. For reasons described earlier in this book, he simply did not look the part.

Michael Foot was, to be sure, competing against a formidable opponent. The only detailed analysis of the party leaders' personal images during the campaign showed that Margaret Thatcher led the others on political virtues, and particularly qualities of leadership.[30] As someone "good in a crisis" she enjoyed a massive advantage over the others—an echo of the Falklands war—and she was also the most likely to be described as "a capable leader" and somebody with "sound judgment" who "understood domestic and world problems." But she also received the most brickbats. Many more described her than the others as somebody who "talked down to people" (54 percent applied this label) and who was "out of touch with ordinary people." The downside of her decisive leadership and strength of personality was a hectoring bossiness and distant arrogance.

Margaret Thatcher was in fact less of an asset to her party than Michael Foot was a liability to his. She was first choice as prime minister (46 percent) by a comfortable but not overwhelming majority over David Steel (35 percent)—and in the eyes of only slightly more people than voted Conservative (44 percent) or chose Callaghan (44 percent) when he went down to defeat in 1979. She aroused intense hostility, moreover, among a substantial minority: 25 percent said she would make the *worst* prime minister. Her abrasive and uncompromising style of politics made almost as many enemies as converts during the campaign. Her combined "best" and "worst" score of +21 easily surpassed Michael Foot's (−50), but did not match David Steel's (+33) who had nearly as many admirers but far fewer detractors.

By this token David Steel, not Margaret Thatcher, was the star of the campaign. In the MORI poll noted earlier almost as many praised him for political virtues, but many more perceived personal qualities such as honesty, trustworthiness, and the absence of inflexibility and narrow-mindedness in him than in Margaret Thatcher. He was not, however, the official leader of the Alliance; Roy Jenkins was, by virtue of being the Alliance's prime-minister-designate. One reason that part of Steel's popularity did not convert into Alliance votes was Roy Jenkins's lackluster campaign. It did not provoke the derision that greeted Michael Foot but it did not inspire warmth or much respect either; it left voters vaguely puzzled, mildly disappointed, or indifferent. The overall impact was fractionally negative: only 10 percent thought he would make the worst prime minister but even fewer—a tiny 6 percent—thought he would make the best. How many votes Roy Jenkins cost the Alliance is difficult to judge. A National Opinion Poll (NOP) survey in early June asked respondents if they would be more or less likely to vote for the Alliance if David Steel rather than Roy Jenkins was its prime-minister-designate: among Conservative and Labour supporters 27 percent said "more likely" and only 2 percent "less likely" (the rest said "no difference").[31] The answer "more likely," however, is not the same as actually switching. Among the 17 percent of the BBC / Gallup respondents who claimed to have seriously considered voting for the Alliance before deciding against a mere 9 percent cited Jenkins—from a set list of nine possible factors—as their reason. Among the 1979 Liberal voters who defected in 1983 only 4 percent gave Jenkins as the reason. The fact that he rather than David Steel was official leader of the Alliance probably cost it, at most, 1 to 2 percent of the vote.

The impact of the party leaders, like much else in the campaign, turned out to be largely negative. The question of who was least wanted as prime minister was especially crucial. It correlated more strongly with the vote than the choice of who would be best. The great majority of Conservatives made Margaret Thatcher their first choice (86 percent), but even more made Michael Foot their last (89 percent). Labour voters were half-loyal to Foot (44 percent) but over-whelmingly hostile to Margaret Thatcher (66 percent). More people wanted to keep another party leader out of 10 Downing Street than put their own in. More people voted against than for.

Party Images and the Impact of Thatcherism

Concentration on issues and the party leaders can overestimate their contribution to an election result by giving an exaggerated impression of specificity and clarity in the motives of voters. The fact that survey respondents answer questions about issues and party leaders does not mean that they enter the polling booths with a specific issue or leader in the forefront of their minds. For one thing, the distinction between a party's policies and its leader is not always clear-cut; it is through the leader, as the party's mouthpiece, that voters judge its past record and future proposals. In advertising terms, it is the leader who gives the party product its brand image. For another, it is not one issue but many, and not one party proposal but the whole package, that counts. What moves voters is a diffuse impression of each party's track record, policy package, and leader rolled into one—in a word, its overall "image."

The predominant images presented by the Labour party were division, "extremism," and weak leadership, each reinforcing the other. The divisions were between the "moderates" and the "extremists" and their persistence reflected Michael Foot's inability, or unwillingness, to unite his party. In the BBC / Gallup survey 33 percent of Labour defectors referred to "extremism in the Labour party" and 25 percent to "disunity" as one of their reasons. Among the smaller number of Conservative defectors, references to Conservative "extremism" and "disunity" were made by only 17 percent and 6 percent respectively. Among late deciders for the Conservatives or the Alliance 38 percent mentioned Labour extremism, 20 percent Labour disunity, as one of the decided factors.

The Labour party's four weeks of campaign shambles—and four years of civil war—had left their mark.

General impressions rather than precise motives helped the Conservatives as much as they hurt Labour. A prominent election poster declared, "Britain Is on the Right Track. Don't Turn Back. Vote Conservative." It hit a popular nerve. Asked to explain their vote, only a third of Conservative voters (34 percent) said it was because of "something in particular they liked"; twice as many (66 percent) said "they saw no need for a change of government." General as opposed to specific factors also accounted for the majority of Conservative recruits and late deciders. Four years earlier the proportion of Labour voters giving the continuation of the Labour government as the reason for their vote had been smaller (52 percent). What was it about Thatcher's government that persuaded so many voters that it was "on the right track?"

The obvious answer is "Thatcherism." But what is Thatcherism? How does it differ from ordinary Conservatism? Thatcher's wing of the party has long been at pains to distance itself from the Conservatism of Butler, Macmillan, and, above all, Heath. Yet neither the manifesto nor the achievements of Thatcher's first government deviated significantly from the staple fare of postwar Conservatism.[32] What distinguishes Thatcherites is not the substance of their government, in fact, but the style of their governing. It is partly a matter of language. In support of established Conservative values they are self-assured, aggressive, and explicit where their predecessors were hesitant, defensive, and mealy-mouthed. It is also a matter of the role of government. Thatcherism stands for the contraction of the state, for the reduction of its responsibilities and its withdrawal from entanglements with organized interests. It stresses the limits of the state's resources, wisdom, and proper sphere of influence. The 1979–83 government kept the CBI and TUC at arm's length and dismantled the tripartite, "corporatist" mode of decision making that had operated for most of the 1970s. Compromise and concession in relation to special interests were spurned, although the government was careful not to take on opponents, like the miners and power workers, it could not necessarily beat. The watchword was not confrontation but nonintervention. In its relations with foreign states Thatcherism displayed parallel instincts. On the one hand, a strident advocacy of Western values and denunciation of the Communist bloc, a distaste for windy internationalism, and an uncompromising nationalism in the EEC and over the Falklands; on the other, realistic concessions in situations, such as Zimbabwe and Hong Kong, where Britain could not win. The overall impression, to critics as much as sympathizers, was of no-nonsense, determined, and firm government.

There is evidence that Thatcherism as a style of government contributed to the swing to the Conservatives. The BBC/Gallup survey asked people to respond to five questions making up a "Thatcherism scale," as shown in Table

Table 7.15 Popular attitudes toward elements of "Thatcherism" (in percentages)

Question	Distribution of responses	
When dealing with political opponents, what is better—sticking firmly to one's political beliefs, or trying to meet them halfway?	Sticking to beliefs [†]	50
	Meet halfway [‡]	39
	Neither/both/don't know	11
In difficult economic times, what is better—for the government to be caring or for the government to be tough?	Tough [†]	46
	Caring [‡]	34
	Neither/both/don't know	20
When governments make decisions about the economy, what is better—to involve major interests like trade unions and business, or to keep them at arm's length?	Keep at arm's length [†]	28
	Involve [‡]	60
	Neither/both/don't know	12
It is sometimes said that no government of any party can in fact do much to create economic prosperity; that it is up to people themselves. Do you agree or disagree?	Agree [†]	48
	Disagree [‡]	37
	Neither/both/don't know	15
In its relations with the rest of the world, what is better—for Britain to stick resolutely to its own position, or for Britain to meet other countries halfway?	Stick to own position [†]	30
	Meet halfway [‡]	58
	Neither/both/don't know	12

Note: [†] Presumed "Thatcherite" response: [‡] presumed anti-Thatcherite response

Degrees of "Thatcherism"	"Thatcherism" Scores [a]	Percentage of Respondents
Very Thatcherite	+4, +5	15
Fairly Thatcherite	+1, +2, +3	26
Intermediate	0	11
Fairly anti-Thatcherite	−1, −2, −3	26
Very anti-Thatcherite	−4, −5	22

[a] Respondents were awareded a score of +1 for each Thatcherite response, 0 for each neutral response, and −1 for each anti-Thatcherite response.
Source: BBC TV/Gallup surveys of 8, 9 June 1983.

7.15. The British electorate was not overwhelmingly Thatcherite. On three of the five questions, the Thatcherite response came out ahead, but not by much. On the other two, dealing with relations with organized interests and with foreign powers, the public strongly rejected the Thatcherite position. On the five questions combined, the figures show that anti-Thatcherites (48 percent) slightly outnumbered Thatcherites (41 percent), whose size was similar to the Conservative vote. However, the two groups were not synonymous: 30 percent of Conservative voters were anti-Thatcherite and 36 percent of Thatcherites did not vote Conservative. The significance of Thatcherism lay in its relation

Table 7.16   Thatcherism and vote switching, 1979–83 (in percentages)

	Thatcherite		Inter-	Anti-Thatcherite	
	Very	Fairly	mediate	Fairly	Very
Voted Conservative in 1979 and					
stayed Con. in 1983	95	88	86	74	59
defected to All.	5	9	14	19	29
defected to Lab.	—	3	—	7	12
$N =$	411	496	156	357	151
Voted Labour in 1979 and					
stayed in Lab. in 1983	53	65	69	65	75
defected to All.	18	20	19	29	24
defected to Con.	29	15	12	6	1
$N =$	75	254	143	348	462
Voted Liberal in 1979 and					
stayed All. in 1983	78	79	67	74	80
defected to Con.	20	20	—	9	9
defected to Lab.	1	2	33	14	11
$N =$	44	77	36	92	94

Source: See note to table 7.3. The wording of the question is given in the text.

to vote switching between 1979 and 1983 (see table 7.16). For example, only 5 percent of very Thatcherite ex-Conservatives defected, all to the Alliance, whereas 41 percent of the very anti-Thatcherite ex-Conservatives (a one-in-ten minority) switched, including 12 percent who bucked the national trend and moved across to Labour. The equivalent pattern occurred among Labour's 1979 supporters, but with greater impact. Most were anti-Thatcherite (63 percent) and of these 29 percent defected, almost all to the Alliance. A quarter were Thatcherites and of these 38 percent defected. Among the small minority who were very Thatcherite, 47 percent changed sides, the majority moving directly to the Conservatives.

Such was the effect of Thatcherism. Whether it reflected no more than the extraordinary but short-lived events of the preceding year or signified a more profound change in the electorate's outlook is discussed in the concluding section.

From Explanation to Interpretation

The Conservative victory was undoubtedly a landslide. But was it more, namely a "realignment" of the British party system? The word "realignment" is becoming overworked. After every decisive election, commentators diagnose a potential realignment. When first used by V. O. Key,[33] the term signified more than a big win and relied on more than the evidence of a single election. It meant, first, a switch of party loyalties, not simply party support, a switch that might last for a generation. Second, it meant a change precipitated by more than an appraisal of the administration's record but by a transformation in the social structure, in the parties' broad positions, and in the relationship between the two. Third, it meant a marked shift not only of voting patterns but in the balance of power among groups and interests and in the intellectual climate surrounding the conduct and discussion of public affairs. A truly realigning election crystallizes a structural change in the mass basis of the political order, much as an earthquake is both cause and effect of a geological shift in the landscape.

Genuine partisan realignments, are, in fact, just about as rare as major earthquakes. Even election landslides usually represent no more than a marked but strictly short-term preference for one party over the other. Nonetheless, the prima facie grounds for believing that the 1983 result betokens a seismic change in British politics is quite strong. Setting aside the margin of victory, proponents of this view make three points.

First, the Conservatives were reelected, not newly elected. In Britain reelection is rare even in normal times; in the midst of deep recession, and in contrast to the electoral defeats of governments elsewhere, it is extraordinary. This argument is in line with recent revisionist analyses of American party realignments,[34] which stress the importance of the period shortly *after* the newly favored party first takes power. It is in this period that an administration can convert a potential realignment into a permanent realignment by delivering the goods, symbolic as well as material, to its new supporters. The test of its success, the evidence for a true realignment, therefore rests on the subsequent election. Without Roosevelt's reendorsement in 1936, the 1932 election would have been described as "deviating" rather than "realigning." As 1936 stands to 1932 in the United States so, it is claimed, 1983 stands to 1979 in Britain.

Those discerning a realignment emphasize next the crucial role of Prime Minister Thatcher. Realignments require skillful and determined leadership. Thatcher personifies the realignment in Britain as Roosevelt did in the United States and de Gaulle in the Fifth Republic. Here a number of claims are being made. One is that her popularity is exceptional, not only in its magnitude, but in its national rather than partisan appeal. She is, it is argued, in tune with the popular mood, indeed she has resurrected a national spirit, in a way that no preceding prime minister since Churchill has managed. A second claim is that Thatcher is unusual for being a politician of conviction and principle rather than consensus and pragmatism. She appeals to people's values, not their interests. She does not trim or dissemble her views to curry popular favor; she leads rather than follows public opinion.

Third, realignments are precipitated by special events as well as by special leaders, notably crises whose impact on the electorate is unusually deep and wide, but which are resolved by resourceful leadership. The Falklands war, and its handling by Thatcher, it is claimed, constituted just such an event. Finally, Thatcher's first administration transformed the balance of power and cultural climate. Power shifted from pressure groups to government, from local to central government, and, above all, from labor to management (the latter as a result of mass unemployment and the reduction in the rights and legal immunities of trade unions). The old postwar consensus was replaced by a new one in which the common ground of political debate moved sharply to the right. Common assumptions and the political atmosphere changed from collective provision to individual self-reliance, from permissive to traditional morals, from middle-class guilt to bourgeois confidence, from national self-doubt to national self-respect, and from pessimism to optimism. Unlike established Conservatism, Thatcherism sought more than the reelection of Conservative governments. It sought—and achieved—a partisan realignment in the fullest sense of the term.

The case for realignment is plausible but the evidence is patchy. This chapter already has recorded that the Conservative vote share in 1983 was small by historical standards and actually lower than in 1979; that the victory owed more to Labour's weaknesses than to the Conservatives' attractions; that Thatcher, although overwhelmingly preferred to Foot, was by no means exceptionally popular by past standards; and that her party's triumph was a landslide by default. To these findings we can add further counterevidence.

First, the electorate did not move to the right between 1979 and 1983. Support for the main planks of the Conservative party's distinctive economic strategy, on which it campaigned in 1979, fell back in the period up to 1983 (see table 7.17). Some of these policies, it is true, continued to receive strong endorsement. The implementation of further laws to regulate trade union activities was supported by 72 percent, but this was a drop from 81 percent in 1979. Sixty-one percent preferred the private sector to central government as a means of tackling unemployment, but this too is a fall from 75 percent in 1979. Approval of tax cuts when they lead to poorer public services always has been low. In 1979 only 29 percent supported the idea but by 1983 the figure had fallen to 20 percent. Keynes might be out of fashion, but Beveridge is not.

Skepticism about a realignment is reinforced by the trend in the single best indicator of long-term party allegiance: party identification (see table 7.18). The proportion identifying themselves as Conservative in 1983 was identical to that in 1979 (38 percent) and, for that matter, to the proportion when measurements were first taken in 1964; it has always been confined to the 35 to 40 percent range. The only particle of evidence in support of realignment is the small rise in the proportion of "very strong" Conservative identifiers (from 9 to 13 per-

Table 7.17 Attitudes toward Conservative positions (in percentages)

Question: "Which of these two statements comes closest to your view: there should be stricter laws to regulate the activities of trade unions; there is no call for stricter laws to regulate the activites of trade unions."

	1979	1983
There should be stricter laws	81	72
There is no call for stricter laws	19	28
Neither / both / don't know	5	8

Question: "Which of these two statements comes closest to your view: the best way to tackle unemployment is to allow private companies to keep more of their profits to create more jobs; it is mainly up to the government to tackle unemployment by using tax money to create jobs."

	1979	1983
Leave it to private companies	75	61
Up to the government	25	39

Question: "Which of these two statements comes closest to your view: cut taxes, even if it means some reduction in government sevices like health, education, and welfare; keep up government services like health, education, and welfare even if it means that taxes cannot be cut."

	1979	1983
Cut taxes	29	20
Maintain government services	71	80

Sources: BBC TV / Gallup surveys of 8–9 June 1983 and 2–3 May 1979, and British Election Study, 1979, for 1979 data on the first two questions.
Note: Respondents answering "neither," "both," and "don't know have been omitted from the percentage base.

cent), a sign perhaps of the enthusiasm engendered in committed Conservatives by Thatcher's brand of government.[35]

Even if the case for realignment remains not proven, the 1983 result has important implications for the Conservative party's future prospects. It has punctured the myth that high rates of unemployment inevitably do electoral damage to the presiding government. Believers in this myth should have known better; after all, the interwar years of the depression were dominated by Conservative governments. It is worth reflecting on some of the reasons—other than Labour's apparently unconvincing approach to the problem—for the failure of unemployment to make an electoral impact.

First, in 1983 the unemployed, even though at unprecedented numbers, remained a small minority: 14 percent of the labor force but only 9 percent of the electorate. The vast majority of British electors are not unemployed. Those in jobs, moreover, saw their living standards rise, albeit modestly: between 1979

Table 7.18   Conservative and Labour party
identification, 1964–83 (in percentages)

	1964	1966	1970	1974[a]	1979	1983
Voters identifying with						
Conservative party	38	35	40	35	38	38
Labour party	43	46	42	40	38	32
Conservatives only						
Very strong identifiers	48	49	50	29	23	34
Fairly strong identifiers	41	39	40	50	53	43
Not very strong identifiers	11	12	10	21	24	23
Labour only						
Very strong identifiers	45	50	47	37	27	32
Fairly strong identifiers	43	41	40	44	50	39
Not very strong identifiers	12	9	13	19	23	29

Sources: 1964, 1966, and 1970: election surveys conducted by David Butler and Donald Stokes
for *Political Change in Britain*, 2d ed.; 1974 and 1979: British Election Studies; 1983: BBC TV /
Gallup survey, 8–9 June 1983.
Note: The figures include respondents who at first said they had no party identification but who,
in answer to a supplementary question, said they were "a little closer" to one or the other party.
[a] The average of the February 1974 and October 1974 figures.

and 1983 real average earnings rose by 4 to 5 percent.[36] Other economic problems directly affect many more people than the unemployed minority. Income
tax is paid by about 60 percent of households and price rises impinge on
everybody. It is therefore in the interests of most electors, including working-
class electors, to give higher priority to stable prices and taxes than to full
employment.

Moreover, only a third of the officially unemployed have been without a job
for over a year.[37] Most of the rest are more accurately described as in transition
between jobs, the period of transition being much longer, more painful, and
involving more people than in the 1970s. In the BBC / Gallup survey 39 percent
of respondents declared that they or a member of their family had been unemployed at some time since 1979, but most were back at work. The sheer
normality of their voting patterns and opinions suggests that the experience
had not left a deep political scar.

Second, the trend in unemployment appears to have stronger electoral re-
percussions than the actual level. Altruists fret over the absolute figures; most
people worry about what they see around them. When unemployment rose
rapidly in 1980 and burst through the 2 million barrier, Conservative support
plummeted in the opinion polls. One reason was that rising unemployment

largely arose from the shedding of labor—factory closures, redundancies, etc. —and was therefore highly visible. When unemployment drifted up to 3 million in 1981–82 there was little change in the government's popularity, partly because the trend was gentler, but also because more of the increase resulted from the entry of school-leavers into the labor market, which is less visible. It is even possible that survival through 1980 made those in jobs feel safer in 1983 than they did three years earlier, when unemployment was a million less.

Third, the typical outlook of the unemployed has been resigned skepticism rather than organized anger, cynicism about politics in general rather than hostility to the government in particular. For every unemployed person on a March for Jobs there are many more at home watching television. A fall 1982 survey of the unemployed found that only 24 percent put the main blame on the government, whereas 47 percent blamed "nobody" or the "world economy," and another 14 percent "politicians generally."[38] One reflection of these attitudes is the below-average electoral turnout of the jobless, especially the young.[39]

The unemployed not only turn out less, they are also less likely to be on the electoral register. A recent study of London found that 14 percent of those working were not registered to vote even though eligible. Among the unemployed, however, the proportion was 30 percent, and among those under thirty without a job as high as 47 percent.[40] Finally, the unemployed who can and do vote are concentrated in safe Labour seats such that a marked anti-Conservative swing would have little effect on the parties' strength at Westminster. Of the fifty seats with the worst unemployment rates in 1983, forty-eight returned Labour MPs, with an average majority of 26 percent.[41] For all these reasons current levels of unemployment—even higher levels—constitute much less of an electoral threat to the Conservatives than was ever anticipated when they came to power.

A party realignment in favor of the Conservatives has probably not occurred. This does not preclude major transformations of a different kind. Our ideas about party realignments are influenced heavily by the American cases of 1896 and 1932 that took place in the unusual circumstances of only two parties competing in an electorate regularly injected with newly enfranchised, or at least newly politicized, citizens. Britain in the 1980s, however, has a multiparty system and a slowly growing electorate with much less scope for major and sudden changes in the electorate's allegiance. We therefore have to examine the possibility of a gradual realignment cumulating over a series of elections rather than in spurting in one. We also have to consider two other possible realignments. One is a realignment toward the center, the other a realignment away from the left.

The history of past Liberal "revivals" inevitably colors interpretations of the Alliance's achievement in 1983. Since the late 1950s each Conservative government has been accompanied by a midterm Liberal boom, only to be followed by a slump at the general election and collapse under Labour administrations. This cycle of surge and decline generally is explained in terms of the "softness" and "shallowness" of the Liberal vote. By and large Liberal voters in the past have been Conservative and Labour renegades, not committed partisans, who returned to their home base after a single protest vote. The postwar Liberal party has failed to secure a distinctive social base or to benefit from new issue conflicts or social cleavages that cut across existing partisan divisions. Its appeal has been negative and diffuse rather than positive and specific, based on its leadership, style, and sheer novelty rather than on its policies or ideology.[42]

Analysis of the SDP's initial rush of support concluded that in structure and motivation it closely resembled the Liberal vote of earlier years.[43] The SDP did not carve out a new social and ideological constituency but instead attracted part of the large, volatile, potential Liberal vote that has existed in Britain for many years. To assess the prospects for a realignment toward the center we therefore need to know whether the Alliance's vote in the 1983 election was as fragile as Liberal support in previous elections or whether it had firmed up.

This chapter already has noted that the Alliance drew its vote from across the social spectrum rather than from one particular social group. Table 7.19 shows that the Alliance's support was less rootedly partisan than the Conservative or Labour vote. Very strong identifiers with the Liberal party, the SDP, or the Alliance together added up to 16 percent, much less than its 26 percent share of the national vote, suggesting that it continued to rely on a substantial "protest vote." The 16 percent proportion of very strong identifiers, moreover, was barely higher than that for Liberal identifiers in 1979 (14 percent) or in the two 1974 elections (15 percent): underlying and enduring allegiance to the center had not grown. Indeed, only half (51 percent) of the Alliance's voters actually identified with it, or one of its component parties, and 38 percent thought of themselves as Conservative or Labour. Among the half identifying with the Alliance, partisanship was much weaker than among their Conservative and Labour counterparts. Like the Liberal party before it, the Alliance is acutely vulnerable to substantial defections back to the major parties by the time of the next election.

Table 7.19 also reveals that policy-based and interest-based loyalty was weaker among Alliance than major party voters. Ninety-three percent of Conservative voters and 83 percent of Labour voters said their own party had the best policies overall; among Alliance voters the proportion was 77 percent. Eighty-six percent of Conservative voters and 88 percent of Labour voters said their own party was "best for people like me"; among Alliance voters the proportion was 68 percent.

Had the Alliance engendered more partisanship among its sympathizers it might have polled more of its potential support. As it was, it suffered from third-party squeeze, like the Liberals in earlier elections. Fifty-eight percent

Table 7.19   Strength of the parties' vote

	Vote in 1983		
	Con.	Lab.	All.
Percentage who			
identified with party voted for in 1983	80	85	51
Proportion of identifiers who were			
very strong identifiers	37	35	16
fairly strong identifiers	44	41	55
not very strong identifiers	19	25	29
said their own party			
had the best policy	93	83	77
had the best team of leaders	94	61	69
was best for "people like me"	86	88	68
decided which way to vote			
in final few days	4	6	17
during campaign	14	16	44

Source: See note to table 7.3.

of putative Alliance voters—respondents claiming that they had at one time seriously considered voting for the Alliance—explained their decision not to in strategic terms: the Alliance could not win, and a vote for it would only let the Conservatives or (mentioned twice as often) Labour in (see table 7.20). Vulnerability to adverse tactical voting will continue until the Alliance establishes itself as Britain's second party. On the survey evidence available it has some way to go before attaining that status.

None of this proves that the Alliance's spectacular successes in 1981–82 and more modest advance in 1983 will be as transient as previous Liberal revivals. For one thing, the Alliance's support in 1983, although less durable than that for the Conservative and Labour parties, was undoubtedly much firmer than in February 1974, the previous occasion of a Liberal surge. For example, in February 1974 there was not a single issue on which the Liberal party was the most preferred party *among Liberal voters*: not even one in four could be mustered to pick the Liberal party as best for any of the eight issues.[44] By contrast in 1983 the Alliance was the most preferred party among its voters on all ten of the issues on which they were questioned. For another thing, the past cycle of Liberal support has moved along an upward spiral. Each successive Liberal peak since the late 1950s has reached higher, lasted longer, and subsided less than its predecessor. The postelection monthly polls, in which support for the Alliance has fallen back to 18 to 20 percent, confirm that pattern: the spring-

Table 7.20 Why the Alliance did not do better

Reason for not voting for the Alliance	Almost voted Alliance[a] (%)
Obvious that Alliance could not win	31
Would have let Labour in	18
Would have let the Conservatives in	9
Roy Jenkins	9
Lack of clear policies	16
Might have voted Liberal, but disliked SDP	8
Might have voted SDP, but disliked Liberals	4
Saw no reason for change from usual party	15
None of these reasons	16

Source: See note to table 7.3.
Notes: Wording of questions "In the last two years have you at any time actually voted, or seriously considered voting, for the Liberal/SDP Alliance?" *If yes but voted for party other than Lib/SDP*, "Which of the reasons on this card explain why, in the end, you decided not to vote for the Liberal/SDP Alliance—you should mention all the reasons that apply." Percentages total to more than 100 because multiple responses were allowed.
[a] "Yes" respondents to first survey question, that is, those who seriously considered voting for the Alliance but did not (16 percent of voters).

board for the next leap in the center's support under a Conservative government is higher now than at any time since the war.[45]

We turn finally to the third possibility, a realignment at Labour's expense. Once again, emphatic pronouncements on the basis of the 1983 election alone —dramatically bad as it was for Labour—would be premature. Labour's dismal performance was due in large part to strictly short-term factors that already have been described: in the eyes of the electorate the Conservatives were the preferred party on most issues; Labour's economic plans were not credible; Michael Foot was the least plausible candidate for prime minister in half a century; and Labour's campaign disintegrated into division and confusion, reviving barely faded memories of its internal battles over the previous four years. The 1983 election was probably the first since 1931 in which all the short-term electoral forces let loose by a campaign combined to push voters in the same direction: away from Labour. Such unusual misfortune is unlikely to strike twice in succession.[46]

The impact of these short-lived factors is underscored by the fact that Labour's vote of 28 percent fell well below its showing on indicators of long-term support. Even in 1983, 33 percent chose Labour as "best for people like me" and 38 percent identified with the Labour party (and these figures will have been depressed by the circumstances of the election). This level of long-term allegiance is close to Labour's support in the week preceding the campaign (when it averaged 34 percent in five polls) and in the local elections of 5

May (35 percent)[47] when its defense policies and Michael Foot's leadership were less relevant to the vote. Labour's recent recovery in the polls, which can be dated precisely to October 1983 when Neil Kinnock replaced Michael Foot as leader, corroborates the view that Labour's "natural" vote is much higher than its June 1983 level and probably within the 35 to 40 percent range.[48]

Nevertheless, the unusually adverse circumstances of the 1983 election reinforced longer-term forces that gradually have moved against Labour in the past thirty years. Since 1951, when the Labour vote reached its peak in this century, Labour's share of the electorate has halved, from 40.3 percent to 20.1 percent, falling in eight of the nine subsequent elections, including each of the last five. Its share of the United Kingdom (U.K.) vote has stayed below 40 percent and its share of the U.K. electorate below 30 percent at each election since 1970. Identification with the Labour party has been reduced in tandem. Since 1964, the first election at which survey measures were taken, the proportion of respondents identifying with Labour has dropped from 43 percent to 32 percent and the proportion identifying very strongly with Labour from 19 percent to 10 percent.[49] Levels of identification with the Conservative party are unchanged and in 1983, for the first time, there were more Conservative than Labour identifiers in the electorate (see table 7.18).

Nothing about a trend, of course, guarantees its continuation. Throughout this century parliamentary landslides at one election have been reversed at the next. The Conservatives' crushing majority of 209 in 1924 was followed by a Labour government in 1929. In 1964 Harold Wilson converted a Conservative majority of 100 into a Labour majority of five. Indeed, reversals are the norm: only once this century, in 1935, has a single-party government with a 100+ majority been reendorsed with a workable majority at the following election.

This is Labour's one crumb of comfort in the grim electoral arithmetic of recovery. To obtain a workable overall majority of twenty or more, Labour needs to gain 127 additional seats. It only came second to the Conservatives in 127 seats altogether (and to the Alliance or the Nationalists in another five). The national swing required would be 11.5 percent (assuming that Labour would gain some seats where it came a close third in 1983). Not since 1945 has any party secured a swing of anything approaching that magnitude at a single election—and the electoral situation of 1945 was quite exceptional.[50] Since 1945 the record swing at any one election is 5.2 percent which, even if repeated in Labour's favor in 1987–88, would be insufficient to deprive the Conservatives of their overall majority, let alone give Labour one.

The task of recovery for Labour will be made more Herculean than the bare statistics suggest by a number of unfavorable electoral and sociodemographic trends. The number of marginal seats is declining, through class-related patterns of mobility and the tendency for third parties to prosper at the expense of the weaker of the two parties, so that ever-increasing swings are needed to turn over the same number of seats.[51] Evidence of a small but clear "incumbency advantage," especially for newly elected MPs seeking their first reelection (of whom there will be many Conservatives in 1987–88), is growing.[52] The inexorable migration from north to south, town to country, and inner city to suburb will continue to move electors from Labour to non-Labour milieux. Through medical advance and the drop in the 1960s birthrate the electorate will age. The spread of owner occupation, through tenants' purchase of their council houses among other means, will widen. The public sector will contract further as the government implements its plans for privatization. Trade union membership will go on declining, especially among manual workers, as a result of unemployment, earlier retirement, and a shift in the economic base from strongly unionized heavy manufacturing to a lightly unionized service sector. The class ratio will proceed to tilt toward nonmanual workers. Moreover, the number of "mixed class" households, typically consisting of a blue-collar husband and "white blouse" wife, will rise at the expense of the wholly working-class household as increasing numbers of women enter the nonmanual labor force.[53]

None of these electoral and social trends make Labour's decline irreversible or completely rule out a Labour government in the late 1980s, but all of them make a Labour recovery more difficult. Even if the political water gets less choppy Labour will be sailing against the current. Favorable winds, a united crew, skillful navigation, and a popular captain could still deliver the party to the port of government. However, if Labour stays half-submerged, or sinks altogether, future historians will point to the 1983 election, and the storms preceding it, as the point at which the party became unsalvageable.

Appendix

Results of the British general election,
9 June 1983

Region	Total	Conservative	Labour	Alliance	Other[b]
England[a]	25,472,922	11,711,980	6,862,622	6,714,908	183,412
Percentage		46	26.9	26.4	0.7
Seats	523	362	148	13	0
London—Outer	2,352,068	1,120,377	604,258	601,815	25,618
Percentage		47.6	25.7	25.6	1.1
Seats	55	44	11	0	0
London—Inner	1,105,717	396,777	427,177	251,517	30,246
Percentage		35.9	38.6	22.7	2.7
Seats	29	12	15	2	0
South Eastern	2,133,602	1,220,321	301,162	593,547	18,572
Percentage		57.2	14.1	27.8	0.9
Seats	42	42	0	0	0
Southern and Wessex	2,494,173	1,359,084	357,301	760,753	17,035
Percentage		54.5	14.3	30.5	0.7
Seats	47	46	0	1	0
South Western	1,886,110	947,409	291,913	634,666	12,122
Percentage		50.2	15.5	33.6	0.6
Seats	36	32	1	3	0
Eastern	2,709,172	1,384,958	530,401	782,922	10,891
Percentage		51.1	19.6	28.9	0.4
Seats	51	48	2	1	0
East Midlands	2,148,394	1,013,406	600,624	517,098	17,266
Percentage		47.2	28	24.1	0.8
Seats	42	34	8	0	0
Midlands	2,804,356	1,261,738	874,172	655,982	12,464
Percentage		45	31.2	23.4	0.4
Seats	58	36	22	0	0

Region	Total	Conservative	Labour	Alliance	Other[b]
North Western	3,516,999	1,405,468	1,266,111	822,241	23,179
Percentage		40	36	23.4	0.7
Seats	73	36	35	2	0
Yorkshire and Humberside	2,621,685	1,013,315	925,483	669,375	13,512
Percentage		38.7	35.3	25.5	0.5
Seats	54	24	28	2	0
Northern	1,700,646	589,127	684,020	424,992	2,507
Percentage		34.6	40.2	25	0.1
Seats	36	8	26	2	0
Scotland	2,824,118	801,312	990,644	692,367	339,795
Percentage		28.4	35.1	24.5	12
Seats	72	21	41	8	2
South Western	711,396	184,777	304,747	160,014	61,858
Percentage		26	42.8	22.5	8.7
Seats	17	4	13	0	0
Central	504,165	127,375	199,161	118,049	59,580
Percentage		25.3	39.5	23.4	11.8
Seats	13	2	11	0	0
Edinburgh and the Border	521,045	177,192	148,746	151,444	43,663
Percentage		34	28.5	29.1	8.4
Seats	13	6	5	2	0
Glasgow	399,961	75,295	207,731	84,724	32,211
Percentage		18.8	51.9	21.2	8.1
Seats	11	0	10	1	0
Northern	687,551	236,673	130,259	178,136	142,483
Percentage		34.4	18.9	25.9	20.7
Seats	18	9	2	5	2
Wales	1,608,940	499,310	603,858	373,312	132,460
Percentage		31	37.5	23.2	8.2
Seats	38	14	20	2	2
Central and Northern	635,525	230,303	165,510	153,636	86,076
Percentage		36.2	26	24.2	13.5
Seats	15	7	4	2	2
Southern	973,415	269,007	438,348	219,676	46,394
Percentage		27.6	45	22.6	4.8
Seats	23	7	16	0	0

Region	Total	Conservative	Labour	Alliance	Other[b]
Northern Ireland	764,925	0	0	0	764,925
Percentage		0	0	0	100
Seats	17	0	0	0	17
United Kingdom	30,670,905	13,012,602	8,457,124	7,780,587	1,420,592
Percentage	100	42.4	27.6	25.4	4.6
Seats	650	397	209	23	21

[a] *Constituency boundary changes between the 1979 and 1983 elections have slightly altered the boundaries of some of the regions in this table. However, these changes in regional lines are minor and the returns remain comparable.*

[b] *"Other" vote in Britain includes: 331,975 Scottish National (2 seats); 125,309 Plaid Cymru (2 seats); 198,383 Other. "Other" vote in Northern Ireland includes: 259,952 Ulster Unionist (11 seatrs); 152,749 Democratic Unionist (3 seats); 137,012 Social Democratic and Labour (1 seat); 102,701 Provisional Sinn Fein (1 seat); 61,275 Alliance; 22,861 Ulster Popular Unionist (1 seat); 28,375 Other.*

Figure A.1 Electoral map of the United Kingdom

Notes

Preface

1   Howard R. Penniman, ed., *Britain at the Polls: The Parliamentary Elections of 1974* (Washington, D.C.: American Enterprise Institute, 1975); and Howard R. Penniman, ed., *Britain at the Polls, 1979: A Study of the General Election* (Washington, D.C. and London: American Enterprise Institute, 1981).

2   See Penniman, *Britain at the Polls, 1979*, table 1.1, p. 4.

3   As we noted in the 1979 volume, "the British term 'redistribution' includes two elements distinguished in American usage: 'reapportionment,' meaning redetermining the number of seats allocated to England, Wales, Scotland, and Northern Ireland; and 'redistricting,' meaning redrawing the boundary lines of constituencies wherever required." Ibid., p. 5 n. 7.

4   Robert J. Waller, "The 1983 Boundary Commission: Policies and Effects," *Electoral Studies* 2 (December 1983), p. 195. The discussion in the text leans heavily on Waller's account.

5   See Waller, "The 1983 Boundary Commission," pp. 200–201.

6   The distribution of votes and seats in all general elections from 1900 to 1979 are presented in David Butler and Anne Sloman, eds., *British Political Facts, 1900–1979*, 5th ed. (London: Macmillan, 1980), pp. 206–10.

7   *Economist*, 19 June 1983, p. 33.

Thatcher's First Term

1   Quoted by Hugh Stephenson, *Mrs. Thatcher's First Year* (London: Jill Norman, 1980), p. 112. The distinction between warriors and healers has been applied to Thatcher by a number of writers. On the circumstances in which Thatcher became prime minister, see Anthony King, "Politics, Economics, and the Trade Unions, 1974–1979," in Howard R. Penniman, ed., *Britain at the Polls, 1979: A Study of the General Election* (Washington, D.C.: American Enterprise Institute, 1981). The quotation attributed to St. Francis is on p. 92. The two most thorough political biographies of Thatcher are Patrick Cosgrave, *Margaret Thatcher, Prime Minister* (London: Arrow Books, 1979), and Nicholas Wapshott and George Brock, *Thatcher* (London: Macdonald, 1983). Slighter but useful are Penny Junor, *Margaret Thatcher: Wife, Mother, Politician* (London: Sidgwick and Jackson, 1983), and Russell Lewis, *Margaret Thatcher: A Personal and Political Biography*, 2d ed. (London: Routledge and Kegan Paul, 1984).

2   On the 1975 leadership contest, see King, "Politics, Economics, and the Trade Unions," pp. 59–69, and the accounts in the various biographies of Thatcher.

3   Thatcher's unusual position inside the Conservative party is discussed by Peter Riddell in *The Thatcher Government* (Oxford: Martin Robertson, 1983), chaps. 1–2. Riddell's account of the evolution of government policy during Thatcher's first term has been drawn on heavily in the writing of the present chapter.

4   On her prime ministerial style, see Anthony King, "Margaret Thatcher: The Style of a Prime Minister," in Anthony King, ed., *The British Prime Minister: A Reader*, 2d ed. (London: Macmillan, forthcoming). See also Martin Burch, "Mrs. Thatcher's Approach to Leadership in Government: 1979–June 1983," *Parliamentary Affairs* 36 (Autumn 1983), pp. 399–416.

5   Stephenson, *Mrs. Thatcher's First Year*, chap. 3.

6   Details of the retail price index in the 1979–83 period are given in *The Campaign Guide 1983* (London: Conservative Research Department, 1983), p. 162. The Conservatives' *Campaign Guide*, published for each general election, is an invaluable compendium of factual information. Unless otherwise noted, all of the economic and other statistics cited in this chapter are drawn from *The Campaign Guide 1983*, esp. chap. 9, "Economic Statistics."

7   On the development of Conservative ideas on monetary policy, and also on prices and incomes policies, see Riddell, *The Thatcher Government*, chap. 2. See also King, "Politics, Economics, and the Trade Unions," pp. 62–70.

8   The importance of this shift in policy is underlined by a retired senior civil servant, Sir Leo Pliatzky, in *Getting and Spending: Public Expenditure, Employment and Inflation* (Oxford: Basil Blackwell, 1982), pp. 176–77. Pliatzky writes, "The Conservative victory in May 1979 was more than just another change of government; in terms of political and economic philosophy, it was a revolution. The first victim of this coup was the commitment to full employment."

9   The 1979 manifesto is reprinted in *The Times Guide to the House of Commons, May 1979* (London: Times Books, 1979), pp. 282–94.

10   *Times Guide to the House of Commons, May 1979*, p. 287.

11   The Conservatives' 1970 manifesto also had been, on paper, a radical document, but the Heath government between 1970 and 1974 had modified—in some cases reversed—many of the policies set out in the manifesto. "Radical" is a more appropriate label than "right-wing," the one often used in Britain, because the fact of change is as important as the direction of change and also because much of the Thatcher government's libertarianism was not right-wing in any conventional sense.

12   On the November 1980 episode, see Wapshott and Brock, *Thatcher*, p.

13   This argument is developed in more detail in King, "Margaret Thatcher: The Style of a Prime Minister."

14   Resistance to privatization from the affected trade unions had been expected but in the event did not amount to a great deal. The trade unions in general were cowed by unemployment and by the government's evident determination. In many cases, the workers either did not care whether they worked for a public or private employer or else positively preferred a private employer. Serious resistance was encountered only to the selling off of British Gas's showrooms (and the sale was in the event postponed) and to the privatization of British Telecom (which was not due to take place until 1984).

15   For the details of the government's privatization and liberalization program, see the large table in Riddell, *The Thatcher Government*, pp. 176–77.

16   Heath had attempted in one operation to transform the whole legal basis of industrial relations in Britain and many aspects of the trade union movement's internal government. For an account of how nearly the Heath government succeeded, but of how completely it failed in the end, see Michael Moran, *The Politics of Industrial Relations: The Origins, Life and Death of the 1971 Industrial Relations Act* (London: Macmillan, 1977). The lessons that the Conservatives under Thatcher learned from this episode are described in Michael Moran, "The Conservative Party and the Trade Unions since 1974," *Political Studies* 27 (March 1979), pp. 38–53.

17 She specialized in chemistry at Oxford, graduating in 1945. She then worked for a time as an industrial chemist before training as a tax lawyer. The government's positive initiatives in the field of industrial policy are described in Riddell, *The Thatcher Government*, chap. 8.

18 On the withdrawal of the threat to close uneconomic pits and Biffen's remark about not being a kamikaze pilot, see King, "Margaret Thatcher: The Style of a Prime Minister."

19 *The Campaign Guide 1983*, chap. 25; Riddell, *The Thatcher Government*, pp. 211–15. By the end of her first term, Thatcher was almost certainly the most disliked head of government in the European Community. She was regarded by most of her colleagues on the continent as aggressive, opinionated, and thoroughly tedious. Thatcher's admirers maintained that she was very effective nonetheless.

20 "Conservative Conference 1979," *Politics Today*, no. 16, p. 321.

21 On the idea of the ratchet, see Sir Keith Joseph, *Stranded on the Middle Ground?— Reflections on Circumstances and Policies* (London: Centre for Policy Studies, 1976).

22 Climates of opinion are hard to measure, especially since the opinions that matter most tend to be those of elites rather than those of the general public, but a survey of British elites, or a content analysis of British elite publications, almost certainly would show, for example, that almost no one outside the Labour party any longer believed that nationalized industries could, except in rare instances, be made to be more efficient than privately owned industries or that the British economy could in any meaningful sense be "planned." The thinking of most educated people in Britain was far more market-oriented in the mid-1980s than it had been five or ten years before.

23 These figures are drawn from Norman Webb and Robert Wybrow, eds., *The Gallup Report* (London: Sphere Books, 1981), pp. 167–85; and Webb and Wybrow, eds., *The Gallup Report: Your Opinions in 1981* (London: Sphere Books, 1982), pp. 191–92. In the remainder of this chapter, Gallup data relating to the period 1979–81 are drawn from these two sources unless otherwise noted.

24 The index of industrial production fell from 104.3 in 1979 (1975 = 100) to 89.4 in 1981. In the last quarter of 1980, and in three of the four quarters of 1981, real disposable income per capita was lower than it had been in the corresponding quarter of the previous year. See *The Campaign Guide 1983*, pp. 164–65.

25 The government's economic record during this period is set out in detail in Riddell, *The Thatcher Government*, chaps. 4–5. On the basis of data collected by the Organization for Economic Cooperation and Development, Riddell reckons (p. 91) that British fiscal policy between 1979 and 1982 was four times as tight as that of the average for Britain, Japan, Canada, West Germany, France, Italy, and the United States. In other words, Britain reduced its budget deficit by a far greater amount than these other countries. To the government's economic difficulties were added, in the summer of 1981, serious riots in the Toxteth district of Liverpool and the Brixton district of south London. There was almost no loss of life, but a great deal of property damage. The riots' causes remain obscure, but opposition politicians were quick to attribute them to the government's economic and social policies.

26 See the discussion in Riddell, *The Thatcher Government*, pp. 91–92.

27 Changes in the level of real spending on a variety of public services are set out in *ibid.*, p. 114.

28 No relevant data are available for the 1979–81 period. However, even after the general election, in August 1982, the Gallup Poll found that 65 percent of its respondents agreed with the statement that "the Conservatives are too rigid and inflexible," 58 percent with the statement that "the Conservatives don't care what hardships their policies cause," and 59 percent with the statement that "the Conservatives look after the interests of the rich, not ordinary people." See *Gallup Political Index*, no. 176 (August 1983), p. 7.

29 The American reader will need to know that "wet" is an English schoolboy term of abuse. Someone who is wet is feeble, timid, lacking in initiative. Thatcher or someone in her entourage began to refer to her critics as wet. They, of course, soon began to describe themselves as wet (or damp, or humid, or soggy). "Dry" was used only as the opposite of wet. The wet-dry distinction solved the problem posed by King in "Politics, Economics, and the Trade Unions," p. 74.

30 Michael Edwarde, *Back from the Brink: An Apocalyptic Experience* (London: Collins, 1983), pp. 273-74.

31 *Times*, 12 November 1980, p. 1.

32 Quoted in Michael White, "A Face-lift for Labour?" *Spectator*, 25 June 1983, p. 7.

33 *Times*, 11 October 1980, p. 1.

34 Riddell, *The Thatcher Government*, p. 44.

35 "Conservative Conference 1981," *Politics Today*, no. 20, pp. 371-72.

36 They did not have a theory as such, but some of them certainly had ideas; see, in particular, Ian Gilmour, *Britain Can Work* (Oxford: Martin Robertson, 1983). Thatcher's critics suffered from the fact that in the British system of government—as in almost every other—it is virtually impossible for a minister not involved in the making of policy in a specific field either to develop ideas in that field or, if he or she has developed ideas, to impose them on reluctant colleagues. The wets in the cabinet were very busy and, apart from the cabinet itself, they lacked forums in which they could have any real impact on economic policy. They could criticize, sometimes effectively, but they could not change the central direction in which the government was moving.

37 The prime minister dismissed only members of the cabinet who she calculated would not cause trouble on the back benches. Gilmour made veiled attacks on the drys while still a minister; out of the government, he made less veiled attacks and wrote the book referred to in fn. 36 of this chapter. However, he was not temperamentally suited to being the leader of an organized oppositional faction.

38 *Times*, 19 June 1981, p. 12.

39 *Economist*, 10 October 1981, p. 21.

40 This is, of course, a simplified account. The complexity of the Labour party's internal affairs is conveyed more fully in Lewis Minkin, *The Labour Party Conference: A Study in the Politics of Intra-party Democracy* (London: Allen Lane, 1978); Dennis Kavanagh, ed., *The Politics of the Labour Party* (London: George Allen and Unwin, 1982); and Geoff Hodgson, *Labour at the Crossroads: The Political and Economic Challenge to the Labour Party in the 1980s* (Oxford: Martin Robertson, 1981). There is no ideal terminology for referring to the various factions in the party. "Left-wing" is reasonably satisfactory, but "moderate" and "right-wing" in the text should be taken to mean little more than "not left-wing." Many moderates and right-wingers in the Labour party are not happy to be described in these terms. "Moderate" suggests that they have no passion, "right-wing" that they are Conservatives (or, at any rate, conservatives) in disguise.

41 This phrase first was used in *Labour's Programme for Britain* (London: Labour Party, 1973) and was then repeated in almost every important statement of Labour policy throughout the following decade.

42 There is not space here to catalog the discrepancies between Labour's 1974 election manifesto and the actions of the subsequent Labour government, but see Hodgson, *Labour at the Crossroads*, chap. 6, and David Coates, *Labour in Power?—A Study of the Labour Government 1974-1979* (London: Longman, 1980).

43 Almost the only people who did take the trouble to find out were David Kogan and Maurice Kogan. See their account, *The Battle for the Labour Party* (London: Kogan Page, 1982),

essential to an understanding of the developments taking place at the grassroots of the Labour party during this period.

44 This conclusion, if correct, has important political implications. If the changes that have taken place in the party are the work of ultraleft, undemocratic, "infiltrators," then someone who objects to the changes can, in principle at least, identify the infiltrators, isolate them, and expel them. All that is required is some kind of surgical operation. If, however, the changes are the work of the majority of active party members, then the task facing someone who wants to reverse them becomes much more formidable. Two books that tend to support the conclusion offered here, in addition to Kogan and Kogan, *Battle for the Labour Party*, are Hugh Jenkins, *Rank and File* (London: Croom Helm, 1980); and Peter Tatchell, *The Battle for Bermondsey* (London: Heretic Books, 1983). Reams have been written about the connections between the Labour party and the extreme left; see, among many other things, Stephen Haseler, *The Tragedy of Labour* (Oxford: Basil Blackwell, 1980); David Webster, "The Labour Party and the New Left," Fabian Tract 477 (London: Fabian Society, 1981); John Tomlinson, *Left, Right: The March of Political Extremism in Britain* (London: John Calder, 1981); Blake Baker, *The Far Left: An Exposé of the Extreme Left in Britain* (London: Weidenfeld and Nicolson, 1981); and Peter Shipley, *The Militant Tendency: Trotskyism in the Labour Party* (Richmond, Surrey: Foreign Affairs Publishing, 1983).

45 The document is referred to in fn. 41 above. On its genesis and reception, see Michael Hatfield, *The House the Left Built: Inside Labour Policy Making 1970-75* (London: Gollancz, 1978).

46 *Labour's Plan: The New Hope for Britain* (London: Labour Party, 1983).

47 The 1983 document emerged a few weeks after it was first published as Labour's 1983 election manifesto. Only the wording of the party leader's foreword had changed significantly. *New Hope for Britain* quickly was dubbed, by Margaret Thatcher, "No Hope for Britain" and, by its critics on the right wing of the Labour party, "the longest suicide note in history." See also chap. 3 of this book.

48 The history of mandatory reselection is recounted in Alison Young, *The Reselection of M.P.s* (London: Heinemann, 1983). See also Kogan and Kogan, *Battle for the Labour Party*.

49 The first person to draw attention to this passivity, and its implications, was Austin Ranney in *Pathways to Parliament: Candidate Selection in Britain* (Madison: University of Wisconsin Press, 1965). See esp. pp. 11, 209.

50 The hard left was, roughly, those who held extreme left-wing opinions and who were unprepared to compromise those opinions either in the interests of party unity or in the interests of electoral success. The soft left consisted of those who perhaps held somewhat less extreme opinions but who, in any case, were readier to compromise. The test of whether someone was hard left or soft left increasingly became his or her attitudes toward Tony Benn, who had emerged as the leader of the left in the early 1970s and who had become more and more unbending in both his opinions and his political style. The hard left was pro-Benn, the soft anti-Benn. The statements in the text about the views of successive cohorts of Labour MPs are based on unpublished data collected by the author, but see also Hugh Berrington, "The Labour Left in Parliament: Maintenance, Erosion and Renewal," in Kavanagh, *Politics of the Labour Party*.

51 A convenient listing of the MPs denied reselection after 1979 is given in *The Campaign Guide 1983*, p. 461. See also Young, *The Reselection of M.P.s*. A ninth centrist MP almost certainly would have been deselected had the 1983 election not intervened.

52 Many in the Labour party subsequently blamed Callaghan for not having resigned immediately after his defeat in 1979. If he had gone then, Foot might well not have been elected

leader. It is also possible that, with a new leader elected by the parliamentary party firmly in place, the pressure for the adoption of an electoral college might not have been so intense.

53 For a brief description of the election of Foot, see Austin Mitchell, *Four Years in the Death of the Labour Party* (London: Methuen, 1983), pp. 49–52. As its title suggests, Mitchell (a Labour MP) has written a mordant history of Labour between 1979 and 1983, with chapter headings like "Launching the Red Titanic" and "Disaster from the Jaws of Defeat." Details of the voting in the two ballots can be found in the *Times*, 5 November 1980, p. 1; 12 November 1980, p. 1; and in *The Campaign Guide 1983*, p. 457.

54 See King, "Politics, Economics, and the Trade Unions," pp. 42–45, 67–69.

55 *Gallup Political Index*, no. 243 (November 1980), p. 6.

56 The left accounted for something like 110–15 of Foot's votes, most of the remainder coming from nonleft MPs who feared that the pugnacious Healey would split the party. An undetermined number of right-wingers voted for Foot because they had their own reasons for wanting to make a bad situation in the party even worse. See Mitchell, *Four Years in the Death of the Labour Party*, p. 51.

57 Frank Johnson, "Oh for when the brave new world was young," *Times*, 19 June 1981, p. 12.

58 Gallup's respondents were asked whether there was anything in particular that they disliked about the Labour party. The question was open-ended, and multiple responses were allowed. Only two negative features of the party were singled out by 10 percent or more of respondents: "left is too strong" and "too tied to unions," both mentioned by 14 percent. *Gallup Political Index*, no. 242 (October 1980), p. 8. The other survey, by Opinion Research and Communications, was published in the *Times*, 9 February 1981, p. 4.

59 Gallup's standard question about party leaders other than the prime minister takes the from: "Do you think _____ is or is not proving a good leader of the _____ party?" It is clear from the pattern of responses that most of those interviewed take this question as a general invitation to express their views about the individual rather than as a specific request for a judgment about the individual's competence as leader of his or her party. The proportion answering yes with regard to Foot in February 1981 was 22 percent; the previous low was Heath's 24 percent in February 1967. See Webb and Wybrow, *The Gallup Report*, pp. 167–85. In his last full month as party leader, September 1983, following the general election, Foot established a record that is unlikely ever to be broken. In that month, a mere 9 percent of Gallup's respondents thought he was doing a good job as Labour leader; 84 percent thought he was not. *Gallup Political Index*, no. 277 (September 1983), p. 3.

60 For the Gallup figures on Labour's disunity, see *Gallup Political Index*, no. 242 (October 1980), p. 9. For the circumstances, and the consequences, of Benn's decision to fight Healey for the deputy leadership, see Mitchell, *Four Years in the Death of the Labour Party*, pp. 56–57. Benn must have known that the contest would be damaging to the party. He evidently calculated that not challenging Healey might well cost him the leadership of the extraparliamentary left and also that, if he beat Healey, his position both inside and outside Parliament would be enormously strengthened. He also conscientiously held the view that the party's deputy leader should not be someone who, like Healey, disagreed more and more with the general thrust of the party's policies.

61 The detailed results of the election can be found in *Report of the Annual Conference of the Labour Party 1981* (London: Labour Party, 1982), p. 26 and appendix 7.

62 On the internal structure and recent history of the Liberal party, see Vernon Bogdanor, ed., *Liberal Party Politics* (Oxford: Clarendon, 1983).

63 Calculated from the figures in David Butler and Anne Sloman, eds., *British Political Facts 1900–1979*, 5th ed. (London: Macmillan, 1980), pp. 208–10.

64 The distinction between the "legitimate" and the "illegitimate" left first was drawn by William Rodgers in a speech in February 1977. The legitimate left, he said, was an essential part of the Labour coalition: "We may disagree with it . . . but we respect its right to exist. But it must not be a Trojan horse for the wreckers." See the *Times*, 21 February 1977, p. 2.

65 A number of books already have appeared on the origins and early history of the Social Democratic party. See, in particular, Ian Bradley, *Breaking the Mould?— The Birth and Prospects of the Social Democratic Party* (Oxford: Martin Robertson, 1981); and Hugh Stephenson, *Claret and Chips: The Rise of the SDP* (London: Michael Joseph, 1982).

66 In his lecture Jenkins alluded only obliquely to the possibility of forming a new party. "The response [to Britain's problems]," he said, "should not be to slog through an unending war of attrition, stubbornly and conventionally defending as much of the old citadel as you can hold, but to break out and mount a battle of movement on new and higher ground." Quoted in Stephenson, *Claret and Chips*, pp. 21–22. Jenkins received a huge volume of correspondence after the lecture, indicating that, were a new party to be launched, it would attract considerable support (at least from the kind of people who write letters to politicians). A life of Jenkins was published shortly before the 1983 election: John Campbell, *Roy Jenkins: A Biography* (London: Weidenfeld and Nicolson, 1983).

67 Owen, Rodgers, and Williams all wrote books during the two years after the 1979 election. They did not deal with the controversies within the Labour party but with the country's problems and possible solutions to them. See David Owen, *Face the Future* (London: Jonathan Cape, 1981); William Rodgers, *The Politics of Change* (London: Secker and Warburg, 1982); and Shirley Williams, *Politics is for People* (London: Allen Lane, 1981). Owen's book was published in an abridged edition by the Oxford University Press later in 1981.

68 Many on the right of the party believed that, despite its defeat in 1979, the Callaghan government had been a considerable success. They were proud of its record in bringing down the rate of inflation, in maintaining spending on the social services at high levels, and in helping Britain to weather (better than many other countries) the world recession of the mid-1970s. Yet the moderate 1974–79 Labour government had been elected on a very left-wing manifesto. Many right-wingers after 1979 believed, or at least hoped, that history in this respect might be made to repeat itself. It was only a minority in the party who found themselves wondering whether the failures of 1974–79 and, even more, the failures of 1964–70, did not perhaps suggest that the central ideas of democratic socialism were fatally flawed.

69 The original intention had been to launch the party later in the year, but the buildup of support for the idea of a new party was so rapid that the gang of four and their friends were compelled to bring the date forward. The launch itself took place in London, but immediately afterward the gang of four fanned out across the country, being interviewed and photographed in places as far apart as Plymouth and Glasgow. The launch was a considerable public relations feat; it was the main news on all of the most important television news programs that night and the lead story in all the national newspapers the next day.

70 There is no way of collecting accurate statistics on attendances at public meetings, but it seems that the gang of four, especially Roy Jenkins and Shirley Williams, had an unusual capacity for drawing crowds. Attendance of as many as two thousand was not uncommon at their meetings. The SDP's leaders, like most politicians, were often in danger of imagining that audience size and response at meetings could be used as a gauge of broader public opinion.

71 See the full list in Stephenson, *Claret and Chips*, pp. 193–94.

72 One, Eric Ogden, the MP for Liverpool West Derby, already had been pushed. He was one

of the eight deselected Labour MPs referred to earlier. A small number of the other defectors might not have been reselected had they remained in the Labour party.

73   The four ex-ministers were John Horam, who had served under William Rodgers at the Department of Transport; Robert MacLennan, who had been a junior minister under Shirley Williams at the (since abolished) Department of Prices and Consumer Protection; John Grant, who had been a junior minister in three different departments; and Dickson Mabon, who also had served in a number of departments, most recently as minister of state under Tony Benn in the Department of Energy. The defection of Callaghan's former aide, Tom McNally, came as a considerable surprise to those who did not know him (and to some who did); he was thought of as being an archetypal Labour loyalist. McNally was under great pressure from the left in his constituency of Stockport South.

74   Quoted in Stephenson, *Claret and Chips*, p. 84.

75   On the differences between Social Democrats and Liberals, see Bogdanor, *Liberal Party Politics*, passim; and Alan Beith, *The Case for the Liberal Party and the Alliance* (London: Longman, 1983), esp. chap. 8.

76   It can be found most conveniently in Bradley, *Breaking the Mould?* p. 96.

77   Details of the results are set out in Anthony King, "Whatever Is Happening to the British Party System?" *Parliamentary Affairs* 35 (Summer 1982), p. 249.

78   Quoted in H. V. Hodson, ed., *The Annual Register: A Record of World Events, 1982* (London: Longman, 1983), p. 16.

79   Max Hastings and Simon Jenkins, *The Battle for the Falklands* (London: Michael Joseph, 1983), p. 316. This is much the most thorough and politically informative of the many accounts of the Falklands war that already have appeared. In addition, see *Falkland Islands Review: Report of a Committee of Privy Councillors* [the Franks report], Cmnd. 8787 (London: Her Majesty's Stationery Office, 1983). The Franks report presents the results of the official inquiry into the circumstances of Argentina's capture of the islands. Most observers agree that its conclusions do not follow from its findings.

80   These data are drawn from the monthly numbers of the *Gallup Political Index*. Gallup data cited later in this chapter are drawn from the same source unless otherwise indicated.

81   See the *Economist*, 17 April 1982, p. 23; 24 April 1982, p. 29; 8 May 1982, p. 31; 29 May 1982, p. 26; 26 June 1982, p. 26.

82   Confession allegedly being good for the soul, I must confess to having been wrong about the political consequences of the Falklands war. I imagined, and said at the time, that the political impact of the Falklands would be short-lived and that voters would quickly revert to assessing the government and the Conservative party in terms of their record on inflation, unemployment, etc. I failed to reckon with one of the factors listed below.

83   "The Dunkirk spirit" is meant to symbolize British patriotism and determination. It is a strange symbol to choose, since the British were defeated at Dunkirk, partly as the result of their own leaders' incompetence.

84   The figures were Beaconsfield, May 1982, 26.8 percent; Merton, Mitcham, and Morden, June 1982, 29.4 percent; Coatbridge and Airdrie, June 1982, 8.2 percent; Gower, September 1982, 25.1 percent; Southwark Peckham, October 1982, 32.9 percent; Birmingham Northfield, October 1982, 26.1 percent; Glasgow Queen's Park, December 1982, 9.4 percent; Southwark Bermondsey, February 1983, 57.7 percent; Darlington, March 1983, 24.5 percent. Complete by-election results for the Parliament are given in *The Times Guide to the House of Commons, June 1983* (London: Times Books, 1983), pp. 284–85.

85   The best data on the Alliance's social and political bases, and on how these differed from those of the other parties, are in Ivor Crewe, "Is Britain's Two-Party System Really About to Crumble?—The Social Democratic–Liberal Alliance and the Prospects for Realignment," *Electoral Studies* 1 (December 1982), pp. 275–313.

86 Why did the flow of defectors dry up? The obvious answer is probably also the correct one, namely that those who were most dissatisfied with the Labour party, and most despairing of it, left the party right at the beginning or within the first year. The MPs who stayed behind were either less dissatisfied or less despairing (or for other reasons were always more disposed to be loyal). In addition, it became more and more difficult to leave as time passed, since someone who left after the autumn of 1981 could plausibly be accused of leaving not out of principle but simply because the SDP bandwagon was rolling. There was also some doubt about how warmly such late defectors would be received into the new party. From the spring of 1982 onward, there was no guarantee that they would be adopted to fight their existing seats; the Liberals and SDP by this time were adopting their own candidates.

87 The leadership election itself had been preceded by a quite bitter dispute within the SDP about whether the party leader should be elected by the party's members of Parliament (as in the old Labour party) or on a one-member-one-vote basis by the party's members in the country. Those who wanted Jenkins to be elected leader tended, for obvious reasons, to favor election by MPs; those who wanted Williams or Owen tended, for equally obvious reasons, to favor election by the members. Jenkins was universally assumed, probably rightly, to be held in higher esteem among the SDP parliamentary group than among the party at large. In the event, Jenkins was elected despite the party's failure to adopt the system that he and his supporters preferred. This controversy was yet another that was reported widely in the press and cannot have done the SDP's reputation much good. For the details, see Stephenson, *Claret and Chips*, chaps. 8, 9.

88 On the curious arrangement whereby Jenkins was prime minister-designate while Steel was "leader of the Alliance campaign," see chap. 4 of this book.

The Conservative Campaign

1 The accounts are shown in the note on Conservative party finances at the end of this chapter.

2 See the *Times* 24, 25 July 1980; 6, 13 March 1981.

3 See Michael Pinto-Duschinsky, "How Tory cash is dwindling," *Times*, 26 February 1982.

4 The term "wets" refers to left-wing Conservatives whose views, particularly on economic policy, were sometimes at variance with those of Thatcher and her close supporters. For a description of doctrinal tendencies within the Conservative party in the period leading up to the 1979 election, see Anthony King, "Politics, Economics, and the Trade Unions, 1974–1979," in Howard R. Penniman, ed., *Britain at the Polls, 1979: A Study of the General Election* (Washington, D.C.: American Enterprise Institute, 1981), pp. 69–75.

5 These statistics are taken from Mary Rosselin, "Sociologie des Elus Depuis 1955: Permanence et Changement," paper presented to the Colloque International: Les Elections Legislatives Britanniques du 9 Juin 1983 (Paris: Association Française de Science Politique et le Centre de Recherche en Civilisation Britannique, 1983).

6 See David Butler and Michael Pinto-Duschinsky, "The Conservative Elite 1918–1978: Does Unrepresentativeness Matter?" in Zig Layton-Henry, ed., *Conservative Party Politics* (London: Macmillan, 1980), p. 207.

7 (Chichester, Sussex: Parliamentary Research Services, 1983).

8 Two hundred and sixty-nine associations had the exclusive services of one agent, twenty agents covered two constituencies, four agents covered three or four constituencies each. In Glasgow one agent was responsible for the eleven constituencies in the city.

9 See the *Times*, 7 May 1983.

10 Senior members of Central Office staff included the vice-chairman, Michael Spicer, MP, who spent part of the campaign accompanying the prime minister on her tours; Alistair

McAlpine, the party treasurer and deputy chairman, who acted as a political adviser as well as a fundraiser; Peter Cropper, director of the Research Department; Anthony Garner, director of organization; Chris Lawson, director of marketing; and Anthony Shrimsley, director of the Press and Publicity Department (a former editor of *Now* magazine, he had joined Central Office on 1 March 1983). Several former Research Department staff, who had become political advisers to ministers, had prominent roles, including Adam Ridley and Stephen Sherbourne. Three retiring members of Parliament, Sir Anthony Royle, Sir John Eden, and Jock Bruce-Gardyne, were constantly present at the headquarters as advisers. The former Central Office publicity director, Gordon Reece, who now worked for Armand Hammer in the United States, was present through most of the election. Together with Stephen Sherbourne, he advised the prime minister on her television appearances. It had been Reece who had introduced Saatchi and Saatchi Garland Compton as the party's advertising agency before the 1979 election. He was regarded by the press as a highly influential figure, but his role may have been less in 1983 than in the previous election.

The prime minister's personal staff included her parliamentary private secretary, Ian Gow, MP (who spent part of the campaign in his own constituency), David Wolfson, and Press Secretary Derek Howe. Help with speeches came from Ferdinand Mount, Thatcher's policy adviser, from playwright Sir Ronald Millar, and John Selwyn Gummer, MP (who later succeeded Parkinson as Conservative party chairman).

Saatchi and Saatchi assigned the Conservative party account to two of its executives, Tim Bell and Michael Dobbs, a former member of the Conservative Research Department and a part-time political adviser to Tebbit at the Department of Employment. The managing director of Harris Research Centre, John Hanvey, took direct charge of the firm's private polling for the party and coordinated his work with Keith Britto, deputy director of marketing.

11　The "tactical committee" was organized by Joan Varley, director of the Local Government Department.

12　Addressing unemployment does not seem to have been part of the basic election strategy. However, it soon became evident that attacking the performance of past Labour governments would not be enough and that the issue couldn't be completely bypassed; new polling materials revealed joblessness as a major continuing anxiety for the public. At the first of her regular press conferences, on 20 May, Thatcher put forward a positive Conservative case: (1) that, of course, the Conservative party cared about the unemployed, (2) that her government's policies offered the best hope to create genuine jobs for the future, and (3) that the government had embarked upon the biggest youth employment scheme ever in an attempt to protect school-leavers during a period of economic transition.

13　*Times*, 17 May 1983.

14　*Times*, 19 May 1983.

15　One Conservative advertisement had shown identical items of the Labour and Communist party manifestos side by side, with the slogan "Like your manifesto, Comrade." Another, entitled "And now, the thoughts of Comrade Wall," quoted the Marxist views of the Labour candidate for Bradford North, Pat Wall, who appeared on the same platform as Foot when the Labour leader campaigned in the city.

To the charge that the Conservative party was as subject to extremist infiltration as Labour, Conservatives pointed out that the problem was widespread in the Labour party; that the Conservative leaders refused to speak in support of extremists, unlike Labour leaders who supported candidates of the far-left militant tendency; that Finnegan had disowned his former opinions while Labour party Marxists clung to theirs.

16　State of the Battle survey, 20–21 May.

17 The only poll to have given the Alliance a higher percentage during 23–26 May had been Audience Selection.

18 See, for example, C. A. E. Goodhart and R. T. Bhansali, "Political Economy," *Political Studies* 18 (March 1970).

19 Harris Research Centre conducted a survey, largely of unemployment, for the Conservative party in April 1983; it was analyzed in May. Further questions on unemployment were included in Harris polls for the Conservative party before and during the campaign, in particular the survey of the Current Political Situation carried out at the end of April and the State of the Battle survey of 20–21 May. These are the sources for statements in the text.

20 It was agreed by 47 percent of respondents and disagreed by 44 percent that "being unemployed is something that a lot of people are going to get used to, and even enjoy." A majority (53 percent) believed that unemployment was caused by factors beyond the government's control, but a large minority (42 percent) blamed Thatcher.

21 Responses varied according to the form in which the question was posed. When asked to name the single most important issue, 80 percent named unemployment while no other issue scored above 5 percent (Gallup Poll, *Daily Telegraph*, 25 May 1983).

The Labour Campaign

1 Data on Labour's "national" electoral support relate to Great Britain and exclude Northern Ireland, whose constituencies are not contested by the mainland parties.

2 Under the new electoral college for electing Labour's leader and deputy leader, MPs have 30 percent of the votes, constituency parties 30 percent, and affiliated organizations—overwhelmingly trade unions—40 percent.

3 *Daily Star*, 30 April 1983, p. 1.

4 *Gallup Political Index* (April 1983), p. 6.

5 Geoff Bish wrote his memorandum, *The 1983 Election Campaign: the failures and some lessons*, for a Labour party heads-of-department meeting held on 30 June 1983 (hereinafter referred to as Bish memorandum).

6 *Labour Party Conference Report, 1982* (London: Labour Party), p. 136.

7 *Labour Party Manifesto, 1983* (London: Labour Party), p. 36 (hereinafter referred to as *Manifesto*).

8 *Guardian*, 20 April 1982.

9 *Manifesto*, p. 11.

10 Ibid., p. 33.

11 *Times*, 4 June 1983.

12 Assistant national agent.

13 Bish memorandum, p. 6.

14 Ibid.

15 *Guardian*, 16 June 1983.

16 The author of this chapter was a member of Labour's smaller polling committee, which met each day at 7:30 A.M. to take a closer look at MORI's figures and discuss future polling requirements.

17 Four polls conducted between 17 and 20 May put Labour's share of support between 34 and 37 percent. Subsequently the highest Labour rating recorded by any poll was 33 percent.

18 *Sunday Times*, 22 May 1983.

19   In the event, Wall failed to win the normally safe Labour seat of Bradford North. The former Labour MP, Ben Ford, stood as an independent Labour candidate; although Ford himself came in a poor fourth, his 4,018 votes were more than enough to deprive Wall of the seat and hand it to the Conservatives.

20   MORI poll for *Sunday Times*, fieldwork 17–18 May; *British Public Opinion* (London: MORI, May–June 1983), p. 13.

21   *Gallup Political Index* (June 1983), p. 5.

22   Transcript of *Weekend World*, broadcast by London Weekend Television, 29 May 1983.

23   *Guardian*, 8 June 1983.

24   *Sunday Times*, 29 May 1983.

25   *Times*, 2 June 1983.

26   BBC TV's *Question Time*, reported in the *Times*, 3 June 1983.

27   *Times*, 7 June 1983. Goose Green was the site of one of the battles in the Falklands where British lives were lost.

28   *Observer*, 9 October 1983; *Daily Mail*, 11 October 1983.

The Alliance Campaign, Watersheds and Landslides

1   Jorgen Rasmussen, "David Steel's Liberals: Too Old to Cry, Too Hurt to Laugh," in Howard R. Penniman, ed., *Britain at the Polls, 1979: A Study of the General Election* (Washington, D.C.: American Enterprise Institute, 1981), p. 176.

2   John Goldthorpe et al., *The Affluent Worker: Political Attitudes and Behaviour* (Cambridge: Cambridge University Press, 1968).

3   Ivor Crewe, Bo Sarlvik, and James Alt, "Partisan Dealignment in Britain 1964–1974," *British Journal of Political Science* 7 (April 1977), pp. 129–90; Anthony King, "Whatever Is Happening to the British Party System?" *Parliamentary Affairs* 35 (Summer 1982), pp. 241–51.

4   For a useful summary of these developments and the events leading up to them see, Ian Bradley, *Breaking the Mould? The Birth and Prospects of the Social Democratic Party* (Oxford: Martin Robertson, 1981). Recent writings on the Liberals and the Social Democrats are surveyed in Jorgen Rasmussen, "L/SD: Neither Pounds, Shillings, and Pence Nor an Illusion," paper presented at the Conference on British Studies (South) meetings held in conjunction with the Southern Historical Association convention, 4–6 November 1982, Memphis, Tennessee.

5   Jorgen Scott Rasmussen, *Retrenchment and Revival: A Study of the Contemporary British Liberal Party* (Tucson: University of Arizona Press, 1964), chaps. 4, 7.

6   Social Democratic MP Richard Crawshaw received only 11.2 percent of the vote in Liverpool Broadgreen, while the rebel Liberal obtained 15.3 percent. The independent Liberal in Hammersmith gained only 5.8 percent and two dissident Liberals in Hackney South and Shoreditch combined for only 11.5 percent.

7   Cf. *Gallup Political Index*, no. 271 (March 1983), pp. 18–21, for public ratings of nine prominent politicians on twelve pairs of characteristics.

8   *Gallup Political Index*, no. 272 (April 1983), p. 8. A poll in Scotland alone a few weeks earlier showed Steel to be first choice among all leaders for the office, preferred by 34 percent to only 23 percent for Thatcher, 21 percent for Foot, and 7 percent for Jenkins. MORI, *Public Opinion in Great Britain*, no. 3 (March 1983), p. 19.

9   MORI, *British Public Opinion*, nos. 5, 6 (May, June 1983), p. 23.

10   Ibid., p. 8.

11   *Guardian*, 28 May 1983 (emphasis added).

12 The Liberals claim that support for them always increases during a general election campaign. As Ivor Crewe pointed out in the *Guardian*, 20 May 1983, this is not strictly accurate. The increase occurs principally when it is a Conservative government that is seeking reelection, although such a gain did occur in 1979, when a Labour government was in power. Rasmussen, "David Steel's Liberals," pp. 168–70.

13 *Gallup Political Index*, no. 274 (June 1983), p. 8.

14 Ibid., p. 31.

15 William Rodgers, "Labour's Predicament: Decline or Recovery?" *Political Quarterly* 50 (October–December 1979), pp. 420–34; and Rodgers, *The Politics of Change* (London: Secker and Warburg, 1982), pp. 107–24.

16 This discussion excludes the MORI panel surveys done for the *Sunday Times* and the Audience Selection polls.

17 While the Alliance did do best in those polls conducted by the firm that was doing its private polling as well, one should note also that Labour's best result came in a poll by MORI, which was doing Labour's private polls also, and the Conservatives' best result appeared in a Harris/ORC poll, also doing the Conservatives' private polls.

18 As for the Conservative response to this effort, Cecil Parkinson's comment on the Audience Selection poll taken on 30 May, that showed a striking 24 percent for the Alliance, was a classic: "I don't think the course of British political history will be altered by a telephone poll taken on a sunny bank holiday."

19 Ron Brown and Richard Crawshaw are excluded, since rebel Liberal candidates stood in their constituencies.

20 Given the extensive boundary changes for the 1983 election, no meaningful comparisons can be made with the 1979 constituency results. A group of experts applied the 1983 boundaries to the 1979 results and by a thorough analysis obtained a notional result for each constituency. *The BBC/ITN Guide to the New Parliamentary Constituencies* (Chichester: Parliamentary Research Services, 1983). In those constituencies where Social Democratic MPS stood, except for Brown, Crawshaw, and Christopher Brocklebank-Fowler (excluded because he formerly had been a Conservative), Labour received only 69 percent of its notional vote.

21 Another forty-two hundred votes, properly distributed, would have returned four more of the SDP MPS.

22 One lost by fewer than eighteen hundred votes and another by less than two thousand.

23 William Pitt, who had won the Croydon Northwest by-election in October 1981, was the one defeated.

24 Jo Grimond retired from Parliament. His replacement had little difficulty in holding the seat for the Liberals, but his margin was smaller than Grimond's had been in 1979. The constituency was one of the few whose boundaries were unchanged.

25 The Liberals received 14.1 percent of the vote in Great Britain. For the whole of the United Kingdom (Northern Ireland included), the Liberals had 13.7 and the SDP 11.6 percent.

26 The Liberals were less than 20 percentage points behind in Ross, Cromarty, and Skye as well, but were in third place. Nonetheless, this constituency was the one new one gained by the SDP.

27 *Gallup Political Index*, no. 273 (May 1983), pp. 5, 7.

28 In seven cases the notional Conservative share exceeded 50 percent. Two other cases, where the Conservative notional share was 49.2 and 49.8, are included with the nontactical group as well, since the Conservatives were within a percentage point of having a majority.

29 Although one of the tactical seconds was fought by the SDP rather than by the Liberals, it has been included.

30   Because its extremely small notional gap—0.1 percentage points—would greatly distort the figures, Roxburgh and Berwickshire has been excluded from this calculation.

31   The constituencies won were first, third, sixth, and eighth on the list of tactical seconds.

32   In two other constituencies, although the Liberals in second place were more than twenty percentage points behind the Conservatives, the Liberal share plus the Labour share in the notional figures did surpass the Conservative share. On the whole the voting pattern in these two resembled the nontactical seconds (the group to which they would properly have been assigned had they been included) more than the tactical seconds. The sixth new seat gained by the Liberals had nothing to do with tactical voting, but was the product of years of hard politicking at the grassroots level. The notional figures put the Liberals a distant third in Leeds West. Nonetheless, they won the seat with 38 percent of the vote, as Labour fell from more than 50 to only 34 percent.

33   This section is based on MORI, *British Public Opinion*, nos. 5, 6 (May, June 1983); unpublished printouts of various MORI surveys during the campaign; and the unpublished printout of the Gallup survey for the BBC conducted on the day before the election and on polling day itself. The cooperation of Robert Worcester of MORI and Robert Wybrow of Gallup is gratefully acknowledged.

34   The way in which age groups are defined affects the pattern of Alliance support. If the oldest group is composed of those 55 and older, then support for the Alliance differs little from its national share of the vote. If pensioners—those 65 and older—are the oldest category, however, then Alliance support falls below 20 percent, the weakest for any age group.

35   Defectors are defined as people who voted for a particular party in 1979 but did not do so in 1983. Recruits are those who did not vote for a particular party in 1979 but did support it in 1983.

36   Since only 13 percent said that they had become more favorable to the SDP, however, only about 4.5 percent of all respondents were citing policy.

37   Since 14 percent said they had become more favorable to the Liberals, the portion of the entire electorate saying Steel had made them more favorable was close to 6 percent.

38   Arthur Cyr, *Liberal Party Politics in Britain* (New Brunswick, N.J.: Transaction, 1977).

Opinion Polls as Feedback Mechanisms

1   See, e.g., C. J. Friedrich, *Constitutional Government and Democracy* (Boston: Little, Brown, 1941), pp. 589ff; Karl W. Deutsch, *The Nerves of Government* (New York: Free Press, 1963).

2   See Richard Rose, "Toward Normality: Public Opinion Polls in the 1979 Election," in Howard R. Penniman, ed., *Britain at the Polls, 1979: A Study of the General Election* (Washington, D.C.: American Enterprise Institute, 1981), pp. 177–209.

3   David Butler, *Governing without a Majority* (London: Collins, 1983), p. 29.

4   See reports in MORI, *Public Opinion in Great Britain*, nos. 4–5, 6 (April–May, June 1982).

5   For the author's review of the evidence at that time, concluding that a June election date was favorable for the Conservatives, see Richard Rose, "What Are the Omens for June?" *Daily Telegraph*, 7 May 1983.

6   See Butler, *Governing without a Majority*; John Curtice and Michael Steed, "Electoral Choice and the Production of Government," *British Journal of Political Science* 12, no. 3 (1982), pp. 249–98.

7   See "The Tatchell Factor," *Sunday Times*, 27 February 1983; and National Opinion Polls, *Political Social Economic Review*, no. 40 (February 1983).

8   See William L. Miller, *The Survey Method in the Social and Political Sciences* (London: Frances Pinter, 1983), esp. pp. 232–36; and weekly reports published in the *Sunday Standard* (Glasgow) during March 1982.

9   For details of these surveys with analyses see Ian McAllister and Richard Rose, *The Nationwide Competition for Votes* (London: Frances Pinter, 1984), chaps. 6–8.

10 David McKie, "Poll Gloom for Labour on Young Electors," *Guardian*, 26 May 1983.

11 "Black voters will back Labour," *Daily Telegraph*, 7 June 1983; "Teachers' Poll Gives Tories 16% Lead," *Times*, 27 May 1983; "The Mums back Maggie," *News of the World*, 5 June 1983.

12 See "Benn blows his top at Sun," *Sun*, 12 May 1983; and "Benn Considers Sueing," *Times*, 14 May 1983.

13 Geoffrey Smith, "Comment," *Times*, 24 May 1983. There were problems with the sales force too. See, e.g., "No Plans for Propaganda," *New Statesman*, 15 July 1983.

14 See Richard Rose, *Do Parties Make a Difference?* expanded 2d ed. (London: Macmillan, 1984), preface table 2.

15 Richard Evans, "MORI Poll Was Right on Election Forecast," *Times*, 11 June 1983.

16 John Clemens, "Hotline to the Consumer," *Campaign*, 13 May 1983.

17 See Richard Rose, *Class Does Not Equal Party: the Decline of a Model of British Voting*, Studies in Public Policy, no. 74 (Glasgow: University of Strathclyde, 1980), table 13. In 1980, NOP similarly concluded that there was an 11 to 13 percent Conservative bias among telephone owners. Even after using an 84-cell weighting matrix, based on sex, age, class, and region, it could only reduce the bias to 6 percent.

18 See Bo Sarlvik and Ivor Crewe, *A Decade of Dealignment* (Cambridge: Cambridge University Press, 1983), pp. 345–60, and sources cited at n. 13 of this chap.

19 Quoted in Evans, "MORI Poll Was Right on Election Forecast."

20 Rose, *Class Does Not Equal Party*, table 27.

21 See Rose, "Toward Normality"; Rose, "The Polls and Election Forecasting in February 1974," and "The Polls and Public Opinion in October 1974," in Howard R. Penniman, ed., *Britain at The Polls: the Parliamentary Elections of 1974* (Washington, D.C.: American Enterprise Institute, 1975) pp. 109–30, 223–39; and Rose, *The Polls and the 1970 Election*, Survey Research Centre Occasional Paper, no. 7 (Glasgow: University of Strathclyde, 1970).

22 By contrast with 1979, speculators in the city of London apparently showed less interest in making use of polls or rumors of poll results. David Lipsey found no relationship between movements in the value of sterling and the Conservative standing in opinion polls from November 1982 to early May 1983. Cf. "There's Still Only One Poll that Matters," *Sunday Times*, 8 May 1983; and Rose, "Toward Normality," pp. 206ff. See also Patrick Lay, "Don't Panic, Check the Worcester Source First," *Daily Express*, 2 June 1983.

23 Quoted in Michael Davie, "Why Pollsters ride high," *Sunday Observer*, 20 March 1983.

24 For fuller details, see the monthly *Gallup Political Index*; the frequently issued MORI digests, prior to the 1983 election published as *Public Opinion in Britain* and since as *British Public Opinion*; and NOP, *Political Social Economic Review*. For summaries of election polls, see especially *British Public Opinion: General Election 1983* (London: MORI, 1983); and *Gallup Political Index*, no. 274 (June 1983).

25 David McKie, "Opinion polls by telephone provoke Labour wrath," *Guardian*, 8 June 1983; Colin Brown, "Alliance Leaders 'Distort Polls Message'," *Guardian*, 8 June 1983.

26 Quoted in Peter Kellner, "How party polls were used to mislead voters," *New Statesman*, 8 July 1983. See also Harold Frayman, "Alliance Credibility Gap," *Labour Weekly*, 8 July 1983; and, on the Birmingham Northfield campaign, "Alliance Discredited by Election Tactics," *Times*, 30 October 1982.

27   See the epilogue of Rose, *Do Parties Make a Difference?* "Reality before Rhetoric."
28   "Foot Scorns Poll Predictions of Tory Landslide," *Daily Telegraph*, 6 June 1983.
29   See "Healey Attacks 'Provos'," *Daily Telegraph*, 6 June 1983; "Foot and Benn Counterblast," *Times*, 3 June 1983.
30   See "Steel Dismisses Poll Making Jenkins a Liability," *Guardian*, 25 May 1983.
31   See *What is Talkback?* (Manchester: Granada Television).
32   See *Gallup Political Index*, no. 273 (May 1983), p. 7.
33   *Gallup Political Index*, no. 274 (June 1983), p. 13.
34   Crewe's remarks quoted in "Where Polls Erred," *Observer*, 12 June 1983.
35   Reprinted in Richard Rose, "Opinion Polls and Election Results," in Rose, ed., *Studies in British Politics*, 3d ed. (London: Macmillan, 1976).
36   See Rose, "Toward Normality," table 5.
37   *Labour Weekly*, 17 June 1983.
38   *Gallup Political Index*, no. 273 (May 1983), p. 7.
39   Quoted in Jim Crace, "How Do Opinion Polls Work?" *Sunday Telegraph Magazine*, 5 June 1983.

The Ethnic Minorities Vote

1   Between 1948 and 30 June 1962 migration from the Commonwealth was totally unrestricted. During that period some three-quarters of a million people came from the developing New Commonwealth.
2   Between 1962 and 1971 a voucher system slowed down the movement of workers. Dependents, however, were allowed to enter.
3   It came into force on 1 January 1983.
4   Only sixty-six seats remain unchanged in any way.
5   Country of birth tables, *Census 1981, Great Britain* (London: HMSO, 1983).
6   Responses showed that the cooperation of Afro-Caribbeans was going to be difficult to obtain; parents often felt that their children, who were born in Britain, should be classified as "Europeans." Immigrants from the Indian subcontinent were dissatisfied with a classification that did not allow them to record their religion and/or their nation of origin.
7   *Population Trends* 28 (Summer 1982), p. 2.
8   Ibid., p. 4.
9   *Ethnic and Racial Questions in the Census: Second Report from the Home Affairs Committee* (London: HMSO, May 1983).
10   The calculations are based on the statistics of total population and under-sixteens contained in the *Labour Force Survey*, 1981.
11   The calculations are based on the figures contained in Robert Waller, *The Almanach of British Politics*, 2d ed. (London: Croom Helm, 1983).
12   Until 1922 the twenty-six counties of Eire were an integral part of the United Kingdom. From 1922 to 1949 Eire was in the Commonwealth.
13   An exception was made in 1973 when Prime Minister Bhutto took Pakistan out of the Commonwealth. Pakistanis in Britain were allowed to register and continue as electors under the *Pakistan Act* of 1973.
14   Dr. Pitt reported in Nicolas Deakin, *Colour and the British Electorate, 1964* (London: Pall Mall, 1965), p. 7.
15   Within which one polling district known for its high number of immigrants was selected. The constituencies were Brent East, Bradford West, Birmingham Sparkbrook, Lambeth Norwood, Leicester South, Rochdale, Croydon North East.

16 Birmingham Sparkbrook, Brent East, Bradford West, Bristol North East, Coventry North East, Croydon North East, Ealing Acton, Glasgow Central, Greenwich, Hackney North and Stoke Newington, Harringay Hornsey, Lambeth Norwood, Leicester South, Manchester Ardwick, Newcastle upon Tyne North, Nuneaton, Preston North, Rochdale, Sheffield Heeley, Southampton Itchen, Walsall South, Wandsworth, Battersea South, City of London: Westminster South, Wolverhampton South West.

17 Personal interviews were carried out between 24 and 30 May 1983 with 527 Asians and 469 Afro-Caribbeans.

18 CRE, *Participation of Ethnic Minorities in the General Election October 1974* (1974), p. 4.

19 Confidential memorandum of a Labour party race relations working party.

20 Under the *London Government Act* of 1963 a Greater London Council was created in April 1965. The population of the council's territory is 8 million. The area is divided into thirty-two boroughs, each of which is as large as a medium-sized town, with populations mostly between 200,000 and 300,000. Borough elections are held every three years and all the seats on all the councils are contested at the same time.

21 Partly because some nonwhites had become more prosperous, partly because the process of gentrification had caused a decline in cheap furnished accommodation.

22 *Observer*, 25 May 1983.

23 Conservative Party, *The Challenge of Our Times* (1983).

24 Liberal-SDP Alliance, *Working Together for Britain* (1983).

25 Labour Party, *The New Hope for Britain* (1983).

26 Launched on 23 May 1983.

27 Other photos also were used in the Greek and Cypriot press.

28 *Daily Mail*, 24 May 1983.

29 23 May 1983.

30 Circulation: 23,000. It is a radical newspaper with a strong influence, particularly in London.

31 *West Indian World*, 25 May 1983.

32 *Voice*, 4 June 1983.

33 M. J. Le Lohe, "Participation in Elections by Asians in Bradford," in Ivor Crewe, ed., *British Sociology Year Book: The Politics of Race*, (London: Croom Helm, 1975), 2: 84–122.

34 *Black on Black/Eastern Eye*, London Weekend Television, Harris Research Centre, 30–31 May 1983.

35 *Times*, 7 June 1983.

36 The sample is very small: thirty-nine Afro-Caribbeans and sixty Asians.

37 Bo Sarlvik and Ivor Crewe, *A Decade of Dealignment* (Cambridge: Cambridge University Press, 1983).

38 Hilde Himmelweit et al, *How Voters Decide* (London: Academic, 1981), p. 197.

39 Estimations by a joint working party set up by the BBC and ITN of what the election result might have been in each constituency in May 1979 had the new boundaries been in operation then.

40 Marian Fitzgerald, *Ethnic Minorities in the 1983 General Election*, (The Runnymede Trust, May 1983).

41 Ivor Crewe, "The Black, Brown and Green Votes," *New Society*, 12 April 1979. On another basis the trust found forty-four marginals.

42 Including Leicester East and Leicester South with nonwhite populations of 26 percent (electorate 17.4 percent).

43 Dadabhai Naoroji represented Central Finsbury from 1892 to 1895; M. Bhownagree, Bethnal Green from 1895 to 1905; and Sapurji Saklatvala North Battersea from 1922 to 1923 and 1924 to 1929. All three were Asians.

44   Quoted in David Butler, *The British General Election of February 1974* (London: Macmillan, 1975), p. 335.
45   Michael Steed quoted in David Butler, *The British General Election of 1970* (London: Macmillan, 1971), p. 408.
46   The Communist party put up two and the Revolutionary Communist party one.
47   Cf. Waller, *Almanach of British Politics*, p. 136.
48   Quoted in David Butler, *The British General Election of 1983* (London: Macmillan, 1984).
49   Michael Steed quoted in David Butler, *The British General Election of October 1974* (London: Macmillan, 1975), p. 351.

How to Win a Landslide without Really Trying

1   See Seymour Martin Lipset, "The Economy, Elections and Public Opinion," *Working Papers in Political Science*, no. P-83-1 (The Hoover Institution, Stanford University, July 1983); and Lipset, "No Room for the Ins: Elections Around the World," *Public Opinion* 5 (October–November 1982), pp. 41–44.
2   However, twenty-one of these fifty-eight gains can be attributed to the constituency boundary revisions. If these are excluded, the Conservatives' achievement does not quite match that of the reelected Labour government in 1966.
3   Vote-to-seat distortion is measured by the mean of the difference between the percentage share of the vote and the percentage share of parliamentary seats obtained by each of the Conservative, Labour, Liberal (plus SDP in 1983), and other parties at an election. For postwar figures see Ivor Crewe, "The Electorate: Partisan Dealignment Ten Years On," *West European Politics* 6 (1983).
4   The national electoral statistics that follow in this first section always refer to the United Kingdom; the survey data in the later sections always refer to Great Britain, i.e., the U.K. minus Northern Ireland.
5   In October 1974 when Labour won a majority of three on 39.2 percent of the vote, and in November 1922 when the Conservatives had a majority of sixty-three on 38.5 percent.
6   However, this was the first election under universal franchise in which the center contested every seat (in Great Britain) and as many seats as the Conservative and Labour parties contested. Had every contest been three-cornered in the 1924 and 1929 elections, the Liberal vote would probably have risen to 26 or 27 percent, i.e., to a level similar to that in 1983.
7   These figures are based on Gallup's question: "If the new Social Democratic party made an Alliance with the Liberals so that a candidate from only one of these parties would stand in each constituency, how would you vote?" This differs from the conventional unprompted vote-intention question, but it proved to be a superior measure in 1981–82 of the three parties' vote. See Ivor Crewe, "Is Britain's Two Party System Really About to Crumble?" *Electoral Studies* 1 (1982), esp. pp. 284–88.
8   See Ivor Crewe, *Times*, 9 October 1981.
9   See MORI, *Public Opinion in Great Britain* (May 1982), pp. 12–13; and *Economist*, 26 June 1982. Support for the landing of troops on the Islands rose from 67 percent on 14 April to 89 percent on 25–26 May; over the same period support for the sinking of Argentinian ships rose from 52 percent to 79 percent. Overall satisfaction with the government's "handling of the situation in the Falkland Islands" grew from 60 percent on 14 April to a massive 84 percent on 21–23 June.
10   These and subsequent figures on the public's perception of the economy are taken from the monthly *Gallup Political Index*.

11 For example, the Conservatives normally win up to a dozen seats at each election simply through their more efficient mobilization of the postal vote. See Geoffrey Alderman, *British Elections: Myth and Reality* (London: Batsford, 1978), pp. 46–48.

12 Michael Pinto-Duschinsky, "Financing the British General Election of 1983," in Ivor Crewe and Martin Harrop, eds., *Political Communications: The General Election Campaign of 1983* (Cambridge: Cambridge University Press, 1985). Figures refer to central and regional (but not local) spending, including grants to candidates, before and during the campaign.

13 Corroboration that the three main parties' PEBs reached very similar numbers is provided by the Broadcasting Audience Research Board's (BARB) figures on the size of PEB audiences. Over the whole campaign period Conservative PEBs were watched by an average of 29.2 percent of the U.K. population aged 4+, Labour PEBs by 28.2 percent, and Alliance PEBs by 27 percent. See MORI, *British Public Opinion, General Election 1983, Final Report*, appendix 7 (hereinafter referred to as *Final Report*).

14 Strictly speaking the proportions were probably slightly lower, because respondents could mention more than one TV broadcast, party advert/poster, or personal contact as influences on their vote; summing the column percentages involves a small amount of double counting.

15 Most of the analysis reported in this chapter is based on a survey commissioned by BBC Television, conducted by Social Surveys (Gallup Poll) Ltd., and designed by the author. Face-to-face interviews were conducted with 4,141 respondents on 8 and 9 June 1983 (i.e., on the preceding day and actual day of the election); 3,174 in England and Wales and 967 in Scotland (weighted down for overall Great Britain figures). Northern Ireland was excluded from the survey. The sample was a quota sample composed of age, sex, and housing. The survey incorporated weighted oversamples of 862 respondents in Labour-held marginal constituencies and 738 in Liberal-Conservative and Conservative-Liberal constituencies. Each interview lasted about thirty minutes. The vote recorded by the survey compared with the actual election result in Great Britain (in parentheses) is as follows: Conservative 43.9 percent (43.5 percent); Labour 28.7 (28.2); Alliance 25.8 (26); and other 1.6 (2.3).

16 See David Butler and Donald Stokes, *Political Change in Britain* (London: Macmillan, 1969), p. 288; and Bo Sarlvik and Ivor Crewe, *Decade of Dealignment* (Cambridge: Cambridge University Press, 1983), p. 45. For data on the voting patterns of new electors see Henry Durant, "Voting Behaviour in Britain, 1945–1964," in Richard Rose, ed., *Studies in British Politics* (London: Macmillan, 1966), pp. 122–28, esp. p. 126; Butler and Stokes, *Political Change in Britain*, 2d ed., chap. 11; and Sarlvik and Crewe, *Decade of Dealignment*, chap. 2.

17 See Crewe, "Is Britain's Two Party System About to Crumble?" pp. 293–94; and MORI *British Public Opinion* 5 (April 1983), p. 4, which confirmed that this age pattern continued until the campaign.

18 Readers might be puzzled that Labour experienced a high defection rate but a low adverse swing among the middle classes in general and the professions and management in particular (cf. tables 7.6 and 7.8). There are two reasons for this apparent paradox. First, "swing" is derived from the *percentage point change* in the Labour (and Conservative) share of a group's vote whereas defection rates describe *proportional* change. The difference of 6 percent in the professional and managerial vote for Labour between 1979 and 1983 represented a relatively small percentage point fall, but a large proportion of what was already a small Labour vote. Second, the percentage point drop in the Conservative vote in this group (−6 percent) was relatively large, thus producing the zero swing.

19 Tony Benn, "Spirit of Labour Reborn," *Guardian*, 20 June 1983. ("For the first time since 1945, a political party with an openly socialist policy has received the support of over 8½

million people. This is a remarkable development by any standards.") For a rebuttal, see Peter Kellner, "Are there really 8½ million socialists in Britain?" *New Statesman*, 24 June 1983.

20   Neither the 1979 BBC TV / Gallup survey nor other surveys and polls conducted then asked for people's preferred party on defense so we cannot measure the change from 1979 to 1983 in party preferences on this issue. The Conservatives traditionally have been regarded as the "strong defense" party and almost certainly would have been the preferred party among the 2 percent in 1979 citing defense as an issue.

21   From mid-1981 until the beginning of the election campaign, different polls consistently found that a majority of the public disapproved of the installation of cruise missiles in Britain. During the campaign, however, an NOP poll reported that approval outweighed disapproval by 48 percent to 38 percent and the BBC / Gallup survey found the same: 50 percent thought it a good idea, 39 percent a bad idea. For detailed trend figures, see Ivor Crewe, "Britain: Two and a Half Cheers for the Atlantic Alliance," in Gregory Flynn and Hans Rattinger, eds., *Public Opinion and Atlantic Defense* (London: Croom Helm, 1984).

22   This figure is arrived at by comparing Labour's advantage on the issue of prices in 1979 (a 13 percent majority among 40 percent of respondents or 5.2 percent of all respondents) with the Conservatives' advantage on the issue in 1983 (a 40 percent majority among 22 percent of respondents, or 8.8 percent).

23   In MORI's panel survey for the *Sunday Times* the proportion mentioning the NHS as an issue they would "take into account when deciding which party to vote for" rose from 13 percent on 21-25 April to 26 percent on 1-2 June. The only issue (out of eleven) to rise in importance by even more was defense. See MORI, *Final Report*, p. 114.

24   This is suggested by the fact that the NHS was cited by 24 percent of late-deciding Labour voters as one of the two issues most influencing their vote. Among last-minute Conservatives and Alliance voters the proportions were 2 percent and 11 percent respectively.

25   See MORI, *Final Report*, p. 62.

26   See ibid., p. 60; *Gallup Political Index*, no. 274 (June 1983), p. 27; Report of Harris poll of two-party marginals commissioned by London Weekend Television (fieldwork 25-26 May 1983), p. 45.

27   MORI, *Final Report*, p. 62.

28   See *Gallup Political Index*, no. 274 (June 1983), pp. 26-27.

29   According to a MORI poll conducted on 6 May for BBC Panorama. See MORI, *British Public Opinion* 5 (May-June 1983), p. 5.

30   See MORI, *Final Report*, pp. 109-12. Thatcher's image also is examined in detail in *Gallup Political Index*, no. 274 (June 1983), pp. 23-24, but unlike the MORI poll this one does not have comparative data on the other party leaders.

31   National Opinion Polls, *Political Social Economic Review*, no. 42 (June 1983), p. 12. See also the MORI poll of Yorkshire marginals conducted on 6 June for Yorkshire Television, which found that 34 percent of respondents said they would be more likely to vote for the Alliance if David Steel rather than Roy Jenkins was its leader, as against 6 percent who would be less likely. MORI, *British Public Opinion* 5 (May-June 1983), p. 6.). A Harris poll of Lib.-Con. and Con.-Lib. marginals conducted on 1-3 June for London Weekend Television found that the single most frequent reason, out of a list of seven, given by respondents for not supporting the Alliance was "Roy Jenkins would be an ineffective prime minister" (21 percent).

32   Two useful accounts of this government's record are Peter Riddell, *The Thatcher Government* (Oxford: Martin Robertson, 1983), esp. chaps. 3, 11; and Nicholas Wapshott and George Brock, *Thatcher* (London: Macdonald, 1983), esp. chaps. 11, 13.

33 V. O. Key, Jr., "A Theory of Critical Elections," *Journal of Politics* 17 (1955), pp. 3–18; and Key, "Secular Realignment and the Party System," *Journal of Politics* 21 (1959), pp. 198–210.

34 See Jerome M. Clubb, William H. Flanigan, and Nancy Z. H. Zingale, *Partisan Realignment* (Beverly Hills and London: Sage, 1980).

35 Note, however, that this could be an artifact of research design. Self-declared strength of party identification tends to be higher in surveys conducted close to general elections than in midterm. See Butler and Stokes, *Political Change in Britain*, 2d ed., p. 470. The interviewing for the election surveys in 1964, 1966, 1970, 1974, and 1979 was done a good few weeks after the election, whereas that for the 1983 election was done on the eve and day of polling.

36 This figure is based on the trend in average earnings, discounted by the trend in the tax and price index over the same period. The data can be found in the Central Statistical Office, *Economic Trends Annual Supplement 1983 Edition* (London: HMSO, 1983), pp. 113, 118. I am grateful to Christopher Huhne of the *Guardian* for assistance on this point.

37 See "Britain's Jobless," *Economist*, 4 December 1982, p. 23.

38 Ibid.

39 In the BBC TV / Gallup survey 45 percent of the unemployed among the 18–22-year-olds did not vote.

40 See Jean Todd and Bob Butcher, *Electoral Registration in 1981* (London: Office of Population Censuses and Surveys, Social Survey Division, 1982), table 10, p. 23.

41 See Ivor Crewe and Anthony Fox, *British Parliamentary Constituencies: A Statistical Compendium* (London: Faber and Faber, 1984), appendix 35.

42 Useful accounts of the Liberal vote can be found in David Butler and Donald Stokes, *Political Change in Britain*, 1st ed., chap. 14; Hilde Himmelweit et al., *How Voters Decide* (London: Academic 1981), chap. 10; and John Curtice, "Liberal Voters and the Alliance: Realignment or Protest?" in Vernon Bogdanor, ed., *Liberal Party Politics* (Oxford: Clarendon, 1983).

43 See Curtice, "Liberal Voters and the Alliance"; and Crewe, "Is Britain's Two Party System Really About to Crumble?" esp. pp. 288–303.

44 See Ivor Crewe, Bo Sarlvik, and James Alt, "The Decline of the Two Party System," paper presented to the Political Studies Association Conference, Oxford, March 1975, p. 6, tables 6 and 7.

45 In the monthly Gallup polls the Alliance's vote share has averaged 20 percent since October 1983 (when the election of Neil Kinnock to the leadership of the Labour party restored Labour's position at the expense of the Alliance). Average support for the Liberals in the Gallup polls for the first nine months after earlier Conservative election victories was 13.7 percent in 1979–80, 7.2 percent in 1970–71, and 9.3 percent in 1959–60. See Norman Webb and Robert Wybrow, eds., *The Gallup Report* (London: Sphere Books, 1981), appendix E.

46 This interpretation of the 1983 election is argued strongly in William MIller, *There Was No Alternative—The British General Election of 1983*, Strathclyde Papers on Government and Politics, no. 19 (Glasgow: Department of Politics, University of Strathclyde, 1984). "Dissension at the top rather than spontaneous desertion at the bottom was the cause of Labour's very poor performance," the author writes. "Everything considered, 1983 was kind to Labour."

47 A MORI poll conducted on 23–24 April found that Conservatives led Labour by 45 to 30 percent for a general election, but by only 40 to 35 percent when respondents were asked how they would vote in the coming local elections. See *Sunday Times*, 1 May 1983, p. 1.

48 In the monthly Gallup polls from July to September 1983 Labour's vote averaged 26 percent. In the October Gallup it shot up to 35.5 percent, at which level it has stayed on average

up to the time of writing (February 1984). Other regular polls record the same jump in October 1983 but put Labour support 1 or 2 percent higher.

49 There is no inconsistency with the preceding paragraph. The proportion of all respondents identifying with Labour was 32 percent; the proportion of respondents who voted, 38 percent.

50 The 1945 election was the first for ten years, in which period a large proportion of the swollen cohort of new electors had been torn away from the influence of family and neighborhood by conscription into the armed forces, military service abroad, or (among young women) entry into the workforce. The government that won the war was a Conservative-Labour coalition; the Labour leaders who campaigned on a program of reconstruction had all held major responsibility in domestic offices of state for a number of years.

51 See John Curtice and Michael Steed, "Electoral Choice and the Production of Government: The Changing Operation of the Electoral System in the United Kingdom since 1955," *British Journal of Political Science* 12, no. 3 (July 1982), esp. pp. 256–82.

52 See John Curtice and Michael Steed, "Appendix 2: An Analysis of the Voting," in David Butler and Dennis Kavanagh, *The British General Election of 1979* (London: Macmillan, 1980), pp. 408–9.

53 See Nicky Britten and Anthony Heath, "Women, Men and Social Class," mimeo (Department of Community Health, University of Bristol, 1982), table 3, diagrams 12, 13; and Anthony Heath, *Social Mobility* (London: Fontana, 1981), pp. 233–45.

Index

Advertising: by national party organizations, 41–42; "negative," 61; effects of, 163–65

Agents, 45

Alliance (Liberal party and Social Democratic party): campaign expenditures, strategy, and results, 92–96, 128, 162–64; composition of electoral support, 97–99; Conservatives' strategy for dealing with, 53–54; "Ettrick Bridge Summit" on leadership problems, 88–89, 92–93; fluctuating support in public opinion polls, 28–29, 45–46, 57, 83–84, 94, 109; formation, 25–27, 83; impact of Falklands war on popularity of, 34–35, 84–85, 159–60; impact of standing in polls on voting support, 57–58, 95–96, 102–3, 118–19, 130–31; leadership tensions between David Steel and Roy Jenkins, 87–89, 92–93, 128–29, 182–83; local Liberal organizations' coolness to, 86–87; manifesto, 90–91; negotiations over allocation of candidatures, 84–87; organizational contribution of Social Democratic party, 162; party political broadcasts, 87; policy agreements and disagreements between Liberals and Social Democrats, 28, 86–92; polls commissioned by, 95, 118–19; position on Falklands war, 159; possible merger of the two parties, 105–6; prospects for the future, 104–7, 191–94; public unawareness of Alliance policies, 100, 129; success in early by-elections, 28–30; successes and failures in the 1983 election, 96–97; weak voter partisanship for, 192–93

Audience Selection Ltd., 57, 58, 59, 113, 120, 129, 134; accuracy of polls, 122–23; controversy with Tony Benn, 115–16; reliance on telephone interviews, 95, 114, 121–22, 135; polls conducted for Alliance, 95, 118–19

Benn, Tony: controversy with Audience Selection poll, 115–16; contest for deputy leader of Labour party, 22, 66; opposition to Falklands war, 37, 78, 159; explanation of election outcome, 175

Bermondsey by-election (1983), 47, 67, 85, 111–12

Bevins, Anthony, 77, 91–92

Biffen, John, 8, 48

Bish, Geoff, 68

Butler, David, 110

By-elections: general significance, 83; Bermondsey (1983), 47, 67, 85, 111–12; Crosby (1981), 84; Croydon North West (1981), 28, 84; Darlington (1983), 47–48, 67, 85, 112; Glasgow Hillhead (1982), 114, 159–60; Warrington (1981), 28–29

Callaghan, James, 15, 18, 20, 56, 65, 66, 110, 138, 181

Campaign for Labour Party Democracy, 16–17

Campaign organization and strategies: Alliance, 92–96, 162–64; Conservative party, 50–59; Labour party, 72–79, 162–64

Candidates and candidate selection, 4, 84–87, 151–54

Class basis of voting, 169–70, 172–73

Clemens, John, 113, 121–22, 123

Common Market. See European Economic Community (EEC)

Conservative party: appeals to ethnic minorities, 144–47; campaign expenditures, organization, strategy, and effects, 50–59, 93, 161, 162–64; direct mail solicitations, 42–43; election of Margaret Thatcher as leader, 2; finances, 61–64, 162; impact of Falklands war on popularity of, 30–34, 109, 158–59, 160–61, 188; manifesto (1979), 4, 5; manifesto (1983), 46, 49, 51;

membership decline, 41; nonwhite candidates, 152; organizational and financial problems, 40–41, 44–45; polls commissioned by, 13, 31–34, 49–50, 52, 57, 58–59, 116–17; public opinion toward, 13, 31–34, 52, 57; record number of seats gained, 155; small increase in party identifiers, 188–89; strategy for dealing with the Alliance, 53–54; "wets" in, 13, 14–15, 40–41
Crewe, Ivor, 132, 149, 150
Crosby by-election (1981), 84
Croydon North West by-election (1981), 28, 84

Darlington by-election (1983), 47–48, 67, 85, 112
Dealignment, 81–82
Defense: as a campaign issue, 176, 178; conflict over in Labour party, 17–18, 69–70, 77–78; Thatcher government policy toward, 9
Deposits lost, 96
Direct mail, 42–43
Dissolution of Parliament, ix–x

Election date, choice of, 46–47, 48–50, 109–11
Electoral volatility, 81–82
Ethnic minorities: candidates from, 151–54; Conservative party appeals to, 144–47; constituencies where most important, 150; numbers and countries of origin, 139–41; party appeals to, 144–47; registration, 142–43; strong preference for Labour, 148–51; turnout, 147–48
"Ettrick Bridge Summit" of Alliance leaders, 88–89, 92–93
European Economic Community (EEC), 8, 18, 71
The Evening Standard, 120–21
Exit polls, 121

Falklands war, 1, 15; Alliance position on, 159; as a campaign issue, 53, 78, 128, 162; impact on popularity of Thatcher government, 30–34, 109, 158–59, 160–61, 188; impact on popularity of Alliance, 34–35, 84–85, 159–60; Labour leaders' positions on, 37–38, 78, 159
Feedback, through elections and public opinion polls, 108–9, 133–34
Foot, Michael: campaign activities, 75–77, 108, 125, 136; and conflict within Labour party, 66–67, 76, 85, 183; as an orator, 75–76; position on defense issues, 68–69, 78, 178; position on Falklands war, 37, 159, 181–82, 194; selection as leader of Labour

party, 20; unpopularity, 21–23, 37, 74, 76–77, 101, 128

Gallup poll, 67, 81, 85, 89, 110, 111, 114, 116–17, 120, 121, 122, 123, 129, 130, 133, 137, 147, 162, 181, 184–85
"Gang of Four" (Roy Jenkins, David Owen, William Rodgers, and Shirley Williams), 25–27, 82
Gender gap, 167–68
Gilmour, Sir Ian, 15, 42
Glasgow Hillhead by-election (1982), 114, 159–60
"Granada 500," 129–30
The Guardian, 58, 59, 124

Harris Research Centre, 52, 57, 58–59, 110, 115, 116, 120, 121, 125, 134
Hattersley, Roy, 71, 74, 79–80, 146
Healey, Denis: loss of contest for Labour party leadership, 20; election as deputy leader of Labour party, 22, 66; position on defense issues, 69; position on the EEC, 71; role in campaign, 58, 74, 78, 117, 128, 161, 181
Heath, Edward, 2, 8, 18, 50, 110, 184
Howe, Sir Geoffrey, 3, 5, 12, 13, 42, 46, 48, 49

Immigrants, 139–41
Inflation: as a campaign issue, 178, 179–80; statistics, 3, 11–12
Issues in the campaign: changes in attitudes toward (1979–83), 177–78; defense, 68–69, 78; Falklands war, 53, 78, 128, 162; foreign policy, 17; incomes policy, 70–71; inflation, 178, 179–80; National Health Service, 70–71, 176, 178–79; Polaris missiles, 69–70, 77, 92; relative importance of in 1983, 129, 176–83; unemployment, 53–60, 70–71, 176, 179

Jenkins, Roy: election in Glasgow Hillhead by-election, 30; narrow loss in Warrington by-election, 28–29; relations with David Steel in Alliance leadership, 87–89, 92–93, 128–29, 182–83; replaced by David Owen as leader of SDP, 105; role in forming SDP, 25–27, 82, 83; selection as leader of SDP, 35–36; voters' perceptions of as a leader, 88, 181, 182–83

Key, V. O., Jr., 187
Kinnock, Neil: role in campaign, 58, 79, 161; selection as Labour party leader, 79–80, 195

Labour party: appeals to ethnic minorities, 144–47; Geoff Bish analysis of reasons for loss, 68, 72; campaign expenditures, organization, strategy, and effects, 72–79, 162–64; contest over selection of deputy party leader, 22, 66; defection of MPs to SDP, 27, 82; defection of voters in 1983 election, 98; defense policy, internal conflict over, 17–18, 69–70, 77–78; European Economic Community policy, 18, 71; foreign policy, 17; incomes policy, 70–71; manifesto (1973), 17; manifesto (1983), 17, 54, 68–71; Militant Tendency movement, 16–22, 67, 76; nonwhite candidates, 151–52; polls commissioned by, 117–18, 128; popular image of, 183–84; press conferences, 73–75; prospects for regaining power, 80–81, 194–95; "reselection" of MPs, 19, 82; secession of right wingers to SDP, 24–26, 82; selection of parliamentary candidates, 19–20; selection of party leaders, 18, 20, 66, 79, 82; standing in public opinion polls, 23, 109; unemployment policy, 70–71; unsuccessful challenge to redistribution of seats, xi; voter defections from, 165–67, 172–73

Lawson, Christopher, 42–43, 116

Liberal party: formation of alliance with SDP, 27–28; local "community" politics as basis of strength, 106–7; local organizations' reluctance about alliance with SDP, 86–97; nonwhite candidates, 152; shares of votes and seats prior to alliance with SDP, 23–24, 191–92; weakness of national organization, 161–62

"Limehouse Declaration," 26, 82

Manifestos: Alliance, 90–91; Conservative, 46, 49, 51; Labour, 17, 54, 68–71

Marginal constituencies, 45

Market and Opinion Research International (MORI), 57, 67, 72, 110, 111, 112, 114, 115, 117–18, 120, 121, 124, 133, 134, 135, 136, 137, 162, 179

Marplan, 58, 59, 110, 113, 120, 134

Militant Tendency movement in the Labour party, 16–22, 67, 76

"Misery index," 155

Monetarism, 3

Mortimer, James, 72, 74–75

National Front, 55

National Health Service, 176, 178–79

National Opinion Polls (NOP), 112, 115

Negative voting, 174–76

Nationalized industries, "privatization" of, 4, 5–6

North Sea oil, 5, 13–14

The Observer, 112, 113, 124

Owen, David: contest for leadership of SDP, 35–36; replaces Roy Jenkins as leader of SDP, 105; role in forming SDP, 25–27, 82, 83

Parkinson, Cecil, 42, 44, 46, 48, 50, 52, 59, 93, 108, 146

Party: election broadcasts, 43, 54, 87, 162, 164–65; identification, 188–90; images, 101–3, 176, 183–86; leaders, relative popularity of, 89, 101, 181–83, 187–88

Polaris missiles, as issue in campaign, 69–70, 77, 92

Prior, James, 2, 14, 15

Public opinion polls: accuracy of forecasts in by-elections, 94–95, 114; accuracy of forecasts in 1983 general election, 119–20, 131–32; basic techniques, 113–14; commissioned by Alliance, 95, 118–19; commissioned by Conservative party, 13, 31–34, 49–50, 52, 57, 58–59, 116–17; commissioned by Labour party, 117–18, 128; commissioned by newspapers, 124–25; commissioned by Social Democratic party, 118–19; commissioned by television broadcasters, 57, 112, 115–16, 121, 124–25; exit polls, 121; impact on voting choices, 57–58, 95–96, 102–3, 111–12, 118–19, 130–31; panel studies used to measure trends during campaign, 123–24; politicians' use of, 136–38; public attitudes toward, 137; public and private, 125–26; record number in 1983, 112; use of "quickie" polls, 134–36

Realignment, 186–89

Redistribution of seats (1983): Labour party's unsuccessful court challenge to, xi; sweeping extent of, x–xi, 44–45, 46–47

Registration, 141–42

Rodgers, William: role in forming SDP, 25–27, 82; role in negotiations with Liberals over allocation of candidatures, 84–85

Saatchi and Saatchi Garland Compton (advertising firm), 43, 48, 54, 59, 60, 162, 165

Seats and votes, ix, xi–xii, 156–57, 197–99

Shore, Peter, 20, 70, 74, 79

Silkin, John, 20, 78

Smith, Geoffrey, 118

Social Democratic party: contest over leadership of, 35–36; defeat of MPs standing for reelection, 96; defection of Labour MPs to, 27; formation of, 24–27, 82; formation of alliance with Liberal party, 27–28; initial support, 192; organizational contribution to Alliance, 162; public opinion polls commissioned by, 118–19

Steed, Michael, 154

Steel, David: leading role in formation of alliance with SDP, 83, 86–87; popularity of, 24, 88, 101, 181, 182–83; relationship with Roy Jenkins in Alliance leadership, 87–89, 92–93, 128–29, 182–83; role in the campaign, 53; television performances, 88

The Sun, 115–16, 123

The Sunday Times, 77, 114, 124, 133

Swing, 165–67, 172–73, 195

Tactical voting, 96–97, 101–3, 111, 130–31

Tatchell, Peter, 47, 67, 85, 111–12

Tebbit, Norman, 42, 48

Television: coverage of campaign by broadcasters, 54, 77, 111; "Granada 500" program, 129–30; party political broadcasts, 43, 54, 87, 162, 164–65; public opinion polls commissioned by, 57, 112, 115–16, 121, 124–25

Thatcher, Margaret: campaign activities, 50–51, 56; economic philosophy and strategy, 3–5, 9–10; election as Conservative party leader, 2; impact on British politics, 187–88; impact of Falklands war on popularity of, 30–34, 160–61; popularity in public opinion polls, 11–12, 101, 182–83; principles and pragmatism, 7–8; relations with cabinet, 5; style, 2–3, 13, 54–55, 74, 184–86

Thatcher government (1979–83): approval in public opinion polls, 10–12, 39–40; attack on inflation, 3–4, 34; cabinet reshuffle, 42; council houses, encouragement of private purchases of, 7; crime and police policies, 7; defense policy, 9; economic recession and recovery, 155, 160; election date decision, 46–47, 48–50, 109–11; foreign policy, 8–9; policy on employment, 4, 34; policy toward trade unions, 4–5, 6–7; position of the "wets," 13, 14–15; privatization of nationalized industries, 4, 5–6; tax policies,

4–5; tenure compared with that of other governments, x

"Thatcherism," 7, 184–86, 187

The Times, 76, 91–92, 112

Timing of election, 46–47, 48–50, 109–11

Trade unions: movement to the left, 16, 59; rejection of incomes policy, 71; Thatcher government policy toward, 4–5, 6–7; voting patterns, 170–71

Turnout: overall, compared with other general elections, ix; differential turnout of parties' supporters, 167; of ethnic minorities, 147–48

Unemployment: as a campaign issue, 53, 60, 176, 179, 189–91; statistics, 11, 12, 34, 59

Voters, behavior by groups in 1983: age groups, 98, 168; home owners and renters, 99, 170–71; men, 98, 167–68; occupation, 97, 170–71; regions, 98; social class, 97–98, 169–70; trade union members, 97; women, 98, 167–68

Votes and seats in 1983, ix, xi–xii, 156–57, 197–99

Voting defections in 1983, 98, 165–67

Warrington by-election (1981), 28–29

"Wets," 13, 14–15, 40–41

Whitelaw, William, 2, 14, 20, 48, 49

Williams, Shirley: elected in Crosby by-election, 29, 84; role in forming SDP, 25–27, 82

Wilson, Sir Harold, 16, 18, 50, 61, 65, 110, 195

Women, distinctive voting patterns, 167–68

Worcester, Robert, 72, 112, 121, 124. See also Market and Opinion Research International

Working class, "new" and "old," 172–73

Youth vote, 168